3
37
169

THE ∙ ART ∙ OF
Dreaming

THE · ART · OF
Dreaming

CARLOS CASTANEDA

HarperCollins*Publishers*

A leatherbound signed first edition of this book has been published by The Easton press.

Grateful acknowledgment is made to the following for permission to use material in this book:

"I Have Longed to Move Away," by Dylan Thomas, from *Poems of Dylan Thomas*. Copyright 1939 by New Directions Publishing Corp. Reprinted by permission of New Directions Publishing Corp.

HarperCollins books may be purchased for educational, business, or sales promotional use. For information, please write: Special Markets Department, HarperCollins Publishers, Inc., 10 East 53rd Street, New York, NY 10022.

FIRST EDITION

Designed by Jessica Shatan

Library of Congress Cataloging-in-Publication Data

Castaneda, Carlos.
  The art of dreaming / Carlos Castaneda.— 1st ed.
    p.   cm.
  ISBN 0-06-017051-4 (cloth)
  1. Dreaming. 2. Juan, Don. I. Title.
BF1091. C34 1993
135'. 3—dc20   92-56194
93 94 95 96 97 ❖/HC 10 9 8 7 6 5 4 3 2 1

CONTENTS

AUTHOR'S NOTE

Over the past twenty years, I have written a series of books about my apprenticeship with a Mexican Yaqui Indian sorcerer, don Juan Matus. I have explained in those books that he taught me sorcery, but not as we understand sorcery in the context of our daily world: the use of supernatural powers over others, or the calling of spirits through charms, spells, or rituals to produce supernatural effects. For don Juan, sorcery was the act of embodying some specialized theoretical and practical premises about the nature and role of perception in molding the universe around us.

Following don Juan's suggestion, I have refrained from using shamanism, a category proper to anthropology, to classify his knowledge. I have called it all along what he himself called it: sorcery. On examination, however, I realized that calling it sorcery obscures even more the already obscure phenomena he presented to me in his teachings.

In anthropological works, shamanism is described as a belief system of some native people of northern Asia—prevailing also among certain native North American Indian tribes—which maintains that an unseen world of ancestral spiritual forces, good and evil, is pervasive around us and that these spiritual forces can be summoned or controlled through the acts of practitioners, who are the intermediaries between the natural and supernatural realms.

Don Juan was indeed an intermediary between the natural world of everyday life and an unseen world, which he called not the supernatural but the second attention. His role as a teacher was to make this configuration accessible to me. I have described in my previous work his teaching methods to this effect, as well as the sorcery arts he made me practice, the most important of which is called the art of dreaming.

Don Juan contended that our world, which we believe to be unique and absolute, is only one in a cluster of consecutive worlds, arranged like the layers of an onion. He asserted that even though we have been energetically conditioned to perceive solely our world, we still have the capability of entering into those other realms, which are as real, unique, absolute, and engulfing as our own world is.

Don Juan explained to me that, for us to perceive those other realms, not only do we have to covet them but we need to have sufficient energy to seize them. Their existence is constant and independent of our awareness, he said, but their inaccessibility is entirely a consequence of our energetic conditioning. In other words, simply and solely because of that conditioning, we are compelled to assume that the world of daily life is the one and only possible world.

Believing that our energetic conditioning is correctable, don Juan stated that sorcerers of ancient times developed a set of practices designed to recondition our energetic capabilities to perceive. They called this set of practices the art of dreaming.

With the perspective time gives, I now realize that the most fitting statement don Juan made about dreaming was to call it the "gateway to infinity." I remarked, at the time he said it, that the metaphor had no meaning to me.

"Let's then do away with metaphors," he conceded. "Let's say that dreaming is the sorcerers' practical way of putting ordinary dreams to use."

"But how can ordinary dreams be put to use?" I asked.

"We always get tricked by words," he said. "In my own case, my teacher attempted to describe dreaming to me by saying that it is the way sorcerers say good night to the world. He was, of course, tailoring his description to fit my mentality. I'm doing the same with you."

On another occasion don Juan said to me, "Dreaming can only be experienced. Dreaming is not just having dreams; neither is it daydreaming or wishing or imagining. Through dreaming we can perceive other worlds, which we can certainly describe, but we can't describe what makes us perceive them. Yet we can feel how dreaming opens up those other realms. Dreaming seems to be a sensation—a process in our bodies, an awareness in our minds."

In the course of his general teachings, don Juan thoroughly explained to me the principles, rationales, and practices of the art of dreaming. His instruction was divided into two parts. One was about dreaming procedures, the other about the purely abstract explanations of these procedures. His teaching method was an interplay between enticing my intellectual curiosity with the abstract principles of dreaming and guiding me to seek an outlet in its practices.

I have already described all this in as much detail as I was able to. And I have also described the sorcerers' milieu in which don Juan placed me in order to teach me his arts. My interaction in this milieu was of special interest to me because it took place exclusively in the second attention. I interacted there with the ten women and five men who were don Juan's sorcerer companions and with the four young men and the four young women who were his apprentices.

Don Juan gathered them immediately after I came into his world. He made it clear to me that they formed a traditional sorcerers' group—a replica of his own party—and that I was supposed to lead them. However, working with me he realized that I was different than he expected. He explained that difference in terms of an energy configuration seen only by sorcerers: instead of having four compartments of energy, as he himself had, I had only three. Such a configuration, which he had mistakenly hoped was a correctable flaw, made me so completely inadequate for interacting with or leading those eight apprentices that it became imperative for don Juan to gather another group of people more akin to my energetic structure.

I have written extensively about those events. Yet I have never mentioned the second group of apprentices; don Juan did not permit me to do so. He argued that they were exclusively in my field and that the agreement I had with him was to write about his field, not mine.

The second group of apprentices was extremely compact. It had only three members: a dreamer, Florinda Grau; a stalker, Taisha Abelar; and a nagual woman, Carol Tiggs.

We interacted with one another solely in the second attention. In the world of everyday life, we did not have even a vague notion of one another. In terms of our relationship with don Juan, however, there was no vagueness; he put enormous effort into training all of us equally. Nevertheless, toward the end, when don Juan's time was about to finish, the psychological pressure of his departure started to collapse the rigid boundaries of the second attention. The result was that our interaction began to lapse into the world of everyday affairs, and we met, seemingly for the first time.

None of us, consciously, knew about our deep and arduous interaction in the second attention. Since all of us were involved in academic studies, we ended up more than shocked when we found out we had met before. This was and still is, of course, intellectually inadmissible to us, yet we know that it was thoroughly within our experience. We have been left, therefore, with the disquieting knowledge that the human psyche is infinitely more complex than our mundane or academic reasoning had led us to believe.

Once we asked don Juan, in unison, to shed light on our predicament. He said that he had two explanatory options. One was to cater to our hurt rationality and patch it up, saying that the second attention is a state of awareness as illusory as elephants flying in the sky and that everything we thought we had experienced in that state was simply a product of hypnotic suggestions. The other option was to explain it the way sorcerer dreamers understand it: as an energetic configuration of awareness.

During the fulfillment of my dreaming tasks, however, the barrier of the second attention remained unchanged. Every time I entered into dreaming, I also entered into the second attention, and waking up from dreaming did not necessarily mean I had left the second attention. For years I could remember only bits of my dreaming experiences. The bulk of what I did was energetically unavailable to me. It took me fifteen years of uninterrupted work, from 1973 to 1988, to store enough energy to rearrange everything linearly in my mind. I remembered then sequences upon sequences of dreaming events, and I was able to fill in, at last, some seeming lapses of memory. In this manner I captured the inherent continuity of don Juan's lessons in the art of dreaming, a continuity that had been lost to me because of his making me weave between the awareness of our everyday life and the awareness of the second attention. This work is a result of that rearrangement.

All this brings me to the final part of my statement: the reason for writing this book. Being in possession of most of the pieces of don Juan's lessons in the art of dreaming, I would like to explain, in a future work, the current position and interest of his last four students: Florinda Grau, Taisha Abelar, Carol Tiggs, and myself. But before I describe and explain the results of don Juan's guidance and influence on us, I must review, in light of what I know now, the parts of don Juan's lessons in dreaming to which I did not have access before.

The definitive reason for this work, however, was given by Carol Tiggs. Her belief is that explaining the world that don Juan made us inherit is the ultimate expression of our gratitude to him and our commitment to his quest.

· 1 ·

SORCERERS OF ANTIQUITY:

AN INTRODUCTION

Don Juan stressed, time and time again, that everything he was teaching me had been envisioned and worked
out by men he referred to as sorcerers of antiquity. He made it
very clear that there was a profound distinction between those
sorcerers and the sorcerers of modern times. He categorized
sorcerers of antiquity as men who existed in Mexico perhaps
thousands of years before the Spanish Conquest, men whose
greatest accomplishment had been to build the structures of
sorcery, emphasizing practicality and concreteness. He rendered them as men who were brilliant but lacking in wisdom.
Modern sorcerers, by contrast, don Juan portrayed as men

renowned for their sound minds and their capacity to rectify the course of sorcery if they deemed it necessary.

Don Juan explained to me that the sorcery premises pertinent to dreaming were naturally envisioned and developed by sorcerers of antiquity. Out of necessity—for those premises are key in explaining and understanding dreaming—I again have to write about and discuss them. The major part of this book is, therefore, a reintroduction and amplification of what I have presented in my previous works.

During one of our conversations, don Juan stated that, in order to appreciate the position of dreamers and dreaming, one has to understand the struggle of modern-day sorcerers to steer sorcery away from concreteness toward the abstract.

"What do you call concreteness, don Juan?" I asked.

"The practical part of sorcery," he said. "The obsessive fixation of the mind on practices and techniques, the unwarranted influence over people. All of these were in the realm of the sorcerers of the past."

"And what do you call the abstract?"

"The search for freedom, freedom to perceive, without obsessions, all that's humanly possible. I say that present-day sorcerers seek the abstract because they seek freedom; they have no interest in concrete gains. There are no social functions for them, as there were for the sorcerers of the past. So you'll never catch them being the official seers or the sorcerers in residence."

"Do you mean, don Juan, that the past has no value to modern-day sorcerers?"

"It certainly has value. It's the taste of that past which we don't like. I personally detest the darkness and morbidity of the mind. I like the immensity of thought. However, regardless of my likes and dislikes, I have to give due credit to the sorcerers of antiquity, for they were the first to find out and do everything we know and do today.

Don Juan explained that their most important attainment

was to perceive the energetic essence of things. This insight was of such importance that it was turned into the basic premise of sorcery. Nowadays, after lifelong discipline and training, sorcerers do acquire the capacity to perceive the essence of things, a capacity they call *seeing*.

"What would it mean to me to perceive the energetic essence of things?" I once asked don Juan.

"It would mean that you perceive energy directly," he replied. "By separating the social part of perception, you'll perceive the essence of everything. Whatever we are perceiving is energy, but since we can't directly perceive energy, we process our perception to fit a mold. This mold is the social part of perception, which you have to separate."

"Why do I have to separate it?"

"Because it deliberately reduces the scope of what can be perceived and makes us believe that the mold into which we fit our perception is all that exists. I am convinced that for man to survive now, his perception must change at its social base."

"What is this social base of perception, don Juan?"

"The physical certainty that the world is made of concrete objects. I call this a social base because a serious and fierce effort is put out by everybody to guide us to perceive the world the way we do."

"How then should we perceive the world?"

"Everything is energy. The whole universe is energy. The social base of our perception should be the physical certainty that energy is all there is. A mighty effort should be made to guide us to perceive energy as energy. Then we would have both alternatives at our fingertips."

"Is it possible to train people in such a fashion?" I asked.

Don Juan replied that it was possible and that this was precisely what he was doing with me and his other apprentices. He was teaching us a new way of perceiving, first, by making us realize we process our perception to fit a mold and, second, by fiercely guiding us to perceive energy directly. He assured me that this method was very much like the one used to teach us to perceive the world of daily affairs.

Don Juan's conception was that our entrapment in processing our perception to fit a social mold loses its power when we realize we have accepted this mold, as an inheritance from our ancestors, without bothering to examine it.

"To perceive a world of hard objects that had either a positive or a negative value must have been utterly necessary for our ancestors' survival," don Juan said. "After ages of perceiving in such a manner, we are now forced to believe that the world is made up of objects."

"I can't conceive the world in any other way, don Juan," I complained. "It is unquestionably a world of objects. To prove it, all we have to do is bump into them."

"Of course it's a world of objects. We are not arguing that."

"What are you saying then?"

"I am saying that this is first a world of energy; then it's a world of objects. If we don't start with the premise that it is a world of energy, we'll never be able to perceive energy directly. We'll always be stopped by the physical certainty of what you've just pointed out: the hardness of objects."

His argument was extremely mystifying to me. In those days, my mind would simply refuse to consider any way to understand the world except the one with which I was familiar. Don Juan's claims and the points he struggled to raise were outlandish propositions that I could not accept but could not refuse either.

"Our way of perceiving is a predator's way," he said to me on one occasion. "A very efficient manner of appraising and classifying food and danger. But this is not the only way we are able to perceive. There is another mode, the one I am familiarizing you with: the act of perceiving the essence of everything, energy itself, directly.

"To perceive the essence of everything will make us understand, classify, and describe the world in entirely new, more exciting, more sophisticated terms." This was don Juan's claim. And the more sophisticated terms to which he was alluding were those he had been taught by his predecessors, terms that correspond to sorcery truths, which have no rational foundation and no relation whatsoever to the facts of our daily world but which are self-evident truths for the sorcerers who perceive energy directly and *see* the essence of everything.

For such sorcerers, the most significant act of sorcery is to *see* the essence of the universe. Don Juan's version was that the sorcerers of antiquity, the first ones to *see* the essence of the universe, described it in the best manner. They said that the essence of the universe resembles incandescent threads stretched into infinity in every conceivable direction, luminous filaments that are conscious of themselves in ways impossible for the human mind to comprehend.

From *seeing* the essence of the universe, the sorcerers of antiquity went on to *see* the energy essence of human beings. Don Juan stated that they depicted human beings as bright shapes that resembled giant eggs and called them luminous eggs.

"When sorcerers *see* a human being," don Juan said, "they *see* a giant, luminous shape that floats, making, as it moves, a deep furrow in the energy of the earth, just as if the luminous shape had a taproot that was dragging."

Don Juan had the impression that our energy shape keeps on changing through time. He said that every seer he knew, himself included, *saw* that human beings are shaped more like balls or even tombstones than eggs. But, once in a while, and for no reason known to them, sorcerers *see* a person whose energy is shaped like an egg. Don Juan suggested that people who are egglike in shape today are more akin to people of ancient times.

In the course of his teachings, don Juan repeatedly discussed and explained what he considered the decisive finding of the sorcerers of antiquity. He called it the crucial feature of human beings as luminous balls: a round spot of intense brilliance, the size of a tennis ball, permanently lodged inside the luminous ball, flush with its surface, about two feet back from the crest of a person's right shoulder blade.

Since I had trouble visualizing this the first time don Juan described it to me, he explained that the luminous ball is much larger than the human body, that the spot of intense brilliance is part of this ball of energy, and that it is located on a place at the height of the shoulder blades, an arm's length from a person's back. He said that the old sorcerers named it the assemblage point after *seeing* what it does.

"What does the assemblage point do?" I asked.

"It makes us perceive," he replied. "The old sorcerers *saw* that, in human beings, perception is assembled there, on that point. *Seeing* that all living beings have such a point of brilliance, the old sorcerers surmised that perception in general must take place on that spot, in whatever pertinent manner."

"What did the old sorcerers *see* that made them conclude that perception takes place on the assemblage point?" I asked.

He answered that, first, they *saw* that out of the millions of the universe's luminous energy filaments passing through the entire luminous ball, only a small number pass directly through the assemblage point, as should be expected since it is small in comparison with the whole.

Next, they *saw* that a spherical extra glow, slightly bigger than the assemblage point, always surrounds it, greatly intensifying the luminosity of the filaments passing directly through that glow.

Finally, they *saw* two things. One, that the assemblage points of human beings can dislodge themselves from the spot where they are usually located. And, two, that when the assemblage point is on its habitual position, perception and awareness seem to be normal, judging by the normal behavior of the subjects being observed. But when their assemblage points and surrounding glowing spheres are on a different position than the habitual one, their unusual behavior seems to be the proof that their awareness is different, that they are perceiving in an unfamiliar manner.

The conclusion the old sorcerers drew from all this was that the greater the displacement of the assemblage point from its customary position, the more unusual the consequent behavior and, evidently, the consequent awareness and perception.

"Notice that when I talk about *seeing*, I always say 'having the appearance of' or 'seemed like,'" don Juan warned me. "Everything one *sees* is so unique that there is no way to talk about it except by comparing it to something known to us."

He said that the most adequate example of this difficulty was the way sorcerers talk about the assemblage point and the glow that surrounds it. They describe them as brightness, yet it cannot be brightness, because seers *see* them without their eyes. They have to fill out the difference, however, and say that the assemblage point is a spot of light and that around it there is a halo, a glow. Don Juan pointed out that we are so visual, so ruled by our predator's perception, that everything we *see* must be rendered in terms of what the predator's eye normally sees.

After *seeing* what the assemblage point and its surrounding glow seemed to be doing, don Juan said that the old sorcerers advanced an explanation. They proposed that in human beings the assemblage point, by focusing its glowing sphere on the universe's filaments of energy that pass directly through it, automatically and without premeditation assembles those filaments into a steady perception of the world.

"How are those filaments you talk about assembled into a steady perception of the world?" I asked.

"No one can possibly know that," he emphatically replied. "Sorcerers *see* the movement of energy, but just *seeing* the movement of energy cannot tell them how or why energy moves."

Don Juan stated that, *seeing* that millions of conscious energy filaments pass through the assemblage point, the old sorcerers postulated that in passing through it they come together, amassed by the glow that surrounds it. After *seeing* that the glow is extremely dim in people who have been rendered unconscious or are about to die, and that it is totally absent from corpses, they were convinced that this glow is awareness.

"How about the assemblage point? Is it absent from a corpse?" I asked.

He answered that there is no trace of an assemblage point on a dead being, because the assemblage point and its surrounding glow are the mark of life and consciousness. The inescapable conclusion of the sorcerers of antiquity was that awareness and perception go together and are tied to the assemblage point and the glow that surrounds it.

"Is there a chance that those sorcerers might have been mistaken about their *seeing*?" I asked.

"I can't explain to you why, but there is no way sorcerers can be mistaken about their *seeing*," don Juan said, in a tone that admitted no argument. "Now, the conclusions they arrive at from their *seeing* might be wrong, but that would be because they are naive, uncultivated. In order to avoid this disaster, sorcerers have to cultivate their minds, in whatever form they can."

He softened up then and remarked that it certainly would be infinitely safer for sorcerers to remain solely at the level of describing what they *see*, but that the temptation to conclude and explain, even if only to oneself, is far too great to resist.

The effect of the assemblage point's displacement was another energy configuration the sorcerers of antiquity were able to *see* and study. Don Juan said that when the assemblage point is displaced to another position, a new conglomerate of millions of luminous energy filaments come together on that point. The sorcerers of antiquity *saw* this and concluded that since the glow of awareness is always present wherever the assemblage point is, perception is automatically assembled there. Because of the different position of the assemblage point, the resulting world, however, cannot be our world of daily affairs.

Don Juan explained that the old sorcerers were capable of distinguishing two types of assemblage point displacement. One was a displacement to any position on the surface or in the interior of the luminous ball; this displacement they called a *shift* of the assemblage point. The other was a displacement to a position outside the luminous ball; they called this displacement a *movement* of the assemblage point. They found out that the difference between a shift and a movement was the nature of the perception each allows.

Since the shifts of the assemblage point are displacements within the luminous ball, the worlds engendered by them, no matter how bizarre or wondrous or unbelievable they might be, are still worlds within the human domain. The human domain is the energy filaments that pass through the entire luminous ball. By contrast, movements of the assemblage point, since they are displacements to positions outside the luminous ball, engage filaments of energy that are beyond the human realm. Perceiving such filaments engenders worlds that are beyond comprehension, inconceivable worlds with no trace of human antecedents in them.

The problem of validation always played a key role in my mind in those days. "Forgive me, don Juan," I said to him on one occasion, "but this business of the assemblage point is an idea so farfetched, so inadmissible that I don't know how to deal with it or what to think of it."

"There is only one thing for you to do," he retorted. "*See* the assemblage point! It isn't that difficult to *see*. The difficulty is in breaking the retaining wall we all have in our minds that holds us in place. To break it, all we need is energy. Once we have energy, *seeing* happens to us by itself. The trick is in abandoning our fort of self-complacency and false security."

"It is obvious to me, don Juan, that it takes a lot of knowledge to *see*. It isn't just a matter of having energy."

"It *is* just a matter of having energy, believe me. The hard part is convincing yourself that it can be done. For this, you need to trust the nagual. The marvel of sorcery is that every sorcerer has to prove everything with his own experience. I am telling you about the principles of sorcery not with the hope that you will memorize them but with the hope that you will practice them."

Don Juan was certainly right about the need for trusting. In the beginning stages of my thirteen-year apprenticeship with him, the hardest thing for me was to affiliate myself with his world and his person. This affiliating meant that I had to learn to trust him implicitly and accept him without bias as the nagual.

Don Juan's total role in the sorcerers' world was synthesized in the title accorded to him by his peers; he was called the *nagual.* It was explained to me that this concept refers to any person, male or female, who possesses a specific kind of energy configuration, which to a seer appears as a double luminous ball. Seers believe that when one of these people enters into the sorcerers' world, that extra load of energy is turned into a measure of strength and the capacity for leadership. Thus, the nagual is the natural guide, the leader of a party of sorcerers.

At first, to feel such a trust for don Juan was quite disturbing to me, if not altogether odious. When I discussed it with him, he assured me that to trust his teacher in such a manner had been just as difficult for him.

"I told my teacher the same thing you are saying to me now," don Juan said. "He replied that without trusting the nagual there is no possibility of relief and thus no possibility of clearing the debris from our lives in order to be free."

Don Juan reiterated how right his teacher had been. And I reiterated my profound disagreement. I told him that being reared in a stifling religious environment had had dreadful effects on me, and that his teacher's statements and his own acquiescence to his teacher reminded me of the obedience dogma that I had to learn as a child and that I abhorred. "It sounds like you're voicing a religious belief when you talk about the nagual," I said.

"You may believe whatever you want," don Juan replied undauntedly. "The fact remains, there is no game without the nagual. I know this and I say so. And so did all the naguals who preceded me. But they didn't say it from the standpoint of self-importance, and neither do I. To say there is no path without the nagual is to refer totally to the fact that the man, the nagual, is a nagual because he can reflect the abstract, the spirit, better than others. But that's all. Our link is with the spirit itself and only incidentally with the man who brings us its message."

I did learn to trust don Juan implicitly as the nagual, and this, as he had stated it, brought me an immense sense of relief and a greater capacity to accept what he was striving to teach me.

In his teachings, he put a great emphasis on explaining and discussing the assemblage point. I asked him once if the assemblage point had anything to do with the physical body.

"It has nothing to do with what we normally perceive as the body," he said. "It's part of the luminous egg, which is our energy self."

"How is it displaced?" I asked.

"Through energy currents. Jolts of energy, originating outside or inside our energy shape. These are usually unpredictable currents that happen randomly, but with sorcerers they are very predictable currents that obey the sorcerer's intent."

"Can you yourself feel these currents?"

"Every sorcerer feels them. Every human being does, for that matter, but average human beings are too busy with their own pursuits to pay any attention to feelings like that."

"What do those currents feel like?"

"Like a mild discomfort, a vague sensation of sadness followed immediately by euphoria. Since neither the sadness nor the euphoria has an explainable cause, we never regard them as veritable onslaughts of the unknown but as unexplainable, ill-founded moodiness."

"What happens when the assemblage point moves outside the energy shape? Does it hang outside? Or is it attached to the luminous ball?"

"It pushes the contours of the energy shape out, without breaking its energy boundaries."

Don Juan explained that the end result of a movement of the assemblage point is a total change in the energy shape of a human being. Instead of a ball or an egg, he becomes something resembling a smoking pipe. The tip of the stem is the assemblage point, and the bowl of the pipe is what remains of the luminous ball. If the assemblage point keeps on moving, a moment comes when the luminous ball becomes a thin line of energy.

Don Juan went on to explain that the old sorcerers were the only ones who accomplished this feat of energy shape transformation. And I asked him whether in their new energetic shape those sorcerers were still men.

"Of course they were still men," he said. "But I think what you want to know is if they were still men of reason, trustworthy persons. Well, not quite."

"In what way were they different?"

"In their concerns. Human endeavors and preoccupations had no meaning whatsoever to them. They also had a definite new appearance."

"Do you mean that they didn't look like men?"

"It's very hard to tell what was what about those sorcerers. They certainly looked like men. What else would they look like? But they were not quite like what you or I would expect. Yet if you pressed me to tell in what way they were different, I would go in circles, like a dog chasing its tail."

"Have you ever met one of those men, don Juan?"

"Yes, I have met one."

"What did he look like?"

"As far as looks, he looked like a regular person. Now, it was his behavior that was unusual."

"In what way was it unusual?"

"All I can tell you is that the behavior of the sorcerer I met is something that defies the imagination. But to make it a matter of merely behavior is misleading. It is really something you must see to appreciate."

"Were all those sorcerers like the one you met?"

"Certainly not. I don't know how the others were, except through sorcerers' stories handed down from generation to generation. And those stories portray them as being quite bizarre."

"Do you mean monstrous?"

"Not at all. They say that they were very likable but extremely scary. They were more like unknown creatures. What makes mankind homogeneous is the fact that we are all luminous balls. And those sorcerers were no longer balls of energy but lines of energy that were trying to bend themselves into circles, which they couldn't quite make."

"What finally happened to them, don Juan? Did they die?"

"Sorcerers' stories say that because they had succeeded in stretching their shapes, they had also succeeded in stretching the duration of their consciousness. So they are alive and conscious to this day. There are stories about their periodic appearances on the earth."

"What do you think of all this yourself, don Juan?"

"It is too bizarre for me. I want freedom. Freedom to retain my awareness and yet disappear into the vastness. In my personal opinion, those old sorcerers were extravagant, obsessive, capricious men who got pinned down by their own machinations.

"But don't let my personal feelings sway you. The old sorcerers' accomplishment is unparalleled. If nothing else, they proved to us that man's potentials are nothing to sneeze at."

Another topic of don Juan's explanations was the indispensability of energetic uniformity and cohesion for the purpose of perceiving. His contention was that mankind perceives the world we know, in the terms we do, only because we share energetic uniformity and cohesion. He said that we automatically attain these two conditions of energy in the course of our rearing and that they are so taken for granted we do not realize their vital importance until we are faced with the possibility of perceiving worlds other than the world we know. At those moments, it becomes evident that we need a new appropriate energetic uniformity and cohesion to perceive coherently and totally.

I asked him what uniformity and cohesion were, and he explained that man's energetic shape has uniformity in the sense that every human being on earth has the form of a ball or an egg. And the fact that man's energy holds itself together as a ball or an egg proves it has cohesion. He said that an example of a new uniformity and cohesion was the old sorcerers' energetic shape when it became a line: every one of them uniformly became a line and cohesively remained a line. Uniformity and cohesion at a line level permitted those old sorcerers to perceive a homogeneous new world.

"How are uniformity and cohesion acquired?" I asked.

"The key is the position of the assemblage point, or rather the fixation of the assemblage point," he said.

He did not want to elaborate any further at that time, so I asked him if those old sorcerers could have reverted to being egglike. He replied that at one point they could have, but that they did not. And then the line cohesion set in and made it impossible for them to go back. He believed that what really crystallized that line cohesion and prevented them from making the journey back was a matter of choice and greed. The scope of what those sorcerers were able to perceive and do as lines of energy was astronomically greater than what an average man or any average sorcerer can do or perceive.

He explained that the human domain when one is an energy ball is whatever energy filaments pass through the space within the ball's boundaries. Normally, we perceive not all the human domain but perhaps only one thousandth of it. He was of the opinion that, if we take this into consideration, the enormity of what the old sorcerers did becomes apparent; they extended themselves into a line a thousand times the size of a man as an energy ball and perceived all the energy filaments that passed through that line.

On his insistence, I made giant efforts to understand the new model of energy configuration he was outlining for me. Finally, after much pounding, I could follow the idea of energy filaments inside the luminous ball and outside it. But if I thought of a multitude of luminous balls, the model broke down in my mind. In a multitude of luminous balls, I reasoned, the energy filaments that are outside one of them will perforce be inside the adjacent one. So in a multitude there could not possibly be any energy filaments outside any luminous ball.

"To understand all this certainly isn't an exercise for your reason," he replied after carefully listening to my arguments. "I have no way of explaining what sorcerers mean by filaments inside and outside the human shape. When seers *see* the human energy shape, they *see* one single ball of energy. If there is another ball next to it, the other ball is *seen* again as a single ball of energy. The idea of a multitude of luminous balls comes from your knowledge of human crowds. In the universe of energy, there are only single individuals, alone, surrounded by the boundless.

"You must *see* that for yourself!"

I argued with don Juan then that it was pointless to tell me to *see* it for myself when he knew I could not. And he proposed that I borrow his energy and use it to *see*.

"How can I do that? Borrow your energy."

"Very simple. I can make your assemblage point shift to another position more suitable to perceiving energy directly."

This was the first time, in my memory, that he deliberately talked about something he had been doing all along: making me enter into some incomprehensible state of awareness that defied my idea of the world and of myself, a state he called the second attention. So, to make my assemblage point shift to a position more suitable to perceiving energy directly, don Juan slapped my back, between my shoulder blades, with such a force that he made me lose my breath. I thought that I must have fainted or that the blow had made me fall asleep. Suddenly, I was looking or I was dreaming I was looking at something literally beyond words. Bright strings of light shot out from everywhere, going everywhere, strings of light which were like nothing that had ever entered my thoughts.

When I recovered my breath, or when I woke up, don Juan expectantly asked me, "What did you *see?*" And when I answered, truthfully, "Your blow made me see stars," he doubled up laughing.

He remarked that I was not ready yet to comprehend any unusual perception I might have had. "I made your assemblage point shift," he went on, "and for an instant you were dreaming the filaments of the universe. But you don't yet have the discipline or the energy to rearrange your uniformity and cohesion. The old sorcerers were the consummate masters of that rearranging. That was how they *saw* everything that can be *seen* by man."

"What does it mean to rearrange uniformity and cohesion?"

"It means to enter into the second attention by retaining the assemblage point on its new position and keeping it from sliding back to its original spot."

Don Juan then gave me a traditional definition of the second attention. He said that the old sorcerers called the result of fixing the assemblage point on new positions the second attention and that they treated the second attention as an area of all-inclusive activity, just as the attention of the daily world is. He pointed out that sorcerers really have two complete areas for their endeavors: a small one, called the first attention or the awareness of our daily world or the fixation of the assemblage point on its habitual position; and a much larger area, the second attention or the awareness of other worlds or the fixation of the assemblage point on each of an enormous number of new positions.

Don Juan helped me to experience inexplicable things in the second attention by means of what he called a sorcerer's maneuver: tapping my back gently or forcefully striking it at the height of my shoulder blades. He explained that with his blows he displaced my assemblage point. From my experiential position, such displacements meant that my awareness used to enter into a most disturbing state of unequaled clarity, a state of superconsciousness, which I enjoyed for short periods of time and in which I could understand anything with minimal pre-ambles. It was not quite a pleasing state. Most of the time it was like a strange dream, so intense that normal awareness paled by comparison.

Don Juan justified the indispensability of such a maneuver, saying that in normal awareness a sorcerer teaches his appren-tices basic concepts and procedures and in the second attention he gives them abstract and detailed explanations.

Ordinarily, apprentices do not remember these explanations at all, yet they somehow store them, faithfully intact, in their memories. Sorcerers have used this seeming peculiarity of memory and have turned remembering everything that hap-pens to them in the second attention into one of the most diffi-cult and complex traditional tasks of sorcery.

Sorcerers explain this seeming peculiarity of memory, and the task of remembering, saying that every time anyone enters into the second attention, the assemblage point is on a different position. To remember, then, means to relocate the assemblage point on the exact position it occupied at the time those entrances into the second attention occurred. Don Juan assured me not only that sorcerers have total and absolute recall but that they relive every experience they had in the second atten-tion by this act of returning their assemblage point to each of those specific positions. He also assured me that sorcerers dedi-cate a lifetime to fulfilling this task of remembering.

In the second attention, don Juan gave me very detailed explanations of sorcery, knowing that the accuracy and fidelity of such instruction will remain with me, faithfully intact, for the duration of my life.

About this quality of faithfulness he said, "Learning something in the second attention is just like learning when we were children. What we learn remains with us for life. 'It's second nature with me,' we say when it comes to something we've learned very early in life."

Judging from where I stand today, I realize that don Juan made me enter, as many times as he could, into the second attention in order to force me to sustain, for long periods of time, new positions of my assemblage point and to perceive coherently in them, that is to say, he aimed at forcing me to rearrange my uniformity and cohesion.

I succeeded countless times in perceiving everything as precisely as I perceive in the daily world. My problem was my incapacity to make a bridge between my actions in the second attention and my awareness of the daily world. It took a great deal of effort and time for me to understand what the second attention is. Not so much because of its intricacy and complexity, which are indeed extreme, but because, once I was back in my normal awareness, I found it impossible to remember not only that I had entered into the second attention but that such a state existed at all.

Another monumental breakthrough that the old sorcerers claimed, and that don Juan carefully explained to me, was to find out that the assemblage point becomes very easily displaced during sleep. This realization triggered another one: that dreams are totally associated with that displacement. The old sorcerers *saw* that the greater the displacement, the more unusual the dream or vice versa: the more unusual the dream, the greater the displacement. Don Juan said that this observation led them to devise extravagant techniques to force the displacement of the assemblage point, such as ingesting plants that can produce altered states of consciousness; subjecting themselves to states of hunger, fatigue, and stress; and especially controlling dreams. In this fashion, and perhaps without even knowing it, they created dreaming.

One day, as we strolled around the plaza in the city of Oaxaca, don Juan gave me the most coherent definition of dreaming from a sorcerer's standpoint.

"Sorcerers view dreaming as an extremely sophisticated art," he said, "the art of displacing the assemblage point at will from its habitual position in order to enhance and enlarge the scope of what can be perceived."

He said that the old sorcerers anchored the art of dreaming on five conditions they *saw* in the energy flow of human beings.

One, they *saw* that only the energy filaments that pass directly through the assemblage point can be assembled into coherent perception.

Two, they *saw* that if the assemblage point is displaced to another position, no matter how minute the displacement, different and unaccustomed energy filaments begin to pass through it, engaging awareness and forcing the assembling of these unaccustomed energy fields into a steady, coherent perception.

Three, they *saw* that, in the course of ordinary dreams, the assemblage point becomes easily displaced by itself to another position on the surface or in the interior of the luminous egg.

Four, they *saw* that the assemblage point can be made to move to positions outside the luminous egg, into the energy filaments of the universe at large.

And, five, they *saw* that through discipline it is possible to cultivate and perform, in the course of sleep and ordinary dreams, a systematic displacement of the assemblage point.

▪ 2 ▪

THE FIRST GATE OF

DREAMING

As a preamble to his first lesson in dreaming, don Juan talked about the second attention as a progression: beginning as an idea that comes to us more like a curiosity than an actual possibility; turning into something that can only be felt, as a sensation is felt; and finally evolving into a state of being, or a realm of practicalities, or a preeminent force that opens for us worlds beyond our wildest fantasies.

When explaining sorcery, sorcerers have two options. One is to speak in metaphorical terms and talk about a world of magical dimensions. The other is to explain their business in abstract terms proper to sorcery. I have always preferred the

latter, although neither option will ever satisfy the rational mind of a Western man.

Don Juan told me that what he meant by his metaphorical description of the second attention as a progression was that, being a by-product of a displacement of the assemblage point, the second attention does not happen naturally but must be intended, beginning with intending it as an idea and ending up with intending it as a steady and controlled awareness of the assemblage point's displacement.

"I am going to teach you the first step to power," don Juan said, beginning his instruction in the art of dreaming. "I'm going to teach you how to set up dreaming."

"What does it mean to set up dreaming?"

"To set up dreaming means to have a precise and practical command over the general situation of a dream. For example, you may dream that you are in your classroom. To set up dreaming means that you don't let the dream slip into something else. You don't jump from the classroom to the mountains, for instance. In other words, you control the view of the classroom and don't let it go until you want to."

"But is it possible to do that?"

"Of course it's possible. This control is no different from the control we have over any situation in our daily lives. Sorcerers are used to it and get it every time they want or need to. In order to get used to it yourself, you must start by doing something very simple. Tonight, in your dreams, you must look at your hands."

Not much more was said about this in the awareness of our daily world. In my recollection of my experiences in the second attention, however, I found out that we had a more extensive exchange. For instance, I expressed my feelings about the absurdity of the task, and don Juan suggested that I should face it in terms of a quest that was entertaining, instead of solemn and morbid.

"Get as heavy as you want when we talk about dreaming,"

he said. "Explanations always call for deep thought. But when you actually dream, be as light as a feather. Dreaming has to be performed with integrity and seriousness, but in the midst of laughter and with the confidence of someone who doesn't have a worry in the world. Only under these conditions can our dreams actually be turned into dreaming."

Don Juan assured me that he had selected my hands arbitrarily as something to look for in my dreams and that looking for anything else was just as valid. The goal of the exercise was not finding a specific thing but engaging my dreaming attention.

Don Juan described the dreaming attention as the control one acquires over one's dreams upon fixating the assemblage point on any new position to which it has been displaced during dreams. In more general terms, he called the dreaming attention an incomprehensible facet of awareness that exists by itself, waiting for a moment when we would entice it, a moment when we would give it purpose; it is a veiled faculty that every one of us has in reserve but never has the opportunity to use in everyday life.

My first attempts at looking for my hands in my dreams were a fiasco. After months of unsuccessful efforts, I gave up and complained to don Juan again about the absurdity of such a task.

"There are seven gates," he said as a way of answering, "and dreamers have to open all seven of them, one at the time. You're up against the first gate that must be opened if you are to dream."

"Why didn't you tell me this before?"

"It would've been useless to tell you about the gates of dreaming before you smacked your head against the first one. Now you know that it is an obstacle and that you have to overcome it."

Don Juan explained that there are entrances and exits in the energy flow of the universe and that, in the specific case of dreaming, there are seven entrances, experienced as obstacles, which sorcerers call the seven gates of dreaming.

"The first gate is a threshold we must cross by becoming aware of a particular sensation before deep sleep," he said. "A sensation which is like a pleasant heaviness that doesn't let us open our eyes. We reach that gate the instant we become aware that we're falling asleep, suspended in darkness and heaviness."

"How do I become aware that I am falling asleep? Are there any steps to follow?"

"No. There are no steps to follow. One just intends to become aware of falling asleep."

"But how does one intend to become aware of it?"

"Intent or intending is something very difficult to talk about. I or anyone else would sound idiotic trying to explain it. Bear that in mind when you hear what I have to say next: sorcerers intend anything they set themselves to intend, simply by intending it."

"That doesn't mean anything, don Juan."

"Pay close attention. Someday it'll be your turn to explain. The statement seems nonsensical because you are not putting it in the proper context. Like any rational man, you think that understanding is exclusively the realm of our reason, of our mind.

"For sorcerers, because the statement I made pertains to intent and intending, understanding it pertains to the realm of energy. Sorcerers believe that if one would intend that statement for the energy body, the energy body would understand it in terms entirely different from those of the mind. The trick is to reach the energy body. For that you need energy."

"In what terms would the energy body understand that statement, don Juan?"

"In terms of a bodily feeling, which it's hard to describe. You'll have to experience it to know what I mean."

I wanted a more precise explanation, but don Juan slapped my back and made me enter into the second attention. At that time, what he did was still utterly mysterious to me. I could have sworn that his touch hypnotized me. I believed he had instantaneously put me to sleep, and I dreamt that I found myself walking with him on a wide avenue lined with trees in some unknown city. It was such a vivid dream, and I was so aware of everything, that I immediately tried to orient myself by reading signs and looking at people. It definitely was not an English- or Spanish-speaking city, but it was a Western city. The people seemed to be northern Europeans, perhaps Lithuanians. I became absorbed in trying to read billboards and street signs.

Don Juan nudged me gently. "Don't bother with that," he said. "We are nowhere identifiable. I've just lent you my energy so you would reach your energy body, and with it you've just crossed into another world. This won't last long, so use your time wisely.

"Look at everything, but without being obvious. Don't let anyone notice you."

We walked in silence. It was a block-long walk, which had a remarkable effect on me. The more we walked, the greater my sensation of visceral anxiety. My mind was curious, but my body was alarmed. I had the clearest understanding that I was not in this world. When we got to an intersection and stopped walking, I saw that the trees on the street had been carefully trimmed. They were short trees with hard-looking, curled leaves. Each tree had a big square space for watering. There were no weeds or trash in those spaces, as one would find around trees in the city, only charcoal black, loose dirt.

The moment I focused my eyes on the curb, before I stepped off it to cross the street, I noticed that there were no cars. I tried desperately to watch the people who milled around us, to discover something about them that would explain my anxiety. As I stared at them, they stared back at me. In one instant a circle of hard blue and brown eyes had formed around us.

A certainty hit me like a blow: this was not a dream at all; we were in a reality beyond what I know to be real. I turned to face don Juan. I was about to realize what was different about those people, but a strange dry wind that went directly to my sinuses hit my face, blurred my view, and made me forget what I wanted to tell don Juan. The next instant, I was back where I had started from: don Juan's house. I was lying on a straw mat, curled up on my side.

"I lent you my energy, and you reached your energy body," don Juan said matter-of-factly.

I heard him talk, but I was numb. An unusual itching on my solar plexus kept my breaths short and painful. I knew that I had been on the verge of finding something transcendental about dreaming and about the people I had seen, yet I could not bring whatever I knew into focus.

"Where were we, don Juan?" I asked. "Was it all a dream? A hypnotic state?"

"It wasn't a dream," he replied. "It was dreaming. I helped you reach the second attention so that you would understand intending as a subject not for your reason but for your energy body.

"At this point, you can't yet comprehend the import of all this, not only because you don't have sufficient energy but because you're not intending anything. If you were, your energy body would comprehend immediately that the only way to intend is by focusing your intent on whatever you want to intend. This time I focused it for you on reaching your energy body."

"Is the goal of dreaming to intend the energy body?" I asked, suddenly empowered by some strange reasoning.

"One can certainly put it that way," he said. "In this particular instance, since we're talking about the first gate of dreaming, the goal of dreaming is to intend that your energy body becomes aware that you are falling asleep. Don't try to force yourself to be aware of falling asleep. Let your energy body do it. To intend is to wish without wishing, to do without doing.

"Accept the challenge of intending," he went on. "Put your silent determination, without a single thought, into convincing yourself that you have reached your energy body and that you are a dreamer. Doing this will automatically put you in the position to be aware that you are falling asleep."

"How can I convince myself that I am a dreamer when I am not?"

"When you hear that you have to convince yourself, you automatically become more rational. How can you convince yourself you are a dreamer when you know you are not? Intending is both: the act of convincing yourself you are indeed a dreamer, although you have never dreamt before, and the act of being convinced."

"Do you mean I have to tell myself I am a dreamer and try my best to believe it? Is that it?"

"No, it isn't. Intending is much simpler and, at the same time, infinitely more complex than that. It requires imagination, discipline, and purpose. In this case, to intend means that you get an unquestionable bodily knowledge that you are a dreamer. You feel you are a dreamer with all the cells of your body."

Don Juan added in a joking tone that he did not have sufficient energy to make me another loan for intending and that the thing to do was to reach my energy body on my own. He assured me that intending the first gate of dreaming was one of the means discovered by the sorcerers of antiquity for reaching the second attention and the energy body.

After telling me this, he practically threw me out of his house, commanding me not to come back until I had intended the first gate of dreaming.

I returned home, and every night for months I went to sleep intending with all my might to become aware that I was falling asleep and to see my hands in my dreams. The other part of the task—to convince myself that I was a dreamer and that I had reached my energy body—was totally impossible for me.

Then, one afternoon while taking a nap, I dreamt I was looking at my hands. The shock was enough to wake me up. It proved to be a unique dream that could not be repeated. Weeks went by, and I was unable either to become aware that I was falling asleep or to find my hands. I began to notice, however, that I was having in my dreams a vague feeling that there was something I should have been doing but could not remember. This feeling became so strong that it kept on waking me up at all hours of the night.

When I told don Juan about my futile attempts to cross the first gate of dreaming, he gave me some guidelines. "To ask a dreamer to find a determined item in his dreams is a subterfuge," he said. "The real issue is to become aware that one is falling asleep. And, strange as it may seem, that doesn't happen by commanding oneself to be aware that one is falling asleep but by sustaining the sight of whatever one is looking at in a dream."

He told me that dreamers take quick, deliberate glances at everything present in a dream. If they focus their dreaming attention on something specific, it is only as a point of departure. From there, dreamers move on to look at other items in the dream's content, returning to the point of departure as many times as possible.

After a great effort, I indeed found hands in my dreams, but they never were mine. They were hands that only seemed to belong to me, hands that changed shape, becoming quite nightmarish at times. The rest of my dreams' content, nonetheless, was always pleasantly steady. I could almost sustain the view of anything I focused my attention on.

It went on like this for months, until one day when my capacity to dream changed seemingly by itself. I had done nothing special besides my constant earnest determination to be aware that I was falling asleep and to find my hands.

I dreamt I was visiting my hometown. Not that the town I was dreaming about looked at all like my hometown, but somehow I had the conviction that it was the place where I was born. It all began as an ordinary, yet very vivid dream. Then the light in the dream changed. Images became sharper. The street where I was walking became noticeably more real than a moment before. My feet began to hurt. I could feel that things were absurdly hard. For instance, on bumping into a door, not only did I experience pain on the knee that hit the door but I also was enraged by my clumsiness.

I realistically walked in that town until I was completely exhausted. I saw everything I could have seen had I been a tourist walking through the streets of a city. And there was no difference whatsoever between that dream walk and any walk I had actually taken on the streets of a city I visited for the first time.

"I think you went a bit too far," don Juan said after listening to my account. "All that was required was your awareness of falling asleep. What you've done is equivalent to bringing a wall down just to squash a mosquito sitting on it."

"Do you mean, don Juan, that I flubbed it?"

"No. But apparently you're trying to repeat something you did before. When I made your assemblage point shift and you and I ended up in that mysterious city, you were not asleep. You were dreaming, but not asleep, meaning that your assemblage point didn't reach that position through a normal dream. I forced it to shift.

"You certainly can reach the same position through dreaming, but I wouldn't advise you to do that at this time."

"Is it dangerous?"

"And how! Dreaming has to be a very sober affair. No false movement can be afforded. Dreaming is a process of awakening, of gaining control. Our dreaming attention must be systematically exercised, for it is the door to the second attention."

"What's the difference between the dreaming attention and the second attention?"

"The second attention is like an ocean, and the dreaming attention is like a river feeding into it. The second attention is the condition of being aware of total worlds, total like our world is total, while the dreaming attention is the condition of being aware of the items of our dreams."

He heavily stressed that the dreaming attention is the key to every movement in the sorcerers' world. He said that among the multitude of items in our dreams, there exist real energetic interferences, things that have been put in our dreams extraneously, by an alien force. To be able to find them and follow them is sorcery.

The emphasis he put on those statements was so pronounced that I had to ask him to explain them. He hesitated for a moment before answering.

"Dreams are, if not a door, a hatch into other worlds," he began. "As such, dreams are a two-way street. Our awareness goes through that hatch into other realms, and those other realms send scouts into our dreams."

"What are those scouts?"

"Energy charges that get mixed with the items of our normal dreams. They are bursts of foreign energy that come into our dreams, and we interpret them as items familiar or unfamiliar to us."

"I am sorry, don Juan, but I can't make heads or tails out of your explanation."

"You can't because you're insisting on thinking about dreams in terms known to you: what occurs to us during sleep. And I am insisting on giving you another version: a hatch into other realms of perception. Through that hatch, currents of unfamiliar energy seep in. Then the mind or the brain or whatever takes those currents of energy and turns them into parts of our dreams."

He paused, obviously to give my mind time to take in what he was telling me. "Sorcerers are aware of those currents of foreign energy," he continued. "They notice them and strive to isolate them from the normal items of their dreams."

"Why do they isolate them, don Juan?"

"Because they come from other realms. If we follow them to

their source, they serve us as guides into areas of such mystery that sorcerers shiver at the mere mention of such a possibility."

"How do sorcerers isolate them from the normal items of their dreams?"

"By the exercise and control of their dreaming attention. At one moment, our dreaming attention discovers them among the items of a dream and focuses on them, then the total dream collapses, leaving only the foreign energy."

Don Juan refused to explain the topic any further. He went back to discussing my dreaming experience and said that, all in all, he had to take my dream as being my first genuine attempt at dreaming, and that this meant I had succeeded in reaching the first gate of dreaming.

During another discussion, at a different time, he abruptly brought up the subject again. He said, "I'm going to repeat what you must do in your dreams in order to pass the first gate of dreaming. First you must focus your gaze on anything of your choice as the starting point. Then shift your gaze to other items and look at them in brief glances. Focus your gaze on as many things as you can. Remember that if you glance only briefly, the images don't shift. Then go back to the item you first looked at."

"What does it mean to pass the first gate of dreaming?"

"We reach the first gate of dreaming by becoming aware that we are falling asleep, or by having, like you did, a gigantically real dream. Once we reach the gate, we must cross it by being able to sustain the sight of any item of our dreams."

"I can almost look steadily at the items of my dreams, but they dissipate too quickly."

"This is precisely what I am trying to tell you. In order to off-set the evanescent quality of dreams, sorcerers have devised the use of the starting point item. Every time you isolate it and look at it, you get a surge of energy, so at the beginning don't look at too many things in your dreams. Four items will suffice. Later on, you may enlarge the scope until you can cover all you want, but as soon as the images begin to shift and you feel you are losing control, go back to your starting point item and start all over again."

"Do you believe that I really reached the first gate of dreaming, don Juan?"

"You did, and that's a lot. You'll find out, as you go along, how easy it'll be to do dreaming now."

I thought don Juan was either exaggerating or giving me incentive. But he assured me he was being on the level.

"The most astounding thing that happens to dreamers," he said, "is that, on reaching the first gate, they also reach the energy body."

"What exactly is the energy body?"

"It's the counterpart of the physical body. A ghostlike configuration made of pure energy."

"But isn't the physical body also made out of energy?"

"Of course it is. The difference is that the energy body has only appearance but no mass. Since it's pure energy, it can perform acts that are beyond the possibilities of the physical body."

"Such as what for example, don Juan?"

"Such as transporting itself in one instant to the ends of the universe. And dreaming is the art of tempering the energy body, of making it supple and coherent by gradually exercising it.

"Through dreaming we condense the energy body until it's a unit capable of perceiving. Its perception, although affected by our normal way of perceiving the daily world, is an independent perception. It has its own sphere."

"What is that sphere, don Juan?"

"Energy. The energy body deals with energy in terms of energy. There are three ways in which it deals with energy in dreaming: it can perceive energy as it flows, or it can use energy to boost itself like a rocket into unexpected areas, or it can perceive as we ordinarily perceive the world."

"What does it mean to perceive energy as it flows?"

"It means to *see*. It means that the energy body *sees* energy directly as a light or as a vibrating current of sorts or as a disturbance. Or it feels it directly as a jolt or as a sensation that can even be pain."

"What about the other way you talked about, don Juan? The energy body using energy as a boost."

"Since energy is its sphere, it is no problem for the energy body to use currents of energy that exist in the universe to propel itself. All it has to do is isolate them, and off it goes with them."

He stopped talking and seemed to be undecided, as if he wanted to add something but was not sure about it. He smiled at me, and, just as I was beginning to ask him a question, he continued his explanation.

"I've mentioned to you before that sorcerers isolate in their dreams scouts from other realms," he said. "Their energy bodies do that. They recognize energy and go for it. But it isn't desirable for dreamers to indulge in searching for scouts. I was reluctant to tell you about it, because of the facility with which one can get swayed by that search."

Don Juan then quickly went on to another subject. He carefully outlined for me an entire block of practices. At the time, I found that on one level it was all incomprehensible to me, yet on another it was perfectly logical and understandable. He reiterated that reaching, with deliberate control, the first gate of dreaming is a way of arriving at the energy body. But to maintain that gain is predicated on energy alone. Sorcerers get that energy by redeploying, in a more intelligent manner, the energy they have and use for perceiving the daily world.

When I urged don Juan to explain it more clearly, he added that we all have a determined quantity of basic energy. That quantity is all the energy we have, and we use all of it for perceiving and dealing with our engulfing world. He repeated various times, to emphasize it, that there is no more energy for us anywhere and, since our available energy is already engaged, there is not a single bit left in us for any extraordinary perception, such as dreaming.

"Where does that leave us?" I asked.

"It leaves us to scrounge energy for ourselves, wherever we can find it," he replied.

Don Juan explained that sorcerers have a scrounging method. They intelligently redeploy their energy by cutting down anything they consider superfluous in their lives. They call this method the sorcerers' way. In essence, the sorcerers' way, as don Juan put it, is a chain of behavioral choices for dealing with the world, choices much more intelligent than those our progenitors taught us. These sorcerers' choices are designed to revamp our lives by altering our basic reactions about being alive.

"What are those basic reactions?" I asked.

"There are two ways of facing our being alive," he said. "One is to surrender to it, either by acquiescing to its demands or by fighting those demands. The other is by molding our particular life situation to fit our own configurations."

"Can we really mold our life situation, don Juan?"

"One's particular life situation can be molded to fit one's specifications," don Juan insisted. "Dreamers do that. A wild statement? Not really, if you consider how little we know about ourselves."

He said that his interest, as a teacher, was to get me thoroughly involved with the themes of life and being alive; that is to say, with the difference between life, as a consequence of biological forces, and the act of being alive, as a matter of cognition.

"When sorcerers talk about molding one's life situation," don Juan explained, "they mean molding the awareness of being alive. Through molding this awareness, we can get enough energy to reach and sustain the energy body, and with it we can certainly mold the total direction and consequences of our lives."

Don Juan ended our conversation about dreaming admonishing me not merely to think about what he had told me but to turn his concepts into a viable way of life by a process of repetition. He claimed that everything new in our lives, such as the sorcerers' concepts he was teaching me, must be repeated to us to the point of exhaustion before we open ourselves to it. He pointed out that repetition is the way our progenitors socialized us to function in the daily world.

As I continued my dreaming practices, I gained the capability of being thoroughly aware that I was falling asleep as well as the capability of stopping in a dream to examine at will anything that was part of that dream's content. To experience this was for me no less than miraculous.

Don Juan stated that as we tighten the control over our dreams, we tighten the mastery over our dreaming attention. He was right in saying that the dreaming attention comes into play when it is called, when it is given a purpose. Its coming into play is not really a process, as one would normally understand a process: an ongoing system of operations or a series of actions or functions that bring about an end result. It is rather an awakening. Something dormant becomes suddenly functional.

▪ 3 ▪

THE SECOND GATE

OF DREAMING

J found out by means of my dreaming practices that a dreaming teacher must create a didactic synthesis in order to emphasize a given point. In essence, what don Juan wanted with my first task was to exercise my dreaming attention by focusing it on the items of my dreams. To this effect he used as a spearhead the idea of being aware of falling asleep. His subterfuge was to say that the only way to be aware of falling asleep is to examine the elements of one's dreams.

I realized, almost as soon as I had begun my dreaming practices, that exercising the dreaming attention is the essential point in dreaming. To the mind, however, it seems impossible that one can train oneself to be aware at the level of dreams. Don Juan said that the active element of such training is persistence, and that the mind and all its rational defenses cannot cope with persistence. Sooner or later, he said, the mind's barriers fall, under its impact, and the dreaming attention blooms.

As I practiced focusing and holding my dreaming attention on the items of my dreams, I began to feel a peculiar self-confidence so remarkable that I sought a comment from don Juan.

"It's your entering into the second attention that gives you that sense of self-assurance," he said. "This calls for even more sobriety on your part. Go slowly, but don't stop, and above all, don't talk about it. Just do it!"

I told him that in practice I had corroborated what he had already told me, that if one takes short glances at everything in a dream, the images do not dissolve. I commented that the difficult part is to break the initial barrier that prevents us from bringing dreams to our conscious attention. I asked don Juan to give me his opinion on this matter, for I earnestly believed that this barrier is a psychological one created by our socialization, which puts a premium on disregarding dreams.

"The barrier is more than socialization," he replied. "It's the first gate of dreaming. Now that you've overcome it, it seems stupid to you that we can't stop at will and pay attention to the items of our dreams. That's a false certainty. The first gate of dreaming has to do with the flow of energy in the universe. It's a natural obstacle."

Don Juan made me agree then that we would talk about dreaming only in the second attention and as he saw fit. He encouraged me to practice in the meantime and promised no interference on his part.

As I gained proficiency in setting up dreaming, I repeatedly experienced sensations that I deemed of great importance, such as the feeling that I was rolling into a ditch just as I was falling asleep. Don Juan never told me that they were nonsensical sensations but let me record them in my notes. I realize now how absurd I must have appeared to him. Today, if I were teaching dreaming, I would definitely discourage such a behavior. Don Juan merely made fun of me, calling me a covert egomaniac who professed to be fighting self-importance yet kept a meticulous, superpersonal diary called "My Dreams."

Every time he had an opportunity, don Juan pointed out that the energy needed to release our dreaming attention from its socialization prison comes from redeploying our existing energy. Nothing could have been truer. The emergence of our dreaming attention is a direct corollary of revamping our lives. Since we have, as don Juan said, no way to plug into any external source for a boost of energy, we must redeploy our existing energy, by any means available.

Don Juan insisted that the sorcerers' way is the best means to oil, so to speak, the wheels of energy redeployment, and that of all the items in the sorcerers' way, the most effective is "losing self-importance." He was thoroughly convinced that this is indispensable for everything sorcerers do, and for this reason he put an enormous emphasis on guiding all his students to fulfill this requirement. He was of the opinion that self-importance is not only the sorcerers' supreme enemy but the nemesis of mankind.

Don Juan's argument was that most of our energy goes into upholding our importance. This is most obvious in our endless worry about the presentation of the self, about whether or not we are admired or liked or acknowledged. He reasoned that if we were capable of losing some of that importance, two extraordinary things would happen to us. One, we would free our energy from trying to maintain the illusory idea of our grandeur; and, two, we would provide ourselves with enough energy to enter into the second attention to catch a glimpse of the actual grandeur of the universe.

It took me more than two years to be able to focus my unwavering dreaming attention on anything I wanted. And I became so proficient that I felt as if I had been doing it all my life. The eeriest part was that I could not conceive of not having had that ability. Yet I could remember how difficult it had been even to think of this as a possibility. It occurred to me that the capability of examining the contents of one's dreams must be the product of a natural configuration of our being, similar perhaps to our capability of walking. We are physically conditioned to walk only in one manner, bipedally, yet it takes a monumental effort for us to learn to walk.

This new capacity of looking in glances at the items of my dreams was coupled with a most insistent nagging to remind myself to look at the elements of my dreams. I knew about my compulsive bent of character, but in my dreams my compulsiveness was vastly augmented. It became so noticeable that not only did I resent hearing my nagging at myself but I also began to question whether it was really my compulsiveness or something else. I even thought I was losing my mind.

"I talk to myself endlessly in my dreams, reminding myself to look at things," I said to don Juan.

I had all along respected our agreement that we would talk about dreaming only when he brought up the subject. However, I thought that this was an emergency.

"Does it sound to you like it's not you but someone else?" he asked.

"Come to think of it, yes. I don't sound like myself at those times."

"Then it's not you. It's not time yet to explain it. But let's say that we are not alone in this world. Let's say that there are other worlds available to dreamers, total worlds. From those other total worlds, energetic entities sometimes come to us. The next time you hear yourself nagging at yourself in your dreams, get really angry and yell a command. Say, Stop it!"

I entered into another challenging arena: to remember in my dreams to shout that command. I believe that, perhaps, out of being so tremendously annoyed at hearing myself nagging, I did remember to shout, Stop it. The nagging ceased instantly and never again was repeated.

"Does every dreamer experience this?" I asked don Juan when I saw him again.

"Some do," he answered, uninterestedly.

I began to rant about how strange it had all been. He cut me off, saying, "You are ready now to get to the second gate of dreaming."

I seized the opportunity to seek answers for questions I had not been able to ask him. What I had experienced the first time he made me dream had been foremost in my mind. I told don Juan that I had observed the elements of my own dreams to my heart's content, and never had I felt anything even vaguely similar in terms of clarity and detail.

"The more I think about it," I said, "the more intriguing it becomes. Watching those people in that dream, I experienced a fear and revulsion impossible to forget. What was that feeling, don Juan?"

"In my opinion, your energy body hooked onto the foreign energy of that place and had the time of its life. Naturally, you felt afraid and revolted; you were examining alien energy for the first time in your life.

"You have a proclivity for behaving like the sorcerers of antiquity. The moment you have the chance, you let your assemblage point go. That time your assemblage point shifted quite a distance. The result was that you, like the old sorcerers, journeyed beyond the world we know. A most real but dangerous journey."

I bypassed the meaning of his statements in favor of my own interest and asked him, "Was that city perhaps on another planet?"

"You can't explain dreaming by way of things you know or suspect you know," he said. "All I can tell you is that the city you visited was not in this world."

"Where was it, then?"

"Out of this world, of course. You're not that stupid. That was the first thing you noticed. What got you going in circles is that you can't imagine anything being out of this world."

"Where is out of this world, don Juan?"

"Believe me, the most extravagant feature of sorcery is that configuration called out of this world. For instance, you assumed that I was seeing the same things you did. The proof is that you never asked me what I saw. You and only you saw a city and people in that city. I didn't see anything of the sort. I *saw* energy. So, out of this world was, for you alone, on that occasion, a city."

"But then, don Juan, it wasn't a real city. It existed only for me, in my mind."

"No. That's not the case. Now you want to reduce something transcendental to something mundane. You can't do that. That journey was real. You saw it as a city. I *saw* it as energy. Neither of us is right or wrong."

"My confusion comes when you talk about things being real. You said before that we reached a real place. But if it was real, how can we have two versions of it?"

"Very simple. We have two versions because we had, at that time, two different rates of uniformity and cohesion. I have explained to you that those two attributes are the key to perceiving."

"Do you think that I can go back to that particular city?"

"You got me there. I don't know. Or perhaps I do know but can't explain it. Or perhaps I can explain it but I don't want to. You'll have to wait and figure out for yourself which is the case."

He refused any further discussion.

"Let's get on with our business," he said. "You reach the second gate of dreaming when you wake up from a dream into another dream. You can have as many dreams as you want or as many as you are capable of, but you must exercise adequate control and not wake up in the world we know."

I had a jolt of panic. "Are you saying that I should never wake up in this world?" I asked.

"No, I didn't mean that. But now that you have pointed it out, I have to tell you that it is an alternative. The sorcerers of antiquity used to do that, never wake up in the world we know. Some of the sorcerers of my line have done it too. It certainly can be done, but I don't recommend it. What I want is for you to wake up naturally when you are through with dreaming, but while you are dreaming, I want you to dream that you wake up in another dream."

I heard myself asking the same question I had asked the first time he told me about setting up dreaming. "But is it possible to do that?"

Don Juan obviously caught on to my mindlessness and laughingly repeated the answer he had given me before. "Of course it's possible. This control is no different from the control we have over any situation in our daily lives."

I quickly got over my embarrassment and was ready to ask more questions, but don Juan anticipated me and began to explain facets of the second gate of dreaming, an explanation that made me yet more uneasy.

"There's one problem with the second gate," he said. "It's a problem that can be serious, depending on one's bent of character. If our tendency is to indulge in clinging to things or situations, we are in for a sock in the jaw."

"In what way, don Juan?"

"Think for a moment. You've already experienced the outlandish joy of examining your dreams' contents. Imagine yourself going from dream to dream, watching everything, examining every detail. It's very easy to realize that one may sink to mortal depths. Especially if one is given to indulging."

"Wouldn't the body or the brain naturally put a stop to it?"

"If it's a natural sleeping situation, meaning normal, yes. But this is not a normal situation. This is dreaming. A dreamer on crossing the first gate has already reached the energy body. So what is really going through the second gate, hopping from dream to dream, is the energy body."

"What's the implication of all this, don Juan?"

"The implication is that on crossing the second gate you must intend a greater and more sober control over your dreaming attention: the only safety valve for dreamers."

"What is this safety valve?"

"You will find out for yourself that the true goal of dreaming is to perfect the energy body. A perfect energy body, among other things of course, has such a control over the dreaming attention that it makes it stop when needed. This is the safety valve dreamers have. No matter how indulging they might be, at a given time, their dreaming attention must make them surface."

I started all over again on another dreaming quest. This time the goal was more elusive and the difficulty even greater. Exactly as with my first task, I could not begin to figure out what to do. I had the discouraging suspicion that all my practice was not going to be of much help this time. After countless failures, I gave up and settled down to simply continue my practice of fixing my dreaming attention on every item of my dreams. Accepting my shortcomings seemed to give me a boost, and I became even more adept at sustaining the view of any item in my dreams.

A year went by without any change. Then one day something changed. As I was watching a window in a dream, trying to find out if I could catch a glimpse of the scenery outside the room, some windlike force, which I felt as a buzzing in my ears, pulled me through the window to the outside. Just before that pull, my dreaming attention had been caught by a strange structure some distance away. It looked like a tractor. The next thing I knew, I was standing by it, examining it.

I was perfectly aware that I was dreaming. I looked around to find out if I could tell from what window I had been looking. The scene was that of a farm in the countryside. No buildings were in sight. I wanted to ponder this. However, the quantity of farm machinery lying around, as if abandoned, took all my attention. I examined mowing machines, tractors, grain harvesters, disk plows, thrashers. There were so many that I forgot my original dream. What I wanted then was to orient myself by watching the immediate scenery. There was something in the distance that looked like a billboard and some telephone poles around it.

The instant I focused my attention on that billboard, I was next to it. The steel structure of the billboard gave me a fright. It was menacing. On the billboard itself was a picture of a building. I read the text; it was an advertisement for a motel. I had a peculiar certainty that I was in Oregon or northern California.

I looked for other features in the environment of my dream. I saw mountains very far away and some green, round hills not too far. On those hills were clumps of what I thought were California oak trees. I wanted to be pulled by the green hills, but what pulled me were the distant mountains. I was convinced that they were the Sierras.

All my dreaming energy left me on those mountains. But before it did, I was pulled by every possible feature. My dream ceased to be a dream. As far as my capacity to perceive was concerned, I was veritably in the Sierras, zooming into ravines, boulders, trees, caves. I went from scarp faces to mountain peaks until I had no more drive and could not focus my dreaming attention on anything. I felt myself losing control. Finally, there was no more scenery, just darkness.

"You have reached the second gate of dreaming," don Juan said when I narrated my dream to him. "What you should do next is to cross it. Crossing the second gate is a very serious affair; it requires a most disciplined effort."

I was not sure I had fulfilled the task he outlined for me, because I had not really woken up in another dream. I asked don Juan about this irregularity.

"The mistake was mine," he said. "I told you that one has to wake up in another dream, but what I meant is that one has to change dreams in an orderly and precise manner, the way you have done it.

"With the first gate, you wasted a lot of time looking exclusively for your hands. This time, you went directly to the solution without bothering to follow the given command: to wake up in another dream."

Don Juan said that there are two ways of properly crossing the second gate of dreaming. One is to wake up in another dream, that is to say, to dream that one is having a dream and then dream that one wakes up from it. The alternative is to use the items of a dream to trigger another dream, exactly as I had done.

Just as he had been doing all along, don Juan let me practice without any interference on his part. And I corroborated the two alternatives he described. Either I dreamt that I was having a dream from which I dreamt I woke up or I zoomed from a definite item accessible to my immediate dreaming attention to another one, not quite accessible. Or I entered into a slight variation of the second: I gazed at any item of a dream, maintaining the gaze until the item changed shape and, by changing shape, pulled me into another dream through a buzzing vortex. Never was I capable, however, of deciding beforehand which of the three I would follow. My dreaming practices always ended by my running out of dreaming attention and finally waking up or by my falling into dark, deep slumber.

Everything went smoothly in my practices. The only disturbance I had was a peculiar interference, a jolt of fear or discomfort I had begun to experience with increasing frequency. My way of discarding it was to believe that it was related to my ghastly eating habits or to the fact that, in those days, don Juan was giving me a profusion of hallucinogenic plants as part of my training. Those jolts became so prominent, however, that I had to ask don Juan's advice.

"You have entered now into the most dangerous facet of the

sorcerers' knowledge," he began. "It is sheer dread, a veritable nightmare. I could joke with you and say that I didn't mention this possibility to you out of regard for your cherished rationality, but I can't. Every sorcerer has to face it. Here is where, I fear, you might very well think you're going off the deep end."

Don Juan very solemnly explained that life and consciousness, being exclusively a matter of energy, are not solely the property of organisms. He said that sorcerers have *seen* that there are two types of conscious beings roaming the earth, the organic and the inorganic, and that in comparing one with the other, they have *seen* that both are luminous masses crossed from every imaginable angle by millions of the universe's energy filaments. They are different from each other in their shape and in their degree of brightness. Inorganic beings are long and candlelike but opaque, whereas organic beings are round and by far the brighter. Another noteworthy difference, which don Juan said sorcerers have *seen*, is that the life and consciousness of organic beings is short-lived, because they are made to hurry, whereas the life of inorganic beings is infinitely longer and their consciousness infinitely more calm and deeper.

"Sorcerers find no problem interacting with them," don Juan went on. "Inorganic beings possess the crucial ingredient for interaction, consciousness."

"But do these inorganic beings really exist? Like you and I exist?" I asked.

"Of course they do," he replied. "Believe me, sorcerers are very intelligent creatures; under no condition would they toy with aberrations of the mind and then take them for real."

"Why do you say they are alive?"

"For sorcerers, having life means having consciousness. It means having an assemblage point and its surrounding glow of awareness, a condition that points out to sorcerers that the being in front of them, organic or inorganic, is thoroughly capable of perceiving. Perceiving is understood by sorcerers as the precondition of being alive."

"Then the inorganic beings must also die. Is that true, don Juan?"

"Naturally. They lose their awareness just like we do, except that the length of their consciousness is staggering to the mind."

"Do these inorganic beings appear to sorcerers?"

"It's very difficult to tell what is what with them. Let's say that those beings are enticed by us or, better yet, compelled to interact with us."

Don Juan peered at me most intently. "You're not taking in any of this at all," he said with the tone of someone who has reached a conclusion.

"It's nearly impossible for me to think about this rationally," I said.

"I warned you that the subject will tax your reason. The proper thing to do then is to suspend judgment and let things take their course, meaning that you let the inorganic beings come to you."

"Are you serious, don Juan?"

"Deadly serious. The difficulty with inorganic beings is that their awareness is very slow in comparison with ours. It will take years for a sorcerer to be acknowledged by inorganic beings. So, it is advisable to have patience and wait. Sooner or later they show up. But not like you or I would show up. Theirs is a most peculiar way to make themselves known."

"How do sorcerers entice them? Do they have a ritual?"

"Well, they certainly don't stand in the middle of the road and call out to them with trembling voices at the stroke of midnight, if that's what you mean."

"What do they do then?"

"They entice them in dreaming. I said that what's involved is more than enticing them; by the act of dreaming, sorcerers compel those beings to interact with them."

"How do sorcerers compel them by the act of dreaming?"

"Dreaming is sustaining the position where the assemblage

point has shifted in dreams. This act creates a distinctive energy charge, which attracts their attention. It's like bait to fish; they'll go for it. Sorcerers, by reaching and crossing the first two gates of dreaming, set bait for those beings and compel them to appear.

"By going through the two gates, you have made your bidding known to them. Now, you must wait for a sign from them."

"What would the sign be, don Juan?"

"Possibly the appearance of one of them, although that seems too soon. I am of the opinion that their sign will be simply some interference in your dreaming. I believe that the jolts of fear you are experiencing nowadays are not indigestion but energy jolts sent to you by the inorganic beings."

"What should I do?"

"You must gauge your expectations."

I could not understand what he meant, and he carefully explained that our normal expectation when engaging in interaction with our fellow men or with other organic beings is to get an immediate reply to our solicitation. With inorganic beings, however, since they are separated from us by a most formidable barrier—energy that moves at a different speed— sorcerers must gauge their expectations and sustain the solicitation for as long as it takes to be acknowledged.

"Do you mean, don Juan, that the solicitation is the same as the dreaming practices?"

"Yes. But for a perfect result, you must add to your practices the intent of reaching those inorganic beings. Send a feeling of power and confidence to them, a feeling of strength, of detachment. Avoid at any cost sending a feeling of fear or morbidity. They are pretty morbid by themselves; to add your morbidity to them is unnecessary, to say the least."

"I'm not clear, don Juan, about the way they appear to sorcerers. What is the peculiar way they make themselves known?"

"They do, at times, materialize themselves in the daily world, right in front of us. Most of the time, though, their invisible presence is marked by a bodily jolt, a shiver of sorts that comes from the marrow of the bones."

"What about in dreaming, don Juan?"

"In dreaming we have the total opposite. At times, we feel them the way you are feeling them, as a jolt of fear. Most of the time, they materialize themselves right in front of us. Since at the beginning of dreaming we have no experience whatsoever with them, they might imbue us with fear beyond measure. That is a real danger to us. Through the channel of fear, they can follow us to the daily world, with disastrous results for us."

"In what way, don Juan?"

"Fear can settle down in our lives, and we would have to be mavericks to deal with it. Inorganic beings can be worse than a pest. Through fear they can easily drive us raving mad."

"What do sorcerers do with inorganic beings?"

"They mingle with them. They turn them into allies. They form associations, create extraordinary friendships. I call them vast enterprises, where perception plays the uppermost role. We are social beings. We unavoidably seek the company of consciousness.

"With inorganic beings, the secret is not to fear them. And this must be done from the beginning. The intent one has to send out to them has to be of power and abandon. In that intent one must encode the message 'I don't fear you. Come to see me. If you do, I'll welcome you. If you don't want to come, I'll miss you.' With a message like this, they'll get so curious that they'll come for sure."

"Why should they come to seek me, or why on earth should I seek them?"

"Dreamers, whether they like it or not, in their dreaming seek associations with other beings. This may come to you as a shock, but dreamers automatically seek groups of beings, nexuses of inorganic beings in this case. Dreamers seek them avidly."

"This is very strange to me, don Juan. Why would dreamers do that?"

"The novelty for us is the inorganic beings. And the novelty for them is one of our kind crossing the boundaries of their realm. The thing you must bear in mind from now on is that inorganic beings with their superb consciousness exert a tremendous pull over dreamers and can easily transport them into worlds beyond description.

"The sorcerers of antiquity used them, and they are the ones who coined the name allies. Their allies taught them to move the assemblage point out of the egg's boundaries into the non-human universe. So when they transport a sorcerer, they transport him to worlds beyond the human domain."

As I heard him talk, I was plagued by strange fears and misgivings, which he promptly realized.

"You are a religious man to the end." He laughed. "Now, you're feeling the devil breathing down your neck. Think about dreaming in these terms: dreaming is perceiving more than what we believe it is possible to perceive."

In my waking hours, I worried about the possibility that inorganic conscious beings really existed. When I was dreaming, however, my conscious worries did not have much effect. The jolts of physical fear continued, but whenever they happened a strange calmness always trailed behind, a calmness that took control of me and let me proceed as if I had no fear at all.

It seemed at that time that every breakthrough in dreaming happened to me suddenly, without warning. The presence of inorganic beings in my dreams was no exception. It happened while I was dreaming about a circus I knew in my childhood. The setting looked like a town in the mountains in Arizona. I began to watch people with the vague hope I always had that I would see again the people I had seen the first time don Juan made me enter into the second attention.

As I watched them, I felt a sizable jolt of nervousness in the pit of my stomach; it was like a punch. The jolt distracted me, and I lost sight of the people, the circus, and the mountain town in Arizona. In their place stood two strange-looking figures. They were thin, less than a foot wide, but long, perhaps seven feet. They were looming over me like two gigantic earthworms.

I knew that it was a dream, but I also knew that I was *seeing*. Don Juan had discussed *seeing* in my normal awareness and in the second attention as well. Although I was incapable of experiencing it myself, I thought I had understood the idea of directly perceiving energy. In that dream, looking at those two strange apparitions, I realized that I was *seeing* the energy essence of something unbelievable.

I remained very calm. I did not move. The most remarkable thing to me was that they didn't dissolve or change into something else. They were cohesive beings that retained their candlelike shape. Something in them was forcing something in me to hold the view of their shape. I knew it because something was telling me that if I did not move, they would not move either.

It all came to an end, at a given moment, when I woke up with a fright. I was immediately besieged by fears. A deep preoccupation took hold of me. It was not psychological worry but rather a bodily sense of anguish, sadness with no apparent foundation.

The two strange shapes appeared to me from then on in every one of my dreaming sessions. Eventually, it was as if I dreamt only to encounter them. They never attempted to move toward me or to interfere with me in any way. They just stood there, immobile, in front of me, for as long as my dream lasted. Not only did I never make any effort to change my dreams but I even forgot the original quest of my dreaming practices.

When I finally discussed with don Juan what was happening to me, I had spent months solely viewing the two shapes.

them closed. Then he guided me to sit down on some rocks. I felt the hardness and the coldness of the rocks. The rocks were slanted; it was difficult to keep my balance.

"Sit here and visualize their shape until they are just like they are in your dreams," don Juan said in my ear. "Let me know when you have them in focus."

It took me very little time and effort to have a complete mental picture of their shape, just like in my dreams. It did not surprise me at all that I could do it. What shocked me was that, although I tried desperately to let don Juan know I had pictured them in my mind, I could not voice my words or open my eyes. I was definitely awake. I could hear everything.

I heard don Juan say, "You can open your eyes now." I opened them with no difficulty. I was sitting cross-legged on some rocks, which were not the same ones I had felt under me when I sat down. Don Juan was just behind me to my right. I tried to turn around to face him, but he forced my head to remain straight. And then I saw two dark figures, like two thin tree trunks, right in front of me.

I stared at them openmouthed; they were not as tall as in my dreams. They had shrunk to half their size. Instead of being shapes of opaque luminosity, they were now two condensed, dark, almost black, menacing sticks.

"Get up and grab one of them," don Juan ordered me, "and don't let go, no matter how it shakes you."

I definitely did not want to do anything of the sort, but some unknown drive made me stand up against my will. I had at that moment the clear realization that I would end up doing what he had ordered me to, although I had no conscious intention of doing so.

Mechanically, I advanced toward the two figures, my heart pounding nearly out of my chest. I grabbed the one to my right. What I felt was an electric discharge that almost made me drop the dark figure.

Don Juan's voice came to me as if he had been yelling from a distance away. "You drop it and you're done for," he said.

I held on to the figure, which twirled and shook. Not like a massive animal would, but like something quite fluffy and light, although strongly electrical. We rolled and turned on the sand of the gully for quite some time. It gave me jolt after jolt of some sickening electric current. I thought it was sickening because I fancied it to be different from the energy I had always encountered in our daily world. When it hit my body, it tickled me and made me yell and growl like an animal, not in anguish but in a strange anger.

It finally became a still, almost solid form under me. It lay inert. I asked don Juan if it was dead, but I did not hear my voice.

"Not a chance," said someone laughing, someone who was not don Juan. "You've just depleted its energy charge. But don't get up yet. Lie there just a moment longer."

I looked at don Juan with a question in my eyes. He was examining me with great curiosity. Then he helped me up. The dark figure remained on the ground. I wanted to ask don Juan if the dark figure was all right. Again, I could not voice my question. Then I did something extravagant. I took it all for real. Up to that moment something in my mind was preserving my rationality by taking what was happening as a dream, a dream induced by don Juan's machinations.

I went to the figure on the ground and tried to lift it up. I could not put my arms around it because it had no mass. I became disoriented. The same voice, which was not don Juan's, told me to lie down on top of the inorganic being. I did it, and both of us got up in one motion, the inorganic being like a dark shadow attached to me. It gently separated from me and disappeared, leaving me with an extremely pleasant feeling of completeness.

It took me more than twenty-four hours to regain total control of my faculties. I slept most of the time. Don Juan checked me from time to time by asking me the same question, "Was the inorganic being's energy like fire or like water?"

My throat seemed scorched. I could not tell him that the energy jolts I had felt were like jets of electrified water. I have never felt jets of electrified water in my life. I am not sure if it is possible to produce them or to feel them, but that was the image playing in my mind every time don Juan asked his key question.

Don Juan was asleep when I finally knew I was completely recovered. Knowing that his question was of great importance, I woke him up and told him what I had felt.

"You are not going to have helping friends among the inorganic beings, but relationships of annoying dependence," he stated. "Be extremely careful. Watery inorganic beings are more given to excesses. The old sorcerers believed that they were more loving, more capable of imitating, or perhaps even having feelings. As opposed to the fiery ones, who were thought to be more serious, more contained than the others, but also more pompous."

"What's the meaning of all this for me, don Juan?"

"The meaning is too vast to discuss at this time. My recommendation is that you vanquish fear from your dreams and from your life, in order to safeguard your unity. The inorganic being you depleted of energy and then recharged again was thrilled out of its candlelike shape with it. It'll come to you for more."

"Why didn't you stop me, don Juan?"

"You didn't give me time. Besides, you didn't even hear me shouting at you to leave the inorganic being on the ground."

"You should have lectured me, beforehand, the way you always do, about all the possibilities."

"I didn't know all the possibilities. In matters of the inorganic beings, I am nearly a novice. I refused that part of the sorcerers' knowledge on the ground that it is too cumbersome and capricious. I don't want to be at the mercy of any entity, organic or inorganic."

That was the end of our exchange. I should have been worried because of his definitely negative reaction, but I was not. I somehow was certain that whatever I had done was all right.

I continued my dreaming practices without any interference from the inorganic beings.

· 4 ·

THE FIXATION OF THE

ASSEMBLAGE POINT

Since our agreement had been to discuss dreaming only when don Juan considered it necessary, I rarely asked him about it and never insisted on continuing my questions beyond a certain point. I was more than eager, therefore, to listen to him whenever he decided to take up the subject. His comments or discussions on dreaming were invariably cushioned in other topics of his teachings, and they were always suddenly and abruptly brought in.

We were engaged in some unrelated conversation once, while I was visiting with him in his house, when without any preamble he said that, by means of their dreaming contacts with inorganic beings, the old sorcerers became immensely well-versed in the manipulation of the assemblage point, a vast and ominous subject.

I immediately grabbed the opportunity and asked don Juan for an estimate of the time when the old sorcerers might have lived. At various opportunities before, I had asked the same question, but he never gave me a satisfactory answer. I was confident, however, that at the moment, perhaps because he had brought up the subject himself, he might be willing to oblige me.

"A most trying subject," he said. The way he said it made me believe he was discarding my question. I was quite surprised when he continued talking. "It'll tax your rationality as much as the topic of inorganic beings. By the way, what do you think about them now?"

"I have let my opinions rest," I said. "I can't afford to think one way or another."

My answer delighted him. He laughed and commented on his own fears of and aversions to the inorganic beings.

"They have never been my cup of tea," he said. "Of course, the main reason was my fear of them. I was unable to get over it when I had to, and then it became fixed."

"Do you fear them now, don Juan?"

"It's not quite fear I feel but revulsion. I don't want any part of them."

"Is there any particular reason for this revulsion?"

"The best reason in the world: we are antithetical. They love slavery, and I love freedom. They love to buy, and I don't sell."

I became inexplicably agitated and brusquely told him that the subject was so farfetched for me that I could not take it seriously.

He stared at me, smiling, and said, "The best thing to do with inorganic beings is what you do: deny their existence but visit with them regularly and maintain that you are dreaming and in dreaming anything is possible. This way you don't commit yourself."

I felt strangely guilty, although I could not figure out why. I felt compelled to ask, "What are you referring to, don Juan?"

"To your visits with the inorganic beings," he replied dryly.

"Are you kidding? What visits?"

"I didn't want to discuss this, but I think it's time I tell you that the nagging voice you heard, reminding you to fix your dreaming attention on the items of your dreams, was the voice of an inorganic being."

I thought don Juan was completely irrational. I became so irritated that I even yelled at him. He laughed at me and asked me to tell him about my irregular dreaming sessions. That request surprised me. I had never mentioned to anyone that every so often I used to zoom out of a dream, pulled by a given item, but instead of my changing dreams, as I should have, the total mood of the dream changed and I would find myself in a dimension unknown to me. I soared in it, directed by some invisible guide, which made me twirl around and around. I always awoke from one of these dreams still twirling, and I continued tossing and turning for a long time before I fully woke up.

"Those are bona fide meetings you are having with your inorganic being friends," don Juan said.

I did not want to argue with him, but neither did I want to agree. I remained silent. I had forgotten my question about the old sorcerers, but don Juan picked up the subject again.

"My understanding is that the old sorcerers existed perhaps as far back as ten thousand years ago," he said, smiling and watching my reaction.

Basing my response on current archaeological data on the migration of Asiatic nomadic tribes to the Americas, I said that I believed his date was incorrect. Ten thousand years was too far back.

"You have your knowledge and I have mine," he said. "My knowledge is that the old sorcerers ruled for four thousand years, from seven thousand to three thousand years ago. Three thousand years ago, they went to nothing. And from then on, sorcerers have been regrouping, restructuring what was left of the old ones."

"How can you be so sure about your dates?" I asked.

"How can you be so sure about yours?" he retorted.

I told him that archaeologists have foolproof methods to establish the date of past cultures. Again he retorted that sorcerers have foolproof methods of their own.

"I'm not trying to be contrary or argue you down," he continued, "but someday soon you may be able to ask someone who knows for sure."

"No one can know this for sure, don Juan."

"This is another of those impossible things to believe, but there is somebody who can verify all this. You'll meet that person someday."

"Come on, don Juan, you've got to be joking. Who can verify what happened seven thousand years ago?"

"Very simple, one of the old sorcerers we've been talking about. The one I met. He's the one who told me all about the old sorcerers. I hope you remember what I am going to tell you about that particular man. He is the key to many of our endeavors, and he's also the one you have to meet."

I told don Juan that I was hanging on every word he said, even though I did not understand what he was saying. He accused me of humoring him and not believing a word about the old sorcerers. I admitted that in my state of daily consciousness, of course, I had not believed those farfetched stories. But neither had I in the second attention, although there I should have had a different reaction.

"Only when you ponder what I said does it become a farfetched story," he remarked. "If you don't involve your common sense, it remains purely a matter of energy."

"Why did you say, don Juan, that I am going to meet one of the old sorcerers?"

"Because you are. It is vital that the two of you meet, someday. But, for the moment, just let me tell you another farfetched story about one of the naguals of my line, the nagual Sebastian."

Don Juan told me then that the nagual Sebastian had been a sexton in a church in southern Mexico around the beginning of the eighteenth century. In his account, don Juan stressed how sorcerers, past or present, seek and find refuge in established institutions, such as the Church. It was his idea that because of their superior discipline, sorcerers are trustworthy employees and that they are avidly sought by institutions that are always in dire need of such persons. Don Juan maintained that as long as no one is aware of the sorcerers' doings, their lack of ideological sympathies makes them appear as model workers.

Don Juan continued his story and said that one day, while Sebastian was performing his duties as a sexton, a strange man came to the church, an old Indian who seemed to be ill. In a weak voice he told Sebastian that he needed help. The nagual thought that the Indian wanted the parish priest, but the man, making a great effort, addressed the nagual. In a harsh and direct tone, he told him that he knew that Sebastian was not only a sorcerer but a nagual.

Sebastian, quite alarmed by this sudden turn of events, pulled the Indian aside and demanded an apology. The man replied that he was not there to apologize but to get specialized help. He needed, he said, to receive the nagual's energy in order to maintain his life, which, he assured Sebastian, had spanned thousands of years but at the moment was ebbing away.

Sebastian, who was a very intelligent man, unwilling to pay attention to such nonsense, urged the Indian to stop clowning around. The old man became angry and threatened Sebastian with exposing him and his group to the ecclesiastical authorities if he did not comply with his request.

Don Juan reminded me that those were the times when the ecclesiastical authorities were brutally and systematically eradicating heretical practices among the Indians of the New World. The man's threat was not something to be taken lightly; the nagual and his group were indeed in mortal danger. Sebastian asked the Indian how he could give him energy. The man explained that naguals, by means of their discipline, gain a peculiar energy that they store in their bodies and that he would get it painlessly from Sebastian's energy center on his navel. In return for it, Sebastian would get not only the opportunity to continue his activities unscathed but also a gift of power.

The knowledge that he was being manipulated by the old Indian did not sit right with the nagual, but the man was inflexible and left him no alternative but to comply with his request.

Don Juan assured me that the old Indian was not exaggerating about his claims at all. He turned out to be one of the sorcerers of ancient times, one of those known as the *death defiers*. He had apparently survived to the present by manipulating his assemblage point in ways that only he knew about.

Don Juan said that what transpired between Sebastian and that man later became the ground for an agreement that had bound all six naguals who followed Sebastian. The death defier kept his word; in exchange for energy from every one of those men, he made a donation to the giver, a gift of power. Sebastian had to accept such a gift, although reluctantly; he had been cornered and had no other choice. All the other naguals who followed him, however, gladly and proudly accepted their gifts.

Don Juan concluded his story, saying that over time the death defier came to be known as the *tenant*. And for over two hundred years, the naguals of don Juan's line honored that binding agreement, creating a symbiotic relationship that changed the course and final goal of their lineage.

Don Juan did not care to explain the story any further, and I was left with a strange sensation of truthfulness, which was more bothersome to me than I could have imagined.

"How did he get to live that long?" I asked.

"No one knows," don Juan replied. "All we've known about him, for generations, is what he tells us. The death defier is the one I asked about the old sorcerers, and he told me that they were at their peak three thousand years ago."

"How do you know he was telling you the truth?" I asked.

Don Juan shook his head in amazement, if not revulsion. "When you're facing that inconceivable unknown out there," he said, pointing all around him, "you don't fool around with petty lies. Petty lies are only for people who have never witnessed what's out there, waiting for them."

"What's waiting for us out there, don Juan?"

His answer, a seemingly innocuous phrase, was more terrifying to me than if he had described the most horrendous thing.

"Something utterly impersonal," he said.

He must have noticed that I was coming apart. He made me change levels of awareness to make my fright vanish.

A few months later, my dreaming practices took a strange turn. I began to get, in my dreams, replies to questions I was planning to ask don Juan. The most impressive part of this oddity was that it quickly lapsed into my waking hours. And one day, while I was sitting at my desk, I got a reply to an unvoiced question about the realness of inorganic beings. I had *seen* inorganic beings in dreams so many times I had begun to think of them as real. I reminded myself I had even touched one, in a state of seminormal consciousness in the Sonoran desert. And my dreams had been periodically deviated to views of worlds I seriously doubted could have been products of my mentality. I wished to give don Juan my best shot, in terms of a concise query, so I molded a question in my mind: if one is to accept that inorganic beings are as real as people, where, in the physicality of the universe, is the realm in which they exist?

After formulating the question to myself, I heard a strange laughter, just as I had the day I wrestled with the inorganic being. Then a man's voice answered me. "That realm exists in a particular position of the assemblage point," it said. "Just like your world exists in the habitual position of the assemblage point."

The last thing I wanted was to enter into a dialogue with a disembodied voice, so I stood up and ran out of my house. The thought occurred to me that I was losing my mind. Another worry to add to my collection of worries.

The voice had been so clear and authoritative that it not only intrigued me but terrified me. I waited with great trepidation for oncoming barrages of that voice, but the event was never repeated. At the first opportunity I had, I consulted with don Juan.

He was not impressed in the least. "You must understand, once and for all, that things like this are very normal in the life of a sorcerer," he said. "You are not going mad; you are simply hearing the voice of the dreaming emissary. Upon crossing the first or second gate of dreaming, dreamers reach a threshold of energy and begin to see things or to hear voices. Not really plural voices, but a singular voice. Sorcerers call it the voice of the dreaming emissary."

"What is the dreaming emissary?"

"Alien energy that has conciseness. Alien energy that purports to aid dreamers by telling them things. The problem with the dreaming emissary is that it can tell only what the sorcerers already know or should know, were they worth their salt."

"To say that it's alien energy that has conciseness doesn't help me at all, don Juan. What kind of energy—benign, malignant, right, wrong, what?"

"It's just what I said, alien energy. An impersonal force that we turn into a very personal one because it has a voice. Some sorcerers swear by it. They even see it. Or, as you yourself have done, they simply hear it as a man's or a woman's voice. And the voice can tell them about the state of things, which most of the time they take as sacred advice."

"Why do some of us hear it as a voice?"

"We see it or hear it because we maintain our assemblage points fixed on a specific new position; the more intense this fixation, the more intense our experience of the emissary. Watch out! You may see it and feel it as a naked woman."

Don Juan laughed at his own remark, but I was too scared for levity.

"Is this force capable of materializing itself?" I asked.

"Certainly," he replied. "And it all depends on how fixed the assemblage point is. But, rest assured, if you are capable of maintaining a degree of detachment, nothing happens. The emissary remains what it is: an impersonal force that acts on us because of the fixation of our assemblage points."

"Is its advice safe and sound?"

"It cannot be advice. It only tells us what's what, and then we draw the inferences ourselves."

I told don Juan then about what the voice had said to me.

"It's just like I said," don Juan remarked. "The emissary didn't tell you anything new. Its statements were correct, but it only seemed to be revealing things to you. What the emissary did was merely repeat what you already knew."

"I'm afraid I can't claim that I knew all that, don Juan."

"Yes, you can. You know now infinitely more about the mystery of the universe than what you rationally suspect. But that's our human malady, to know more about the mystery of the universe than we suspect."

Having experienced this incredible phenomenon all by myself, without don Juan's coaching, made me feel elated. I wanted more information about the emissary. I began to ask don Juan whether he also heard the emissary's voice.

He interrupted me and with a broad smile said, "Yes, yes. The emissary also talks to me. In my youth I used to see it as a friar with a black cowl. A talking friar who used to scare the daylights out of me, every time. Then, when my fear was more manageable, it became a disembodied voice, which tells me things to this day."

"What kinds of things, don Juan?"

"Anything I focus my intent on, things I don't want to take the trouble of following up myself. Like, for example, details about the behavior of my apprentices. What they do when I am not around. It tells me things about you, in particular. The emissary tells me everything you do."

At that point, I really did not care for the direction our conversation had taken. I frantically searched my mind for questions about other topics while he roared with laughter.

"Is the dreaming emissary an inorganic being?" I asked.

"Let's say that the dreaming emissary is a force that comes from the realm of inorganic beings. This is the reason dreamers always encounter it."

"Do you mean, don Juan, that every dreamer hears or sees the emissary?"

"Everyone hears the emissary; very few see it or feel it."

"Do you have any explanation for this?"

"No. Besides, I really don't care about the emissary. At one point in my life, I had to make a decision whether to concentrate on the inorganic beings and follow in the footsteps of the old sorcerers or to refuse it all. My teacher, the nagual Julian, helped me make up my mind to refuse it. I've never regretted that decision."

"Do you think I should refuse the inorganic beings myself, don Juan?"

He did not answer me; instead, he explained that the whole realm of inorganic beings is always poised to teach. Perhaps because inorganic beings have a deeper consciousness than ours, they feel compelled to take us under their wings.

"I didn't see any point in becoming their pupil," he added. "Their price is too high."

"What is their price?"

"Our lives, our energy, our devotion to them. In other words, our freedom."

"But what do they teach?"

"Things pertinent to their world. The same way we ourselves would teach them, if we were capable of teaching them, things pertinent to our world. Their method, however, is to take our basic self as a gauge of what we need and then teach us accordingly. A most dangerous affair!"

"I don't see why it would be dangerous."

"If someone was going to take your basic self as a gauge, with all your fears and greed and envy, et cetera, et cetera, and teach you what fulfills that horrible state of being, what do you think the result would be?"

I had no comeback. I thought I understood perfectly well the reasons for his rejection.

"The problem with the old sorcerers was that they learned wonderful things, but on the basis of their unadulterated lower selves," don Juan went on. "The inorganic beings became their allies, and, by means of deliberate examples, they taught the old sorcerers marvels. Their allies performed the actions, and the old sorcerers were guided step by step to copy those actions, without changing anything about their basic nature."

"Do these relationships with inorganic beings exist today?"

"I can't answer that truthfully. All I can say is that I can't conceive of having a relationship like that myself. Involvements of this nature curtail our search for freedom by consuming all our available energy. In order to really follow their allies' example, the old sorcerers had to spend their lives in the realm of the inorganic beings. The amount of energy needed to accomplish such a sustained journey is staggering."

"Do you mean, don Juan, that the old sorcerers were able to exist in those realms like we exist here?"

"Not quite like we exist here, but certainly they lived: they retained their awareness, their individuality. The dreaming emissary became the most vital entity for those sorcerers. If a sorcerer wants to live in the realm of the inorganic beings, the emissary is the perfect bridge; it speaks, and its bent is to teach, to guide."

"Have you ever been in that realm, don Juan?"

"Countless times. And so have you. But there is no point in talking about it now. You haven't cleared all the debris from your dreaming attention yet. We'll talk about that realm some-day."

"Do I gather, don Juan, that you don't approve of or like the emissary?"

"I neither approve of it nor like it. It belongs to another mood, the old sorcerers' mood. Besides, its teachings and guid-ance in our world are nonsense. And for that nonsense the emissary charges us enormities in terms of energy. One day you will agree with me. You'll see."

In the tone of don Juan's words, I caught a veiled implication of his belief that I disagreed with him about the emissary. I was about to confront him with it when I heard the emissary's voice in my ears. "He's right," the voice said. "You like me because you find nothing wrong with exploring all possibilities. You want knowledge; knowledge is power. You don't want to remain safe in the routines and beliefs of your daily world."

The emissary said all that in English with a marked Pacific Coast intonation. Then it shifted into Spanish. I heard a slight Argentine accent. I had never heard the emissary speaking like this before. It fascinated me. The emissary told me about fulfill-ment, knowledge; about how far away I was from my birth-place; about my craving for adventure and my near obsession with new things, new horizons. The voice even talked to me in Portuguese, with a definite inflection from the southern pam-pas.

To hear that voice pouring out all this flattery not only scared me but nauseated me. I told don Juan, right on the spot, that I had to stop my dreaming training. He looked up at me, caught by surprise. But when I repeated what I had heard, he agreed I should stop, although I sensed he was doing it only to appease me.

A few weeks later, I found my reaction a bit hysterical and

my decision to withdraw unsound. I went back to my dreaming practices. I was sure don Juan was aware that I had canceled out my withdrawal.

On one of my visits to him, quite abruptly, he spoke about dreams. "Just because we haven't been taught to emphasize dreams as a genuine field for exploration doesn't mean they are not one," he began. "Dreams are analyzed for their meaning or are taken as portents, but never are they taken as a realm of real events.

"To my knowledge, only the old sorcerers did that," don Juan went on, "but at the end they flubbed it. They got greedy, and when they came to a crucial crossroads, they took the wrong fork. They put all their eggs in one basket: the fixation of the assemblage point on the thousands of positions it can adopt."

Don Juan expressed his bewilderment at the fact that out of all the marvelous things the old sorcerers learned exploring those thousands of positions, only the art of dreaming and the art of stalking remain. He reiterated that the art of dreaming is concerned with the displacement of the assemblage point. Then he defined stalking as the art that deals with the fixation of the assemblage point on any location to which it is displaced.

"To fixate the assemblage point on any new spot means to acquire cohesion," he said. "You have been doing just that in your dreaming practices."

"I thought I was perfecting my energy body," I said, somehow surprised at his statement.

"You are doing that and much more; you are learning to have cohesion. Dreaming does it by forcing dreamers to fixate the assemblage point. The dreaming attention, the energy body, the second attention, the relationship with inorganic beings, the dreaming emissary are but by-products of acquiring cohesion; in other words, they are all by-products of fixating the assemblage point on a number of dreaming positions."

"What is a dreaming position, don Juan?"

"Any new position to which the assemblage point has been displaced during sleep."

"How do we fixate the assemblage point on a dreaming position?"

"By sustaining the view of any item in your dreams, or by changing dreams at will. Through your dreaming practices, you are really exercising your capacity to be cohesive; that is to say, you are exercising your capacity to maintain a new energy shape by holding the assemblage point fixed on the position of any particular dream you are having."

"Do I really maintain a new energy shape?"

"Not exactly, and not because you can't but only because you are shifting the assemblage point instead of moving it. Shifts of the assemblage point give rise to minute changes, which are practically unnoticeable. The challenge of shifts is that they are so small and so numerous that to maintain cohesiveness in all of them is a triumph."

"How do we know we are maintaining cohesion?"

"We know it by the clarity of our perception. The clearer the view of our dreams, the greater our cohesion."

He said then that it was time for me to have a practical application of what I had learned in dreaming. Without giving me a chance to ask anything, he urged me to focus my attention, as if I were in a dream, on the foliage of a desert tree growing nearby: a mesquite tree.

"Do you want me to just gaze at it?" I asked.

"I don't want you to just gaze at it; I want you to do something very special with that foliage," he said. "Remember that, in your dreams, once you are able to hold the view of any item, you are really holding the dreaming position of your assemblage point. Now, gaze at those leaves as if you were in a dream, but with a slight yet most meaningful variation: you are going to hold your dreaming attention on the leaves of the mesquite tree in the awareness of our daily world."

My nervousness made it impossible for me to follow his line

of thought. He patiently explained that by staring at the foliage, I would accomplish a minute displacement of my assemblage point. Then, by summoning my dreaming attention through staring at individual leaves, I would actually fixate that minute displacement, and my cohesion would make me perceive in terms of the second attention. He added, with a chuckle, that the process was so simple it was ridiculous.

Don Juan was right. All I needed was to focus my sight on the leaves, maintain it, and in one instant I was drawn into a vortex-like sensation, extremely like the vortexes in my dreams. The foliage of the mesquite tree became a universe of sensory data. It was as if the foliage had swallowed me, but it was not only my sight that was engaged; if I touched the leaves, I actually felt them. I could also smell them. My dreaming attention was multisensorial instead of solely visual, as in my regular dreaming.

What had begun as gazing at the foliage of the mesquite tree had turned into a dream. I believed I was in a dreamt tree, as I had been in trees of countless dreams. And, naturally, I behaved in this dreamt tree as I had learned to behave in my dreams; I moved from item to item, pulled by the force of a vortex that took shape on whatever part of the tree I focused my multisensorial dreaming attention. Vortexes were formed not only on gazing but also on touching anything with any part of my body.

In the midst of this vision or dream, I had an attack of rational doubts. I began to wonder if I had really climbed the tree in a daze and was actually hugging the leaves, lost in the foliage, without knowing what I was doing. Or perhaps I had fallen asleep, possibly mesmerized by the fluttering of leaves in the wind, and was having a dream. But just like in dreaming, I didn't have enough energy to ponder for too long. My thoughts were fleeting. They lasted an instant; then the force of direct experience blanketed them out completely.

A sudden motion around me shook everything and virtually

made me emerge from a clump of leaves, as if I had broken away from the tree's magnetic pull. I was facing then, from an elevation, an immense horizon. Dark mountains and green vegetation surrounded me. Another jolt of energy made me shake from my bones out; then I was somewhere else. Enormous trees loomed everywhere. They were bigger than the Douglas firs of Oregon and Washington State. Never had I seen a forest like that. The scenery was such a contrast to the aridness of the Sonoran desert that it left me with no doubt that I was having a dream.

I held on to that extraordinary view, afraid to let go, knowing that it was indeed a dream and would disappear once I had run out of dreaming attention. But the images lasted, even when I thought I should have run out of dreaming attention. A horrifying thought crossed my mind then: what if this was neither a dream nor the daily world?

Frightened, as an animal must experience fright, I recoiled into the clump of leaves I had emerged from. The momentum of my backward motion kept me going through the tree foliage and around the hard branches. It pulled me away from the tree, and in one split second I was standing next to don Juan, at the door of his house, in the desert in Sonora.

I instantly realized I had entered again into a state in which I could think coherently, but I could not talk. Don Juan told me not to worry. He said that our speech faculty is extremely flimsy and attacks of muteness are common among sorcerers who venture beyond the limits of normal perception.

My gut feeling was that don Juan had taken pity on me and had decided to give me a pep talk. But the voice of the dreaming emissary, which I clearly heard at that instant, said that in a few hours and after some rest I was going to be perfectly well.

Upon awakening I gave don Juan, at his request, a complete description of what I had seen and done. He warned me that it was not possible to rely on my rationality to understand my experience, not because my rationality was in any way impaired but because what had taken place was a phenomenon outside the parameters of reason.

I, naturally, argued that nothing can be outside the limits of reason; things can be obscure, but sooner or later reason always finds a way to shed light on anything. And I really believed this.

Don Juan, with extreme patience, pointed out that reason is only a by-product of the habitual position of the assemblage point; therefore, knowing what is going on, being of sound mind, having our feet on the ground—sources of great pride to us and assumed to be a natural consequence of our worth—are merely the result of the fixation of the assemblage point on its habitual place. The more rigid and stationary it is, the greater our confidence in ourselves, the greater our feeling of knowing the world, of being able to predict.

He added that what dreaming does is give us the fluidity to enter into other worlds by destroying our sense of knowing this world. He called dreaming a journey of unthinkable dimensions, a journey that, after making us perceive everything we can humanly perceive, makes the assemblage point jump outside the human domain and perceive the inconceivable.

"We are back again, harping on the most important topic of the sorcerers' world," he went on, "the position of the assemblage point. The old sorcerers' curse, as well as mankind's thorn in the side."

"Why do you say that, don Juan?"

"Because both, mankind in general and the old sorcerers, fell prey to the position of the assemblage point: mankind, because by not knowing that the assemblage point exists we are obliged to take the by-product of its habitual position as something final and indisputable. And the old sorcerers because, although they knew all about the assemblage point, they fell for its facility to be manipulated.

"You must avoid falling into those traps," he continued. "It'd be really disgusting if you sided with mankind, as if you didn't know about the existence of the assemblage point. But it'd be even more insidious if you sided with the old sorcerers and cynically manipulate the assemblage point for gain."

"I still don't understand. What is the connection of all this with what I experienced yesterday?"

"Yesterday, you were in a different world. But if you ask me where that world is, and I tell you that it is in the position of the assemblage point, my answer won't make any sense to you."

Don Juan's argument was that I had two choices. One was to follow mankind's rationales and be faced with a predicament: my experience would tell me that other worlds exist, but my reason would say that such worlds do not and cannot exist. The other choice was to follow the old sorcerers' rationales, in which case I would automatically accept the existence of other worlds, and my greed alone would make my assemblage point hold on to the position that creates those worlds. The result would be another kind of predicament: that of having to move physically into visionlike realms, driven by expectations of power and gain.

I was too numb to follow his argument, but then I realized I did not have to follow it because I agreed with him completely, despite the fact that I did not have a total picture of what I was agreeing about. Agreeing with him was rather a feeling that came from far away, an ancient certainty I had lost, which was now slowly finding its way back to me.

The return to my dreaming practices eliminated these turmoils, but created new ones. For example, after months of hearing it daily, I stopped finding the dreaming emissary's voice an annoyance or a wonder. It became a matter of course for me. And I made so many mistakes influenced by what it said that I almost understood don Juan's reluctance to take it seriously. A psychoanalyst would have had a field day interpreting the emissary according to all the possible permutations of my intrapersonal dynamics.

Don Juan maintained a steadfast view on it: it is an impersonal but constant force from the realm of inorganic beings; thus, every dreamer experiences it, in more or less the same terms. And if we choose to take its words as advice, we are incurable fools.

I was definitely one of them. There was no way I could have remained impassive being in direct contact with such an extraordinary event: a voice that clearly and concisely told me in three languages hidden things about anything or anyone I focused my attention on. Its only drawback, which was of no consequence to me, was that we were not synchronized. The emissary used to tell me things about people or events when I had honestly forgotten I had been interested in them.

I asked don Juan about this oddity, and he said that it had to do with the rigidity of my assemblage point. He explained that I had been reared by old adults and that they had imbued me with old people's views; therefore, I was dangerously righteous. His urge to give me potions of hallucinogenic plants was but an effort, he said, to shake my assemblage point and allow it to have a minimal margin of fluidity.

"If you don't develop this margin," he went on, "either you'll become more righteous or you'll become a hysterical sorcerer. My interest in telling you about the old sorcerers is not to bad-mouth them but to pit them against you. Sooner or later, your assemblage point will be more fluid, but not fluid enough to offset your facility to be like them: righteous and hysterical."

"How can I avoid all that, don Juan?"

"There is only one way. Sorcerers call it sheer understanding. I call it a romance with knowledge. It's the drive sorcerers use to know, to discover, to be bewildered."

Don Juan changed the subject and continued to explain the fixation of the assemblage point. He said that *seeing* children's assemblage points constantly fluttering, as if moved by tremors, changing their place with ease, the old sorcerers came to the conclusion that the assemblage point's habitual location is not innate but brought about by habituation. *Seeing* also that only in adults is it fixed on one spot, they surmised that the specific location of the assemblage point fosters a specific way of perceiving. Through usage, this specific way of perceiving becomes a system of interpreting sensory data.

Don Juan pointed out that, since we are drafted into that system by being born into it, from the moment of our birth we imperatively strive to adjust our perceiving to conform to the demands of this system, a system that rules us for life. Consequently, the old sorcerers were thoroughly right in believing that the act of countermanding it and perceiving energy directly is what transforms a person into a sorcerer.

Don Juan expressed wonder at what he called the greatest accomplishment of our human upbringing: to lock our assemblage point on its habitual position. For, once it is immobilized there, our perception can be coached and guided to interpret what we perceive. In other words, we can then be guided to perceive more in terms of our system than in terms of our senses. He assured me that human perception is universally homogeneous, because the assemblage points of the whole human race are fixed on the same spot.

He went on to say that sorcerers prove all this to themselves when they *see* that at the moment the assemblage point is displaced beyond a certain threshold, and new universal filaments of energy begin to be perceived, there is no sense to what we perceive. The immediate cause is that new sensory data has rendered our system inoperative; it can no longer be used to interpret what we are perceiving.

"Perceiving without our system is, of course, chaotic," don Juan continued. "But strangely enough, when we think we have truly lost our bearings, our old system rallies; it comes to our rescue and transforms our new incomprehensible perception into a thoroughly comprehensible new world. Just like what happened to you when you gazed at the leaves of the mesquite tree."

"What exactly happened to me, don Juan?"

"Your perception was chaotic for a while; everything came to you at once, and your system for interpreting the world didn't function. Then, the chaos cleared up, and there you were in front of a new world."

"We are again, don Juan, at the same place we were before. Does that world exist, or is it merely my mind that concocted it?"

"We certainly are back, and the answer is still the same. It exists in the precise position your assemblage point was at that moment. In order to perceive it, you needed cohesion, that is, you needed to maintain your assemblage point fixed on that position, which you did. The result was that you totally perceived a new world for a while."

"But would others perceive that same world?"

"If they had uniformity and cohesion, they would. Uniformity is to hold, in unison, the same position of the assemblage point. The old sorcerers called the entire act of acquiring uniformity and cohesion outside the normal world stalking perception.

"The art of stalking," he continued, "as I have already said, deals with the fixation of the assemblage point. The old sorcerers discovered, through practice, that important as it is to displace the assemblage point, it is even more important to make it stay fixed on its new position, wherever that new position might be."

He explained that if the assemblage point does not become stationary, there is no way that we can perceive coherently. We would experience then a kaleidoscope of disassociated images. This is the reason the old sorcerers put as much emphasis on dreaming as they did on stalking. One art cannot exist without the other, especially for the kinds of activities in which the old sorcerers were involved.

"What were those activities, don Juan?"

"The old sorcerers called them the intricacies of the second attention or the grand adventure of the unknown."

Don Juan said that these activities stem from the displacements of the assemblage point. Not only had the old sorcerers learned to displace their assemblage points to thousands of positions on the surface or on the inside of their energy masses but they had also learned to fixate their assemblage points on those positions, and thus retain their cohesiveness, indefinitely.

"What was the benefit of that, don Juan?"

"We can't talk about benefits. We can talk only about end results."

He explained that the cohesiveness of the old sorcerers was such that it allowed them to become perceptually and physically everything the specific position of their assemblage points dictated. They could transform themselves into anything for which they had a specific inventory. An inventory is, he said, all the details of perception involved in becoming, for example, a jaguar, a bird, an insect, et cetera, et cetera.

"It's very hard for me to believe that this transformation can be possible," I said.

"It is possible," he assured me. "Not so much for you and me, but for them. For them, it was nothing."

He said that the old sorcerers had superb fluidity. All they needed was the slightest shift of their assemblage points, the slightest perceptual cue from their dreaming, and they would instantaneously stalk their perception, rearrange their cohesiveness to fit their new state of awareness, and be an animal, another person, a bird, or anything.

"But isn't that what mentally ill people do? Make up their own reality as they go along?" I said.

"No, it isn't the same. Insane people imagine a reality of their own because they don't have any preconceived purpose at all. Insane people bring chaos into the chaos. Sorcerers, on the contrary, bring order to the chaos. Their preconceived, transcendental purpose is to free their perception. Sorcerers don't make up the world they are perceiving; they perceive energy directly, and then they discover that what they are perceiving is an unknown new world, which can swallow them whole, because it is as real as anything we know to be real."

Don Juan then gave me a new version of what had happened to me as I gazed at the mesquite tree. He said that I began by perceiving the energy of the tree. On the subjective level, however, I believed I was dreaming because I employed dreaming techniques to perceive energy. He asserted that to use dreaming techniques in the world of everyday life was one of the old sorcerers' most effective devices. It made perceiving energy directly dreamlike, instead of totally chaotic, until a moment when something rearranged perception and the sorcerer found himself facing a new world—the very thing that had happened to me.

I told him about the thought I'd had, which I had barely dared to think: that the scenery I was viewing was not a dream, nor was it our daily world.

"It wasn't," he said. "I've been saying this to you over and over, and you think that I am merely repeating myself. I know how difficult it is for the mind to allow mindless possibilities to become real. But new worlds exist! They are wrapped one around the other, like the skins of an onion. The world we exist in is but one of those skins."

"Do you mean, don Juan, that the goal of your teaching is to prepare me to go into those worlds?"

"No. I don't mean that. We go into those worlds only as an exercise. Those journeys are the antecedents of the sorcerers of today. We do the same dreaming that the old sorcerers used to do, but at one moment we deviate into new ground. The old sorcerers preferred the shifts of the assemblage point, so they were always on more or less known, predictable ground. We prefer the movements of the assemblage point. The old sorcerers were after the human unknown. We are after the nonhuman unknown."

"I haven't gotten to that yet, have I?"

"No. You are only beginning. And at the beginning everyone

has to go through the old sorcerers' steps. After all, they were the ones who invented dreaming."

"At what point will I then begin to learn the new sorcerers' brand of dreaming?"

"You have enormous ground yet to cover. Years from now perhaps. Besides, in your case, I have to be extraordinarily careful. In character, you are definitely linked to the old sorcerers. I've said this to you before, but you always manage to avoid my probes. Sometimes I even think that some alien energy is advising you, but then I discard the idea. You are not devious."

"What are you talking about, don Juan?"

"You've done, unwittingly, two things that worry the hell out of me. You traveled with your energy body to a place outside this world the first time you dreamt. And you walked there! And then you traveled with your energy body to another place outside this world, but parting from the awareness of the daily world."

"Why would that worry you, don Juan?"

"Dreaming is too easy for you. And that is a damnation if we don't watch it. It leads to the human unknown. As I said to you, modern-day sorcerers strive to get to the nonhuman unknown."

"What can the nonhuman unknown be?"

"Freedom from being human. Inconceivable worlds that are outside the band of man but that we still can perceive. This is where modern sorcerers take the side road. Their predilection is what's outside the human domain. And what are outside that domain are all-inclusive worlds, not merely the realm of birds or the realm of animals or the realm of man, even if it be the unknown man. What I am talking about are worlds, like the one where we live; total worlds with endless realms."

"Where are those worlds, don Juan? In different positions of the assemblage point?"

"Right. In different positions of the assemblage point, but

positions sorcerers arrive at with a movement of the assemblage point, not a shift. Entering into those worlds is the type of dreaming only sorcerers of today do. The old sorcerers stayed away from it, because it requires a great deal of detachment and no self-importance whatsoever. A price they couldn't afford to pay.

"For the sorcerers who practice dreaming today, dreaming is freedom to perceive worlds beyond the imagination."

"But, what's the point of perceiving all that?"

"You already asked me, today, the same question. You speak like a true merchant. What's the risk? you ask, What's the percentage gain to my investment? Is it going to better me?

"There is no way to answer that. The merchant mind does commerce. But freedom cannot be an investment. Freedom is an adventure with no end, in which we risk our lives and much more for a few moments of something beyond words, beyond thoughts or feelings."

"I didn't ask that question in that spirit, don Juan. What I want to know is what can be the driving force to do all this for a lazy bum like myself?"

"To seek freedom is the only driving force I know. Freedom to fly off into that infinity out there. Freedom to dissolve; to lift off; to be like the flame of a candle, which, in spite of being up against the light of a billion stars, remains intact, because it never pretended to be more than what it is: a mere candle."

5

THE WORLD OF

INORGANIC BEINGS

Faithful to my agreement to wait for don Juan to initiate any comment on dreaming, only in cases of necessity did I ask him for advice. Ordinarily, though, he not only seemed reluctant to touch the subject but was somehow displeased with me about it. In my estimation, a confirmation of his disapproval was the fact that whenever we talked about my dreaming activities, he always minimized the import of anything I had accomplished.

For me, at that time, the animate existence of inorganic beings had become the most crucial aspect of my dreaming practices. After encountering them in my dreams, and especially after my bout with them in the desert around don Juan's house, I should have been more willing to take their existence as a serious affair. But all these events had quite the opposite effect on me. I became adamant and doggedly denied the possibility that they existed.

Then I had a change of heart and decided to conduct an objective inquiry about them. The method of this inquiry required that I first compile a record of everything that transpired in my dreaming sessions, then use that record as a matrix to find out if my dreaming proved or disproved anything about the inorganic beings. I actually wrote down hundreds of pages of meticulous but meaningless details, when it should have been clear to me that the evidence of their existence had been gathered almost as soon as I had started my inquiry.

It took but a few sessions for me to discover that what I thought to be don Juan's casual recommendation—to suspend judgment and let the inorganic beings come to me—was, in fact, the very procedure used by the sorcerers of antiquity to attract them. By leaving me to find it out for myself, don Juan was simply following his sorcery training. He had remarked time and time again that it is very difficult to make the self give up its strongholds except through practice. One of the self's strongest lines of defense is indeed our rationality, and this is not only the most durable line of defense when it comes to sorcery actions and explanations but also the most threatened. Don Juan believed that the existence of inorganic beings is a foremost assailant of our rationality.

In my dreaming practices, I had an established course, which I followed every single day without deviation. I aimed first at observing every conceivable item of my dreams, then at changing dreams. I can say in sincerity that I observed universes of detail in dreams upon dreams. As a matter of course, at one given moment my dreaming attention began to wane, and my dreaming sessions ended either in my falling asleep and having regular dreams, in which I had no dreaming attention whatsoever, or in my waking up and not being able to sleep at all.

From time to time, however, as don Juan had described it, a current of foreign energy, a scout, as he called it, was injected into my dreams. Being forewarned helped me to adjust my dreaming attention and be on the alert. The first time I noticed foreign energy, I was dreaming about shopping in a department store. I was going from counter to counter looking for antiques. I finally found one. The incongruence of looking for antiques in a department store was so obvious that it made me chuckle, but since I had found one, I forgot about that incongruence. The antique was the handle of a walking stick. The salesman told me that it was made of iridium, which he called one of the hardest substances in the world. It was a carved piece: the head and shoulders of a monkey. It looked like jade to me. The salesman was insulted when I insinuated that it might be jade, and to prove his point he hurled the object, with all his strength, against the cement floor. It did not break but bounced like a ball and then sailed away, spinning like a Frisbee. I followed it. It disappeared behind some trees. I ran to look for it, and I found it, stuck on the ground. It had been transformed into an extraordinarily beautiful, deep green and black, full-length walking stick.

I coveted it. I grabbed it and struggled to pull it out of the ground before anyone else came along. But, hard as I tried, I could not make it budge. I was afraid I would break it if I attempted to pry it loose by shaking it back and forth. So I began to dig around it with my bare hands. As I kept on digging, it kept on melting, until only a puddle of green water was left in its place. I stared at the water; it suddenly seemed to explode. It turned into a white bubble, and then it was gone. My dream continued into other images and details, which were not outstanding, although they were crystal clear.

When I told don Juan about this dream, he said, "You isolated a scout. Scouts are more numerous when our dreams are average, normal ones. The dreams of dreamers are strangely free from scouts. When they appear, they are identifiable by the strangeness and incongruity surrounding them."

"Incongruity, in what manner, don Juan?"

"Their presence doesn't make any sense."

"Very few things make sense in a dream."

"Only in average dreams are things nonsensical. I would say that this is so because more scouts are injected then, because average people are subject to a greater barrage from the unknown."

"Do you know why is that so, don Juan?"

"In my opinion, what takes place is a balance of forces. Average people have stupendously strong barriers to protect themselves against those onslaughts. Barriers such as worries about the self. The stronger the barrier, the greater the attack.

"Dreamers, by contrast, have fewer barriers and fewer scouts in their dreams. It seems that in dreamers' dreams nonsensical things disappear, perhaps to ensure that dreamers catch the presence of scouts."

Don Juan advised me to pay close attention and remember every single possible detail of the dream I had had. He even made me repeat what I had told him.

"You baffle me," I said. "You don't want to hear anything about my dreaming, and then you do. Is there any order to your refusals and acceptances?"

"You bet there is order behind all this," he said. "Chances are, you'll do the same someday to another dreamer. Some items are of key importance because they are associated with the spirit. Others are entirely unimportant by reason of being associated with our indulging personality.

"The first scout you isolate will always be present, in any form, even iridium. By the way, what's iridium?"

"I don't really know," I said in total sincerity.

"There you are! And what will you say if it turns out to be one of the strongest substances in the world?"

Don Juan's eyes shone with delight, while I nervously

laughed at that absurd possibility, which, I learned later, is true.

I began to notice from then on the presence of incongruous items in my dreams. Once I had accepted don Juan's categorization of foreign energy in dreams, I totally agreed with him that incongruous items were foreign invaders of my dreams. Upon isolating them, my dreaming attention always focused on them with an intensity that did not occur under any other circumstances.

Another thing I noticed was that every time foreign energy invaded my dreams, my dreaming attention had to work hard to turn it into a known object. The handicap of my dreaming attention was its inability to accomplish fully such a transformation; the end result was a bastardized item, nearly unknown to me. The foreign energy then dissipated quite easily; the bastardized item vanished, turning into a blob of light, which was quickly absorbed by other pressing details of my dreams.

When I asked don Juan to comment on what was happening to me, he said, "At this point in your dreaming, scouts are reconnoiterers sent by the inorganic realm. They are very fast, meaning that they don't stay long."

"Why do you say that they are reconnoiterers, don Juan?"

"They come in search of potential awareness. They have consciousness and purpose, although it is incomprehensible to our minds, comparable perhaps to the consciousness and purpose of trees. The inner speed of trees and inorganic beings is incomprehensible to us because it is infinitely slower than ours."

"What makes you say that, don Juan?"

"Both trees and inorganic beings last longer than we do. They are made to stay put. They are immobile, yet they make everything move around them."

"Do you mean, don Juan, that inorganic beings are stationary like trees?"

"Certainly. What you see in dreaming as bright or dark sticks are their projections. What you hear as the voice of the dreaming emissary is equally their projection. And so are their scouts."

For some unfathomable reason, I was overwhelmed by these statements. I was suddenly filled with anxiety. I asked don Juan if trees also had projections like that.

"They do," he said. "Their projections are, however, even less friendly to us than those of the inorganic beings. Dreamers never seek them, unless they are in a state of profound amenity with trees, which is a very difficult state to attain. We have no friends on this earth, you know." He chuckled and added, "It's no mystery why."

"It may not be a mystery to you, don Juan, but it certainly is to me."

"We are destructive. We have antagonized every living being on this earth. That's why we have no friends."

I felt so ill at ease that I wanted to stop the conversation altogether. But a compulsive urge made me return to the subject of inorganic beings. "What do you think I should do to follow the scouts?" I asked.

"Why in the world would you want to follow them?"

"I am conducting an objective inquiry about inorganic beings."

"You're pulling my leg, aren't you? I thought you were unmovable on your stand that inorganic beings don't exist."

His scoffing tone and cackling laughter told me what his thoughts and feelings about my objective inquiry were.

"I've changed my mind, don Juan. Now I want to explore all those possibilities."

"Remember, the realm of inorganic beings was the old sorcerers' field. To get there, they tenaciously fixed their dreaming attention on the items of their dreams. In that fashion, they were able to isolate the scouts. And when they had the scouts in focus, they shouted their intent to follow them. The instant the old sorcerers voiced that intent, off they went, pulled by that foreign energy."

"Is it that simple, don Juan?"

He did not answer. He just laughed at me as if daring me to do it.

At home, I tired of searching for don Juan's true meanings. I was thoroughly unwilling to consider that he might have described an actual procedure. After running out of ideas and patience, one day I let my guard down. In a dream I was having then, I was baffled by a fish that had suddenly jumped out of a pond I was walking by. The fish twitched by my feet, then flew like a colored bird, perching on a branch, still being a fish. The scene was so outlandish that my dreaming attention was galvanized. I instantly knew it was a scout. A second later, when the fish-bird turned into a point of light, I shouted my intent to follow it, and, just as don Juan had said, off I went into another world.

I flew through a seemingly dark tunnel as if I were a weightless flying insect. The sensation of a tunnel ended abruptly. It was exactly as if I had been spewed out of a tube and the impulse had left me smack against an immense physical mass; I was almost touching it. I could not see the end of it in any direction I looked. The entire thing reminded me so much of science fiction movies that I was utterly convinced I was constructing the view of that mass myself, as one constructs a dream. Why not? The thought I had was that, after all, I was asleep, dreaming.

I settled down to observe the details of my dream. What I was viewing looked very much like a gigantic sponge. It was porous and cavernous. I could not feel its texture, but it looked rough and fibrous. It was dark brownish in color. Then I had a momentary jolt of doubt about that silent mass being just a dream. What I was facing did not change shape. It did not move either. As I looked at it fixedly, I had the complete impression of something real but stationary; it was planted somewhere, and it had such a powerful attraction that I was incapable of deviating my dreaming attention to examine anything else, including myself. Some strange force, which I had never before encountered in my dreaming, had me riveted down.

Then I clearly felt that the mass released my dreaming attention; all my awareness focused on the scout that had taken me there. It looked like a firefly in the darkness, hovering over me, by my side. In its realm, it was a blob of sheer energy. I was able to *see* its energetic sizzling. It seemed to be conscious of me. Suddenly, it lurched onto me and tugged me or prodded me. I did not feel its touch, yet I knew it was touching me. That sensation was startling and new; it was as if a part of me that was not there had been electrified by that touch; ripples of energy went through it, one after another.

From that moment on, everything in my dreaming became much more real. I had a very difficult time keeping the idea that I was dreaming a dream. To this difficulty, I had to add the certainty I had that with its touch the scout had made an energetic connection with me. I knew what it wanted me to do the instant it seemed to tug me or shove me.

The first thing it did was to push me through a huge cavern or opening into the physical mass I had been facing. Once I was inside that mass, I realized that the interior was as homogeneously porous as the outside but much softer looking, as if the roughness had been sanded down. What I was facing was a structure that looked something like the enlarged picture of a beehive. There were countless geometric-shaped tunnels going in every direction. Some went up or down, or to my left or my right; they were at angles with one another, or going up or down on steep or mild inclines.

The light was very dim, yet everything was perfectly visible. The tunnels seemed to be alive and conscious; they sizzled. I stared at them, and the realization that I was *seeing* hit me. Those were tunnels of energy. At the instant of this realization, the voice of the dreaming emissary roared inside my ears, so loudly I could not understand what it said.

"Lower it down," I yelled with unusual impatience and

became aware that if I spoke I blocked my view of the tunnels and entered into a vacuum where all I could do was hear.

The emissary modulated its voice and said, "You are inside an inorganic being. Choose a tunnel and you can even live in it." The voice stopped for an instant, then added, "That is, if you want to do it."

I could not bring myself to say anything. I was afraid that any statement of mine might be construed as the opposite of what I meant.

"There are endless advantages for you," the emissary's voice continued. "You can live in as many tunnels as you want. And each one of them will teach something different. The sorcerers of antiquity lived in this manner and learned marvelous things."

I sensed without any feeling that the scout was pushing me from behind. It appeared to want me to move onward. I took the tunnel to my immediate right. As soon as I was in it, something made me aware that I was not walking on the tunnel; I was hovering in it, flying. I was a blob of energy no different from the scout.

The voice of the emissary sounded inside my ears again. "Yes, you are just a blob of energy," it said. Its redundancy brought me an intense relief. "And you are floating inside one inorganic being," it went on. "This is the way the scout wants you to move in this world. When it touched you, it changed you forever. You are practically one of us now. If you want to stay here, just voice your intent." The emissary stopped talking, and the view of the tunnel returned to me. But when it spoke again, something had been adjusted; I did not lose sight of that world and I still could hear the emissary's voice. "The ancient sorcerers learned everything they knew about dreaming by staying here among us," it said.

I was going to ask if they had learned everything they knew by just living inside those tunnels, but before I voiced my question the emissary answered it.

"Yes, they learned everything by just living inside the inorganic beings," it said. "To live inside them, all the old sorcerers had to do was say they wanted to, just like all it took for you to get here was to voice your intent, loud and clear."

The scout pushed against me to signal me to continue moving. I hesitated, and it did something equivalent to shoving me with such a force that I shot like a bullet through endless tunnels. I finally stopped because the scout stopped. We hovered for an instant; then we dropped into a vertical tunnel. I did not feel the drastic change of direction. As far as my perception was concerned, I was still moving seemingly parallel to the ground.

We changed directions many times with the same perceptual effect on me. I began to formulate a thought about my incapacity to feel that I was moving up or down when I heard the emissary's voice. "I think you'll be more comfortable if you crawl rather than fly," it said. "You can also move like a spider or a fly, straight up or down or upside down."

Instantaneously, I settled down. It was as if I had been fluffy and suddenly I got some weight, which grounded me. I could not feel the tunnel's walls, but the emissary was right about my being more comfortable when crawling.

"In this world you don't have to be pinned down by gravity," it said. Of course, I was able to realize that myself. "You don't have to breathe either," the voice went on. "And, for your convenience alone, you can retain your eyesight and see as you see in your world." The emissary seemed to be deciding whether to add more. It coughed, just like a man clearing his throat, and said, "The eyesight is never impaired; therefore, a dreamer always speaks about his dreaming in terms of what he sees."

The scout pushed me into a tunnel to my right. It was somehow darker than the others. To me, at a preposterous level, it seemed cozier than the others, more friendly or even known to me. The thought crossed my mind that I was like that tunnel or that the tunnel was like me.

"You two have met before," the emissary's voice said.

"I beg your pardon," I said. I had understood what it said, but the statement was incomprehensible.

"You two wrestled, and because of that you now carry each other's energy." I thought that the emissary's voice carried a touch of malice or even sarcasm.

"No, it isn't sarcasm," the emissary said. "I am glad that you have relatives here among us."

"What do you mean by relatives?" I asked.

"Shared energy makes kinship," it replied. "Energy is like blood."

I was unable to say anything else. I clearly felt pangs of fear.

"Fear is something that is absent in this world," the emissary said. And that was the only statement that was not true.

My dreaming ended there. I was so shocked by the vividness of everything, and by the impressive clarity and continuity of the emissary's statements, that I could not wait to tell don Juan. It surprised and disturbed me that he did not want to hear my account. He did not say so, but I had the impression that he believed all of it had been a product of my indulging personality.

"Why are you behaving like this with me?" I asked. "Are you displeased with me?"

"No. I am not displeased with you," he said. "The problem is that I can't talk about this part of your dreaming. You are completely by yourself in this case. I have said to you that inorganic beings are real. You are finding out how real they are. But what you do with this finding is your business, yours alone. Someday you'll see the reason for my staying away."

"But isn't there something you can tell me about that dream?" I insisted.

"What I can say is that it wasn't a dream. It was a journey into the unknown. A necessary journey, I may add, and an ultrapersonal one."

He changed the subject then and began to talk about other aspects of his teachings.

From that day on, in spite of my fear and don Juan's reluctance to advise me, I became a regular dream traveler to that spongy world. I discovered right away that the greater my capacity to observe the details of my dreams, the greater my facility to isolate the scouts. If I chose to acknowledge the scouts as foreign energy, they remained within my perceptual field for a while. Now, if I chose to turn the scouts into quasi known objects, they stayed even longer, changing shapes erratically. But if I followed them, by revealing out loud my intent to go with them, the scouts veritably transported my dreaming attention to a world beyond what I can normally imagine.

Don Juan had said that inorganic beings are always poised to teach. But he had not told me that dreaming is what they are poised to teach. He had stated that the dreaming emissary, since it is a voice, is the perfect bridge between that world and ours. I found out that the dreaming emissary was not only a teacher's voice but the voice of a most subtle salesman. It repeated on and on, at the proper time and occasion, the advantages of its world. Yet it also taught me invaluable things about dreaming. Listening to what it said, I understood the old sorcerers' preference for concrete practices.

"For perfect dreaming, the first thing you have to do is shut off your internal dialogue," it said to me one time. "For best results in shutting it off, put between your fingers some two- or three-inch-long quartz crystals or a couple of smooth, thin river pebbles. Bend your fingers slightly, and press the crystals or pebbles with them."

The emissary said that metal pins, if they were the size and width of one's fingers, were equally effective. The procedure consisted of pressing at least three thin items between the fingers of each hand and creating, an almost painful pressure in the hands. This pressure had the strange property of shutting off the internal dialogue. The emissary's expressed preference was for quartz crystals; it said that they gave the best results, although with practice anything was suitable.

"Falling asleep at a moment of total silence guarantees a perfect entrance into dreaming," said the emissary's voice, "and it also guarantees the enhancing of one's dreaming attention."

"Dreamers should wear a gold ring," said the emissary to me another time, "preferably fitted a bit tight."

The emissary's explanation was that such a ring serves as a bridge for surfacing from dreaming back into the daily world or for sinking from our daily awareness into the inorganic beings' realm.

"How does this bridge work?" I asked. I had not understood what was involved.

"The contact of the fingers on the ring lays the bridge down," the emissary said. "If a dreamer comes into my world wearing a ring, that ring attracts the energy of my world and keeps it; and when it's needed, that energy transports the dreamer back to this world, by the ring releasing it into the dreamer's fingers.

"The pressure of that ring around a finger serves equally well to ensure a dreamer's return to his world. It gives him a constant, familiar sense on his finger."

During another dreaming session, the emissary said that our skin is the perfect organ for transposing energy waves from the mode of the daily world to the mode of the inorganic beings and vice versa. It recommended that I keep my skin cool and free from pigments or oils. It also recommended that dreamers wear a tight belt or headband or necklace to create a pressure point that serves as a skin center of energy exchange. The emissary explained that the skin automatically screens energy, and that what we need to do to make the skin not only screen but exchange energy from one mode to the other is to express our intent out loud, in dreaming.

One day the emissary's voice gave me a fabulous bonus. It said that, in order to ensure the keenness and accuracy of our dreaming attention, we must bring it from behind the roof of the mouth, where an enormous reservoir of attention is located in all human beings. The emissary's specific directions were to practice and learn the discipline and control necessary to press the tip of the tongue on the roof of the mouth while dreaming. This task is as difficult and consuming, the emissary said, as finding one's hands in a dream. But, once it is accomplished, this task gives the most astounding results in terms of controlling the dreaming attention.

I received a profusion of instructions on every conceivable subject, instructions that I promptly forgot if they were not endlessly repeated to me. I sought don Juan's advice on how to resolve this problem of forgetting.

His comment was as brief as I had expected. "Focus only on what the emissary tells you about dreaming," he said.

Whatever the emissary's voice repeated enough times, I grasped with tremendous interest and fervor. Faithful to don Juan's recommendation, I only followed its guidance when it referred to dreaming and I personally corroborated the value of its instruction. The most vital piece of information for me was that the dreaming attention comes from behind the roof of the mouth. It took a great deal of effort on my part to feel in dreaming that I was pressing the roof of my mouth with the tip of my tongue. Once I accomplished this, my dreaming attention took on a life of its own and became, I may say, keener than my normal attention to the daily world.

It did not take much for me to deduce how deep must have been the involvement of the old sorcerers with the inorganic beings. Don Juan's commentaries and warnings about the danger of such an involvement became more vital than ever. I tried my best to live up to his standards of self-examination with no indulgence. Thus, the emissary's voice and what it said became a superchallenge for me. I had to avoid, at all cost, succumbing to the temptation of the emissary's promise of knowledge, and I had to do this all by myself since don Juan continued to refuse to listen to my accounts.

"You must give me at least a hint about what I should do," I insisted on one occasion when I was bold enough to ask him.

"I can't," he said with finality, "and don't ask again. I've told you, in this instance, dreamers have to be left alone."

"But you don't even know what I want to ask you."

"Oh yes I do. You want me to tell you that it is all right to live in one of those tunnels, if for no other reason than just to know what the emissary's voice is talking about."

I admitted that this was exactly my dilemma. If nothing else, I wanted to know what was implied in the statement that one can live inside those tunnels.

"I went through the same turmoil myself," don Juan went on, "and no one could help me, because this is a superpersonal and final decision, a final decision made the instant you voice your desire to live in that world. In order to get you to voice that desire, the inorganic beings are going to cater to your most secret wishes."

"This is really diabolical, don Juan."

"You can say that again. But not just because of what you are thinking. For you, the diabolical part is the temptation to give in, especially when such great rewards are at stake. For me, the diabolical nature of the inorganic beings' realm is that it might very well be the only sanctuary dreamers have in a hostile universe."

"Is it really a haven for dreamers, don Juan?"

"It definitely is for some dreamers. Not for me. I don't need props or railings. I know what I am. I am alone in a hostile universe, and I have learned to say, So be it!"

That was the end of our exchange. He had not said what I wanted to hear, yet I knew that even the desire to know what it was like to live in a tunnel meant almost to choose that way of life. I was not interested in such a thing. I made my decision right then to continue my dreaming practices without any further implications. I quickly told don Juan about it.

"Don't say anything," he advised me. "But do understand

that if you choose to stay, your decision is final. You'll stay there forever."

It is impossible for me to judge objectively what took place during the countless times I dreamt of that world. I can say that it appeared to be a world as real as any dream can be real. Or I can say that it appeared to be as real as our daily world is real. Dreaming of that world, I became aware of what don Juan had said to me many times: that under the influence of dreaming, reality suffers a metamorphosis. I found myself then facing the two options which, according to don Juan, are the options faced by all dreamers: either we carefully revamp or we completely disregard our system of sensory input interpretation.

For don Juan, to revamp our interpretation system meant to intend its reconditioning. It meant that one deliberately and carefully attempts to enlarge its capabilities. By living in accordance with the sorcerers' way, dreamers save and store the necessary energy to suspend judgment and thus facilitate that intended revamping. He explained that if we choose to recondition our interpretation system, reality becomes fluid, and the scope of what can be real is enhanced without endangering the integrity of reality. Dreaming, then, indeed opens the door into other aspects of what is real.

If we choose to disregard our system, the scope of what can be perceived without interpretation grows inordinately. The expansion of our perception is so gigantic that we are left with very few tools for sensory interpretation and, thus, a sense of an infinite realness that is unreal or an infinite unrealness that could very well be real but is not.

For me, the only acceptable option was reconstructing and enlarging my interpretation system. In dreaming the inorganic beings' realm, I was faced with the consistence of that world from dream to dream, from isolating the scouts through listening to the dreaming emissary's voice to going through tunnels. I went through them without feeling anything, yet being aware that space and time were constant, although not in terms discernible by rationality under normal conditions. However, by noticing the difference or the absence or profusion of detail in each tunnel, or by noticing the sense of distance between tunnels, or by noticing the apparent length or width of each tunnel in which I traveled, I arrived at a sense of objective observation.

The area where this reconstruction of my interpretation system had the most dramatic effect was the knowledge of how I related to the world of the inorganic beings. In that world, which was real to me, I was a blob of energy. Thus, I could whiz in the tunnels, like a fast-moving light, or I could crawl on their walls, like an insect. If I flew, a voice told me not arbitrary but consistent information about details on the walls on which I had focused my dreaming attention. Those details were intricate protuberances, like the Braille system of writing. When I crawled on the walls, I could see the same details with greater accuracy and hear the voice giving me more complex descriptions.

The unavoidable consequence for me was the development of a dual stand. On the one hand, I knew I was dreaming a dream; on the other, I knew I was involved in a pragmatic journey, as real as any journey in the world. This bona fide split was a corroboration of what don Juan had said: that the existence of inorganic beings is the foremost assailant of our rationality.

Only after I had really suspended judgment did I get any relief. At one moment, when the tension of my untenable position—seriously believing in the attestable existence of inorganic beings, while seriously believing that it was only a dream—was about to destroy me, something in my attitude changed drastically, but without any solicitation on my part.

Don Juan maintained that my energy level, which had been steadily growing, one day reached a threshold that allowed me to disregard assumptions and prejudgments about the nature of man, reality, and perception. That day I became enamored with knowledge, regardless of logic or functional value, and, above all, regardless of personal convenience.

When my objective inquiry into the subject of inorganic beings no longer mattered to me, don Juan himself brought up the subject of my dream journey into that world. He said, "I don't think you are aware of the regularity of your meetings with inorganic beings."

He was right. I had never bothered to think about it. I commented on the oddity of my oversight.

"It isn't an oversight," he said. "It's the nature of that realm to foster secretiveness. Inorganic beings veil themselves in mystery, darkness. Think about their world: stationary, fixed to draw us like moths to a light or a fire.

"There is something the emissary hasn't dared to tell you so far: that the inorganic beings are after our awareness or the awareness of any being that falls into their nets. They'll give us knowledge, but they'll extract a payment: our total being."

"Do you mean, don Juan, that the inorganic beings are like fishermen?"

"Exactly. At one moment, the emissary will show you men who got caught in there or other beings that are not human that also got caught in there."

Revulsion and fear should have been my response. Don Juan's revelations affected me deeply, but in the sense of creating uncontainable curiosity. I was nearly panting.

"Inorganic beings can't force anyone to stay with them," don Juan went on. "To live in their world is a voluntary affair. Yet they are capable of imprisoning any one of us by catering to our desires, by pampering and indulging us. Beware of awareness that is immobile. Awareness like that has to seek movement, and it does this, as I've told you, by creating projections, phantasmagorical projections at times."

I asked don Juan to explain what "phantasmagorical projections" meant. He said that inorganic beings hook onto dreamers' innermost feelings and play them mercilessly. They create phantoms to please dreamers or frighten them. He reminded me that I had wrestled with one of those phantoms. He explained that inorganic beings are superb projectionists, who delight in projecting themselves like pictures on the wall.

"The old sorcerers were brought down by their inane trust in those projections," he continued. "The old sorcerers believed their allies had power. They overlooked the fact their allies were tenuous energy projected through worlds, like in a cosmic movie."

"You are contradicting yourself, don Juan. You yourself said that the inorganic beings are real. Now you tell me that they are mere pictures."

"I meant to say that the inorganic beings, in our world, are like moving pictures projected on a screen; and I may even add that they are like moving pictures of rarefied energy projected through the boundaries of two worlds."

"But what about inorganic beings in their world? Are they also like moving pictures?"

"Not a chance. That world is as real as our world. The old sorcerers portrayed the inorganic beings' world as a blob of caverns and pores floating in some dark space. And they portrayed the inorganic beings as hollow canes bound together, like the cells of our bodies. The old sorcerers called that immense bundle the labyrinth of penumbra."

"Then every dreamer sees that world in the same terms, right?"

"Of course. Every dreamer sees it as it is. Do you think you are unique?"

I confessed that something in that world had been giving me all along the sensation I was unique. What created this most pleasant and clear feeling of being exclusive was not the voice of the dreaming emissary, or anything I could consciously think about.

"That's exactly what floored the old sorcerers," don Juan

said. "The inorganic beings did to them what they are doing to you now; they created for them the sense of being unique, exclusive; plus a more pernicious sense yet: the sense of having power. Power and uniqueness are unbeatable as corrupting forces. Watch out!"

"How did you avoid that danger yourself, don Juan?"

"I went to that world a few times, and then I never went back."

Don Juan explained that in the opinion of sorcerers, the universe is predatorial, and sorcerers more than anyone else have to take this into account in their daily sorcery activities. His idea was that consciousness is intrinsically compelled to grow, and the only way it can grow is through strife, through life-or-death confrontations.

"The awareness of sorcerers grows when they do dreaming," he went on. "And the moment it grows, something out there acknowledges its growth, recognizes it and makes a bid for it. The inorganic beings are the bidders for that new, enhanced awareness. Dreamers have to be forever on their toes. They are prey the moment they venture out in that predatorial universe."

"What do you suggest I do to be safe, don Juan?"

"Be on your toes every second! Don't let anything or anybody decide for you. Go to the inorganic beings' world only when you want to go."

"Honestly, don Juan, I wouldn't know how to do that. Once I isolate a scout, a tremendous pull is exerted on me to go. I don't have a chance in hell to change my mind."

"Come on! Who do you think you're kidding? You can definitely stop it. You haven't tried to, that's all."

I earnestly insisted that it was impossible for me to stop. He did not pursue the subject any longer, and I was thankful for that. A disturbing feeling of guilt had begun to gnaw at me. For some unknown reason, the thought of consciously stopping the pull of the scouts had never occurred to me.

As usual, don Juan was correct. I found out that I could change the course of my dreaming by intending that course. After all, I did intend for the scouts to transport me to their world. It was feasible that if I deliberately intended the opposite, my dreaming would follow the opposite course.

With practice, my capacity to intend my journeys into the inorganic beings' realm became extraordinarily keen. An increased capacity to intend brought forth an increased control over my dreaming attention. This additional control made me more daring. I felt that I could journey with impunity, because I could stop the journey any time I wanted to.

"Your confidence is very scary" was don Juan's comment when I told him, at his request, about the new aspect of my control over my dreaming attention.

"Why should it be scary?" I asked. I was truly convinced of the practical value of what I had found out.

"Because yours is the confidence of a fool," he said. "I am going to tell you a sorcerers' story that is apropos. I didn't witness it myself, but my teacher's teacher, the nagual Elias, did."

Don Juan said that the nagual Elias and the love of his life, a sorceress named Amalia, were lost, in their youth, in the inorganic beings' world.

I had never heard don Juan talk about sorcerers being the love of anybody's life. His statement startled me. I asked him about this inconsistency.

"It's not an inconsistency. I have simply refrained all along from telling you stories of sorcerers' affection," he said. "You've been so oversaturated with love all your life that I wanted to give you a break.

"Well, the nagual Elias and the love of his life, the witch Amalia, got lost in the inorganic beings' world," don Juan went on. "They went there not in dreaming but with their physical bodies."

"How did that happen, don Juan?"

"Their teacher, the nagual Rosendo, was very close in temperament and practice to the old sorcerers. He intended to help Elias and Amalia, but instead he pushed them across some deadly boundaries. The nagual Rosendo didn't have that crossing in mind. What he wanted to do was to put his two disciples into the second attention, but what he got as a result was their disappearance."

Don Juan said that he was not going to go into the details of that long and complicated story. He was only going to tell me how they became lost in that world. He stated that the nagual Rosendo's miscalculation was to assume that the inorganic beings are not, in the slightest, interested in women. His reasoning was correct and was guided by the sorcerers' knowledge that the universe is markedly female and that maleness, being an offshoot of femaleness, is almost scarce, thus, coveted.

Don Juan made a digression and commented that perhaps that scarcity of males is the reason for men's unwarranted dominion on our planet. I wanted to remain on that topic, but he went ahead with his story. He said that the nagual Rosendo's plan was to give instruction to Elias and Amalia exclusively in the second attention. And to that effect, he followed the old sorcerers' prescribed technique. He engaged a scout, in dreaming, and commanded it to transport his disciples into the second attention by displacing their assemblage points on the proper position.

Theoretically, a powerful scout could displace their assemblage points on the proper position with no effort at all. What the nagual Rosendo did not take into consideration was the trickery of the inorganic beings. The scout did displace the assemblage points of his disciples, but it displaced them on a position from which it was easy to transport them bodily into the realm of the inorganic beings.

"Is this possible, to be transported bodily?" I asked.

"It is possible," he assured me. "We are energy that is kept in a specific shape and position by the fixation of the assemblage point on one location. If that location is changed, the shape and position of that energy will change accordingly. All the inorganic beings have to do is to place our assemblage point on the right location, and off we go, like a bullet, shoes, hat, and all."

"Can this happen to any one of us, don Juan?"

"Most certainly. Especially if our sum total of energy is right. Obviously, the sum total of the combined energies of Elias and Amalia was something the inorganic beings couldn't overlook. It is absurd to trust the inorganic beings. They have their own rhythm, and it isn't human."

I asked don Juan what exactly the nagual Rosendo did to send his disciples to that world. I knew it was stupid of me to ask, knowing that he was going to ignore my question. My surprise was genuine when he began to tell me.

"The steps are simplicity itself," he said. "He put his disciples inside a very small, closed space, something like a closet. Then he went into dreaming, called a scout from the inorganic beings' realm by voicing his intent to get one, then voiced his intent to offer his disciples to the scout.

"The scout, naturally, accepted the gift and took them away, at an unguarded moment, when they were making love inside that closet. When the nagual opened the closet, they were no longer there."

Don Juan explained that making gifts of their disciples to the inorganic beings was precisely what the old sorcerers used to do. The nagual Rosendo did not mean to do that, but he got swayed by the absurd belief that the inorganic beings were under his control.

"Sorcerers' maneuvers are deadly," don Juan went on. "I beseech you to be extraordinarily aware. Don't get involved in having some idiotic confidence in yourself."

"What finally happened to the nagual Elias and Amalia?" I asked.

"The nagual Rosendo had to go bodily into that world and look for them," he replied.

"Did he find them?"

"He did, after untold struggles. However, he could not totally bring them out. So the two young people were always semiprisoners of that realm."

"Did you know them, don Juan?"

"Of course I knew them, and I assure you, they were very strange."

6

THE SHADOWS' WORLD

Y ou must be extremely careful, for you are about to fall prey to the inorganic beings," don Juan said to me, quite unexpectedly, after we had been talking about something totally unrelated to dreaming.

His statement caught me by surprise. As usual, I attempted to defend myself. "You don't have to warn me. I'm very careful," I assured him.

"The inorganic beings are plotting," he said. "I sense that, and I can't console myself by saying that they set traps at the beginning and, in this manner, undesirable dreamers are effectively and permanently screened out."

The tone of his voice was so urgent that I immediately had to reassure him I was not going to fall into any trap.

"You must seriously consider that the inorganic beings have astounding means at their disposal," he went on. "Their awareness is superb. In comparison, we are children, children with a lot of energy, which the inorganic beings covet."

I wanted to tell him that, on an abstract level, I had understood his point and his concern, but, on a concrete plane, I saw no reason for his warning, because I was in control of my dreaming practices.

A few minutes of uneasy silence followed before don Juan spoke again. He changed the subject and said that he had to bring to my attention a very important issue of his dreaming instruction, an issue that had, so far, bypassed my awareness.

"You already understand that the gates of dreaming are specific obstacles," he said, "but you haven't understood yet that whatever is given as the exercise to reach and cross a gate is not really what that gate is all about."

"This is not clear to me at all, don Juan."

"I mean that it's not true to say, for example, that the second gate is reached and crossed when a dreamer learns to wake up in another dream, or when a dreamer learns to change dreams without waking up in the world of daily life."

"Why isn't it true, don Juan?"

"Because the second gate of dreaming is reached and crossed only when a dreamer learns to isolate and follow the foreign energy scouts."

"Why then is the idea of changing dreams given at all?"

"Waking up in another dream or changing dreams is the drill devised by the old sorcerers to exercise a dreamer's capacity to isolate and follow a scout."

Don Juan stated that following a scout is a high accomplishment and that when dreamers are able to perform it, the second gate is flung open and the universe that exists behind it becomes accessible to them. He stressed that this universe is there all the time but that we cannot go into it because we lack energetic prowess and that, in essence, the second gate of dreaming is the door into the inorganic beings' world, and dreaming is the key that opens that door.

"Can a dreamer isolate a scout directly, without having to go through the drill of changing dreams?" I asked.

"No, not at all," he said. "The drill is essential. The question here is whether this is the only drill that exists. Or can a dreamer follow another drill?"

Don Juan looked at me quizzically. It seemed that he actually expected me to answer the question. "It's too difficult to come up with a drill as complete as the one the old sorcerers devised," I said, without knowing why but with irrefutable authority.

Don Juan admitted that I was absolutely right and said that the old sorcerers had devised a series of perfect drills to go through the gates of dreaming into the specific worlds that exist behind every gate. He reiterated that dreaming, being the old sorcerers' invention, has to be played by their rules. He described the rule of the second gate in terms of a series of three steps: one, through practicing the drill of changing dreams, dreamers find out about the scouts; two, by following the scouts, they enter into another veritable universe; and three, in that universe, by means of their actions, dreamers find out, on their own, the governing laws and regulations of that universe.

Don Juan said that in my dealings with the inorganic beings, I had followed the rule so well that he feared devastating consequences. He thought that the unavoidable reaction on the part of the inorganic beings was going to be an attempt to keep me in their world.

"Don't you think that you are exaggerating, don Juan?" I asked. I could not believe that the picture was as bleak as he was painting it.

"I am not exaggerating at all," he said, in a dry, serious tone.

"You'll see. The inorganic beings don't let anyone go, not without a real fight."

"But what makes you think they want me?"

"They've already shown you too many things. Do you really believe that they are going to all this trouble just to entertain themselves?"

Don Juan laughed at his own remark. I did not find him amusing. A strange fear made me ask him whether he thought I should interrupt or even discontinue my dreaming practices.

"You have to continue your dreaming until you have gone through the universe behind the second gate," he said. "I mean that you alone must either accept or reject the lure of the inorganic beings. That is why I remain aloof and hardly ever comment on your dreaming practices."

I confessed to him that I had been at a loss to explain why he was so generous in elucidating other aspects of his knowledge and so miserly with dreaming.

"I was forced to teach you dreaming," he said, "only because that is the pattern set out by the old sorcerers. The path of dreaming is filled with pitfalls, and to avoid those pitfalls or to fall into them is the personal and individual affair of each dreamer, and I may add that it is a final affair."

"Are those pitfalls the result of succumbing to adulation or to promises of power?" I asked.

"Not only succumbing to those, but succumbing to anything offered by the inorganic beings. There is no way for sorcerers to accept anything offered by them, beyond a certain point."

"And what is that certain point, don Juan?"

"That point depends on us as individuals. The challenge is for each of us to take only what is needed from that world, nothing more. To know what's needed is the virtuosity of sorcerers, but to take only what's needed is their highest accomplishment. To fail to understand this simple rule is the surest way of plummeting into a pitfall."

"What happens if you fall, don Juan?"

"If you fall, you pay the price, and the price depends on the circumstances and the depth of the fall. But there is really no way of talking about an eventuality of this sort, because we are not facing a problem of punishment. Energetic currents are at stake here, energetic currents which create circumstances that are more dreadful than death. Everything in the sorcerers' path is a matter of life or death, but in the path of dreaming this matter is enhanced a hundred fold."

I reassured don Juan that I always exercised the utmost care in my dreaming practices, and that I was extremely disciplined and conscientious.

"I know that you are," he said. "But I want you to be even more disciplined and handle everything related to dreaming with kid gloves. Be, above all, vigilant. I can't foretell where the attack will come from."

"Are you *seeing*, as a seer, imminent danger for me, don Juan?"

"I have *seen* imminent danger for you since the day you walked in that mysterious city, the first time I helped you round up your energy body."

"But do you know specifically what I should do and what I should avoid?"

"No, I don't. I only know that the universe behind the second gate is the closest to our own, and our own universe is pretty crafty and heartless. So the two can't be that different."

I persisted in asking him to tell me what was in store for me. And he insisted that, as a sorcerer, he sensed a state of general danger but that he could not be more specific.

"The universe of the inorganic beings is always ready to strike," he went on. "But so is our own universe. That's why you have to go into their realm exactly as if you were venturing into a war zone."

"Do you mean, don Juan, that dreamers always have to be afraid of that world?"

"No. I don't mean that. Once a dreamer goes through the

universe behind the second gate, or once a dreamer refuses to consider it as a viable option, there are no more headaches."

Don Juan stated that only then are dreamers free to continue. I was not sure what he meant; he explained that the universe behind the second gate is so powerful and aggressive that it serves as a natural screen or a testing ground where dreamers are probed for their weaknesses. If they survive the tests, they can proceed to the next gate; if they do not, they remain forever trapped in that universe.

I was left choking with anxiety but, in spite of my coaxing, that was all he said. When I went home, I continued my journeys to the inorganic beings' realm, exerting great care. My carefulness seemed only to increase my sense of enjoying those journeys. I got to the point that the mere contemplation of the inorganic beings' world was enough to create an exultation impossible to describe. I feared that my delight was going to end sooner or later, but it was not so. Something unexpected made it even more intense.

On one occasion, a scout guided me very roughly through countless tunnels, as if searching for something, or as if it were trying to draw all my energy out and exhaust me. By the time it finally stopped, I felt as if I had run a marathon. I seemed to be at the edge of that world. There were no more tunnels, only blackness all around me. Then something lit up the area right in front of me; there, light shone from an indirect source. It was a subdued light that rendered everything diffusely gray or brownish. When I became used to the light, I vaguely distinguished some dark, moving shapes. After a while, it seemed to me that focusing my dreaming attention on those moving shapes made them substantial. I noticed that there were three types: some of them were round, like balls; others were like bells; and others yet like gigantic, undulating candle flames. All of them were basically round and the same size. I judged that they were three to four feet in diameter. There were hundreds, perhaps even thousands of them.

I knew that I was having a strange, sophisticated vision, yet those shapes were so real that I found myself reacting with genuine queasiness. I got the nauseating feeling of being over a nest of giant, round, brown and grayish bugs. I felt somehow safe, though, hovering above them. I discarded all these considerations, however, the moment I realized that it was idiotic of me to feel safe or ill at ease, as if my dream were a real-life situation. However, as I observed those buglike shapes squirm, I became very disturbed at the idea that they were about to touch me.

"We are the mobile unit of our world," the emissary's voice said, all of a sudden. "Don't be afraid. We are energy, and, for sure, we're not intending to touch you. It would be impossible anyway. We are separated by real boundaries."

After a long pause, the voice added, "We want you to join us. Come down to where we are. And don't be ill at ease. You are not ill at ease with the scouts and certainly not with me. The scouts and I are just like the others. I am bell-shaped, and scouts are like candle flames."

That last statement was definitely a cue of sorts for my energy body. On hearing it, my queasiness and fear vanished. I descended to their level, and the balls and bells and candle flames surrounded me. They came so close to me that they would have touched me had I had a physical body. Instead, we went through one another, like encapsulated air puffs.

I had, at that point, an unbelievable sensation. Although I did not feel anything with or in my energy body, I was feeling and recording the most unusual tickling somewhere else; soft, airlike things were definitely going through me, but not right there. The sensation was vague and fast and did not give me time to catch it fully. Instead of focusing my dreaming attention on it, I became entirely absorbed in watching those oversized bugs of energy.

At the level where we were, it seemed to me that there was a commonality between the shadow entities and myself: size.

Perhaps it was because I judged them to be the same size as my energy body that I felt almost cozy with them. On examining them, I concluded that I did not mind them at all. They were impersonal, cold, detached, and I liked that immensely. I wondered for an instant whether my disliking them one minute and liking them the next was a natural consequence of dreaming or a product of some energetic influence those entities were exerting on me.

"They are most likable," I said to the emissary, at the very moment I was overpowered by a wave of profound friendship or even affection for them.

No sooner had I spoken my mind than the dark shapes scurried away, like bulky guinea pigs, leaving me alone in semi-darkness.

"You projected too much feeling and scared them off," the emissary's voice said. "Feeling is too hard for them, and for me for that matter." The emissary actually laughed shyly.

My dreaming session ended there. On awakening, my first reaction was to pack my bag to go to Mexico and see don Juan. However, an unexpected development in my personal life made it impossible for me to travel, in spite of my frantic preparations to leave. The anxiety resulting from this setback interrupted my dreaming practices altogether. I did not engage my conscious volition to stop them; I had unwittingly put so much emphasis on this specific dream that I simply knew if I could not get to don Juan there was no point in continuing dreaming.

After an interruption that lasted over half a year, I became more and more mystified by what had happened. I had no idea that my feelings alone were going to stop my practices. I wondered then if the desire would be sufficient to reinstate it. It was! Once I had formulated the thought of reentering dreaming, my practices continued as if they had never been interrupted. The scout picked up where we had left off and took me directly to the vision I'd had during my last session.

"This is the shadows' world," the emissary's voice said as soon as I was there. "But, even though we are shadows, we shed light. Not only are we mobile but we are the light in the tunnels. We are another kind of inorganic being that exists here. There are three kinds: one is like an immobile tunnel, the other is like a mobile shadow. We are the mobile shadows. The tunnels give us their energy, and we do their bidding."

The emissary stopped talking. I felt it was daring me to ask about the third kind of inorganic being. I also felt that if I did not ask, the emissary would not tell me.

"What's the third kind of inorganic being?" I said.

The emissary coughed and chuckled. To me, it sounded like it relished being asked. "Oh, that's our most mysterious feature," it said. "The third kind is revealed to our visitors only when they choose to stay with us."

"Why is that so?" I asked.

"Because it takes a great deal of energy to see them," the emissary answered. "And we would have to provide that energy."

I knew that the emissary was telling me the truth. I also knew that a horrendous danger was lurking. Yet I was driven by a curiosity without limits. I wanted to see that third kind.

The emissary seemed to be aware of my mood. "Would you like to see them?" it asked casually.

"Most certainly," I said.

"All you have to do is to say out loud that you want to stay with us," the emissary said with a nonchalant intonation.

"But if I say that, I have to stay, right?" I asked.

"Naturally," the emissary said in a tone of ultimate conviction. "Everything you say out loud in this world is for keeps."

I could not help thinking that, if the emissary had wanted to trick me into staying, all it had to do was lie to me. I would not have known the difference.

"I cannot lie to you, because a lie doesn't exist," the emissary said, intruding into my thoughts. "I can tell you only about what exists. In my world, only intent exists; a lie has no intent behind it; therefore, it has no existence."

I wanted to argue that there is intent even behind lies, but before I could voice my argument, the emissary said that behind lies there is intention but that intention is not intent.

I could not keep my dreaming attention focused on the argument the emissary was posing. It went to the shadow beings. Suddenly, I noticed that they had the appearance of a herd of strange, childlike animals. The emissary's voice warned me to hold my emotions in check, for sudden bursts of feelings had the capacity to make them disperse, like a flock of birds.

"What do you want me to do?" I asked.

"Come down to our side and try to push or pull us," the emissary's voice urged me. "The quicker you learn to do that, the quicker you'll be able to move things around in your world by merely looking at them."

My merchant's mind went berserk with anticipation. I was instantly among them, desperately trying to push them or pull them. After a while, I thoroughly exhausted my energy. I had then the impression that I had been trying to do something equivalent to lifting a house with the strength of my teeth.

Another impression I had was that the more I exerted myself, the greater the number of shadows. It was as if they were coming from every corner to watch me, or to feed on me. The moment I had that thought, the shadows again scurried away.

"We are not feeding on you," the emissary said. "We all come to feel your energy, very much like what you do with sunlight on a cold day."

The emissary urged me to open up to them by canceling out my suspicious thoughts. I heard the voice, and, as I listened to what it was saying, I realized that I was hearing, feeling, and thinking exactly as I do in my daily world. I slowly turned to see around me. Taking the clarity of my perception as a gauge, I concluded that I was in a real world.

The emissary's voice sounded in my ears. It said that for me the only difference between perceiving my world and perceiving theirs was that perceiving their world started and ended in the blink of an eye; perceiving mine did not, because my awareness—together with the awareness of an immense number of beings like me, who held my world in place with their intent—was fixed on my world. The emissary added that perceiving my world started and ended the same way for the inorganic beings, in the blink of an eye, but perceiving their world did not, because there were immense numbers of them holding it in place with their intent.

At that instant the scene started to dissolve. I was like a diver, and waking up from that world was like swimming up to reach the surface.

In the following session, the emissary began its dialogue with me by restating that a totally coordinated and coactive relationship existed between mobile shadows and stationary tunnels. It finished its statement saying, "We can't exist without each other."

"I understand what you mean," I said.

There was a touch of scorn in the emissary's voice when it retorted that I could not possibly understand what it means to be related in that fashion, which was infinitely more than being dependent. I intended to ask the emissary to explain what it meant by that, but the next instant I was inside of what I can only describe as the very tissue of the tunnel. I saw some grotesquely merged, glandlike protuberances that emitted an opaque light. The thought crossed my mind that those were the same protuberances that had given me the impression of being like Braille. Considering that they were energy blobs three to four feet in diameter, I began to wonder about the actual size of those tunnels.

"Size here is not like size in your world," the emissary said. "The energy of this world is a different kind of energy; its features don't coincide with the features of the energy of your world, yet this world is as real as your own."

The emissary went on to say that it had told me everything about the shadow beings when it described and explained the protuberances on the tunnels' walls. I retorted that I had heard the explanations but I had not paid attention to them because I believed that they did not pertain directly to dreaming.

"Everything here, in this realm, pertains directly to dreaming," the emissary stated.

I wanted to think about the reason for my misjudgment, but my mind became blank. My dreaming attention was waning. I was having trouble focusing it on the world around me. I braced myself for waking up. The emissary started to speak again, and the sound of its voice propped me up. My dreaming attention perked up considerably.

"Dreaming is the vehicle that brings dreamers to this world," the emissary said, "and everything sorcerers know about dreaming was taught to them by us. Our world is connected to yours by a door called dreams. We know how to go through that door, but men don't. They have to learn it."

The emissary's voice went on explaining what it had already explained to me before.

"The protuberances on the tunnels' walls are shadow beings," it said. "I am one of them. We move inside the tunnels, on their walls, charging ourselves with the energy of the tunnels, which is our energy."

An idle thought crossed my mind: I was really incapable of conceiving a symbiotic relationship such as the one I was witnessing.

"If you would stay among us, you would certainly learn to feel what it is like to be connected as we are connected," the emissary said.

The emissary seemed to be waiting for my reply. I had the feeling that what it really wanted was for me to say that I had decided to stay.

"How many shadow beings are in each tunnel?" I asked to change the mood and immediately regretted it because the emissary began to give me a detailed account of the numbers and functions of the shadow beings in each tunnel. It said that each tunnel had a specific number of dependent entities, which performed specific functions having to do with the needs and expectations of the supporting tunnels.

I did not want the emissary to go into more detail. I reasoned that the less I knew about the tunnel and shadow beings the better off I was. The instant I formulated that thought, the emissary stopped, and my energy body jerked as if it had been pulled by a cable. The next moment, I was fully awake, in my bed.

From then on, I had no more fears that could have interrupted my practices. Another idea had begun to rule me: the idea that I had found unparalleled excitation. I could hardly wait every day to start dreaming and have the scout take me to the shadows' world. The added attraction was that my visions of the shadows' world became even more true to life than before. Judged by the subjective standards of orderly thoughts, orderly visual and auditory sensory input, orderly responses on my part, my experiences, for as long as they lasted, were as real as any situation in our daily world. Never had I had perceptual experiences in which the only difference between my visions and my everyday world was the speed with which my visions ended. One instant I was in a strange, real world, and the next instant I was in my bed.

I craved don Juan's commentaries and explanations, but I was still marooned in Los Angeles. The more I considered my situation, the greater my anxiety; I even began to sense that something in the inorganic beings' realm was brewing at tremendous speed.

As my anxiety grew, my body entered into a state of profound fright, although my mind was ecstatic in the contemplation of the shadows' world. To make things worse, the dreaming emissary's voice lapsed into my daily consciousness. One day while I was attending a class at the university, I heard the voice say, over and over, that any attempt on my part to end my dreaming practices would be deleterious to my total aims. It argued that warriors do not shy away from a challenge and that I had no valid rationale for discontinuing my practices. I agreed with the emissary. I had no intention of stopping anything, and the voice was merely reaffirming what I felt.

Not only did the emissary change but a new scout appeared on the scene. On one occasion, before I had begun to examine the items of my dream, a scout literally jumped in front of me and aggressively captured my dreaming attention. The notable feature of this scout was that it did not need to go through any energetic metamorphosis; it was a blob of energy from the start. In the blink of an eye, the scout transported me, without my having to voice my intent to go with it, to another part of the inorganic beings' realm: the world of the saber-toothed tigers.

I have described in my other works glimpses of those visions. I say glimpses because I did not have sufficient energy then to render these perceived worlds comprehensible to my linear mind.

My nightly visions of the saber-toothed tigers occurred regularly for a long time, until one night when the aggressive scout that had taken me for the first time to that realm suddenly appeared again. Without waiting for my consent, it took me to the tunnels.

I heard the emissary's voice. It immediately went into the longest and most poignant sales pitch I had heard so far. It told me about the extraordinary advantages of the inorganic beings' world. It spoke of acquiring knowledge that would definitely stagger the mind and about acquiring it by the simplest act, of staying in those marvelous tunnels. It spoke of incredible mobility, of endless time to find things, and, above all, of being pampered by cosmic servants that would cater to my slightest whims.

"Aware beings from the most unbelievable corners of the cosmos stay with us," the emissary said, ending its talk. "And they love their stay with us. In fact, no one wants to leave."

The thought that crossed my mind at that moment was that servitude was definitely antithetical to me. I had never been at ease with servants or with being served.

The scout took over and made me glide through many tunnels. It came to a halt in a tunnel that seemed somehow larger than the others. My dreaming attention became riveted on the size and configuration of that tunnel, and it would have stayed glued there had I not been made to turn around. My dreaming attention focused then on a blob of energy a bit bigger than the shadow entities. It was blue, like the blue in the center of a candle's flame. I knew that this energy configuration was not a shadow entity and that it did not belong there.

I became absorbed in sensing it. The scout signaled me to leave, but something was making me impervious to its cues. I remained, uneasily, where I was. However, the scout's signaling broke my concentration, and I lost sight of the blue shape.

Suddenly, a considerable force made me spin around and put me squarely in front of the blue shape. As I gazed at it, it turned into the figure of a person: very small, slender, delicate, almost transparent. I desperately attempted to determine whether it was a man or a woman, but, hard as I tried, I could not.

My attempts to ask the emissary failed. It flew away quite abruptly, leaving me suspended in that tunnel, facing now an unknown person. I tried to talk to that person the way I talked to the emissary. I got no response. I felt a wave of frustration at not being able to break the barrier that separated us. Then I was besieged by the fear of being alone with someone who might have been an enemy.

I had a variety of reactions triggered by the presence of that stranger. I even felt elation, because I knew that the scout had finally shown me another human being caught in that world. I only despaired at the possibility that we were not able to communicate perhaps because that stranger was one of the sorcerers of antiquity and belonged to a time different from mine.

The more intense my elation and curiosity, the heavier I became, until a moment in which I was so massive that I was back in my body, and back in the world. I found myself in Los Angeles, in a park by the University of California. I was standing on the grass, right in the line of people playing golf.

The person in front of me had solidified at the same rate. We stared at each other for a fleeting instant. It was a girl, perhaps six or seven years old. I thought I knew her. On seeing her, my elation and curiosity grew so out of proportion that they triggered a reversal. I lost mass so fast that in another instant I was again a blob of energy in the inorganic beings' realm. The scout came back for me and hurriedly pulled me away.

I woke up with a jolt of fright. In the process of surfacing into the daily world, something had let a message slip through. My mind went into a frenzy trying to put together what I knew or thought I knew. I spent more than forty-eight continuous hours attempting to get at a hidden feeling or a hidden knowledge that had gotten stuck to me. The only success I had was to sense a force—I fancied it to be outside my mind or my body—that told me not to trust my dreaming anymore.

After a few days, a dark and mysterious certainty began to get hold of me, a certainty that grew by degrees until I had no doubt about its authenticity: I was sure that the blue blob of energy was a prisoner in the inorganic beings' realm.

I needed don Juan's advice more desperately than ever. I knew that I was throwing years of work out the window, but I couldn't help it; I dropped everything I was doing and ran to Mexico.

"What do you really want?" don Juan asked me as a way to contain my hysterical babbling.

I could not explain to him what I wanted because I did not know it myself.

"Your problem must be very serious to make you run like this," don Juan said with a pensive expression.

"It is, in spite of the fact that I can't figure out what my problem really is," I said.

He asked me to describe my dreaming practices in all the detail that was pertinent. I told him about my vision of the little girl and how it had affected me at an emotional level. He instantly advised me to ignore the event and regard it as a blatant attempt, on the part of the inorganic beings, to cater to my fantasies. He remarked that if dreaming is overemphasized, it becomes what it was for the old sorcerers: a source of inexhaustible indulging.

For some inexplicable reason, I was unwilling to tell don Juan about the realm of the shadow entities. It was only when he discarded my vision of the little girl that I felt obliged to describe to him my visits to that world. He was silent for a long time, as if he were overwhelmed.

When he finally spoke, he said, "You are more alone than I thought, because I can't discuss your dreaming practices at all. You are at the position of the old sorcerers. All I can do is to repeat to you that you must exercise all the care you are able to muster up."

"Why do you say that I am at the position of the old sorcerers?"

"I've told you repeatedly that your mood is dangerously like the old sorcerers'. They were very capable beings; their flaw was that they took to the inorganic beings' realm like fish take to the water. You are in the same boat. You know things about it that none of us can even conceive. For instance, I never knew about the shadows' world; neither did the nagual Julian or the nagual Elias, in spite of the fact that he spent a long time in the world of the inorganic beings."

"But what difference does knowing the shadows' world make?"

"A great deal of difference. Dreamers are taken there only when the inorganic beings are sure the dreamers are going to stay in that world. We know this through the old sorcerers' stories."

"I assure you, don Juan, that I have no intention whatsoever of staying there. You talk as if I am just about to be lured by promises of service or promises of power. I am not interested in either, and that's that."

"At this level, it isn't that easy anymore. You've gone beyond the point where you could simply quit. Besides, you had the misfortune of being singled out by a watery inorganic being. Remember how you tumbled with it? And how it felt? I told you then that watery inorganic beings are the most annoying. They are dependent and possessive, and once they sink their hooks, they never give up."

"And what does that mean in my case, don Juan?"

"It means real trouble. The specific inorganic being who's running the show is the one you grabbed that fatal day. Over the years, it has grown familiar with you. It knows you intimately."

I sincerely remarked to don Juan that the mere idea that an inorganic being knew me intimately made me sick to my stomach.

"When dreamers realize that the inorganic beings have no appeal," he said, "it is usually too late for them, because by then the inorganic beings have them in the bag."

I felt in the depths of me that he was talking abstractly, about dangers that might exist theoretically but not in practice. I was secretly convinced there was no danger of any sort.

"I am not going to allow the inorganic beings to lure me in any way, if that's what you're thinking," I said.

"I am thinking that they are going to trick you," he said. "Like they tricked the nagual Rosendo. They are going to set you up, and you won't see the trap or even suspect it. They are smooth operators. Now they have even invented a little girl."

"But there is no doubt in my mind that the little girl exists," I insisted.

"There is no little girl," he snapped. "That bluish blob of energy is a scout. An explorer caught in the inorganic beings' realm. I've said to you that the inorganic beings are like fisher-men; they attract and catch awareness."

Don Juan said that he believed, without a doubt, that the bluish blob of energy was from a dimension entirely different from ours, a scout that got stranded and caught like a fly in a spider's web.

I did not appreciate his analogy. It worried me to the point of physical discomfort. I did mention this to don Juan, and he told me that my concern with the prisoner scout was making him feel very close to despair.

"Why does this bother you?" I asked.

"Something is brewing in that confounded world," he said. "And I can't figure out what it is."

While I remained with don Juan and his companions, I did not dream at all about the inorganic beings' world. As usual, my practice was to focus my dreaming attention on the items of my dreams and to change dreams. As a way to offset my concerns, don Juan made me gaze at clouds and at faraway mountain peaks. The result was an immediate feeling of being level with the clouds, or the feeling that I was actually at the faraway mountain peaks.

"I am very pleased, but very worried," don Juan said as a comment on my effort. "You are being taught marvels, and you don't even know it. And I don't mean that you are being taught by me."

"You are talking about the inorganic beings, true?"

"Yes, the inorganic beings. I recommend that you don't gaze at anything; gazing was the old sorcerers' technique. They were able to get to their energy bodies in the blink of an eye, simply by gazing at objects of their predilection. A very impressive technique, but useless to modern sorcerers. It does nothing to increase our sobriety or our capacity to seek freedom. All it does is pin us down to concreteness, a most undesirable state."

Don Juan added that, unless I kept myself in check, by the time I had merged the second attention with the attention of my everyday life, I was going to be an insufferable man. There was, he said, a dangerous gap between my mobility in the second attention and my insistence on immobility in my awareness of the daily world. He remarked that the gap between the two was so great that in my daily state I was nearly an idiot, and in the second attention I was a lunatic.

Before I went home, I took the liberty of discussing my dreaming visions of the shadows' world with Carol Tiggs, although don Juan had advised me not to discuss them with anybody. She was most understanding and most interested, since she was my total counterpart. Don Juan was definitely annoyed with me for having revealed my troubles to her. I felt worse than ever. Self-pity possessed me, and I began to complain about always doing the wrong thing.

"You haven't done anything yet," don Juan snapped at me. "That much, I know."

Was he right! On my next dreaming session, at home, all hell broke loose. I reached the shadows' world, as I had done on countless occasions; the difference was the presence of the blue energy shape. It was among the other shadow beings. I felt it was possible that the blob had been there before and I hadn't noticed it. As soon as I spotted it, my dreaming attention was inescapably attracted to that blob of energy. In a matter of seconds, I was next to it. The other shadows came to me, as usual, but I paid no attention to them.

All of a sudden, the blue, round shape turned into the little girl I had seen before. She craned her thin, delicate, long neck to one side and said in a barely audible whisper, "Help me!" Either she said that or I fantasized that she said it. The result was the same: I stood frozen, galvanized by genuine concern. I experienced a chill, but not in my energy mass. I felt a chill in another part of me. This was the first time I was completely aware that my experience was thoroughly separate from my sensorial feelings. I was experiencing the shadows' world, with all the implications of what I normally consider experiencing: I

was able to think, to assess, to make decisions; I had psychological continuity; in other words, I was myself. The only part
of me that was missing was my sensorial self. I had no bodily
sensations. All my input came through seeing and hearing. My
rationality then considered a strange dilemma: seeing and
hearing were not physical faculties but qualities of the visions I
was having.

"You are really seeing and hearing," the emissary's voice
said, erupting into my thoughts. "That is the beauty of this
place. You can experience everything through seeing and hearing, without having to breathe. Think of it! You don't have to
breathe! You can go anywhere in the universe and not breathe."

A most disquieting ripple of emotion went through me, and,
again, I did not feel it there, in the shadows' world. I felt it in
another place. I became enormously agitated by the obvious
yet veiled realization that there was a live connection between
the me that was experiencing and a source of energy, a source
of sensorial feeling located somewhere else. It occurred to me
that this somewhere else was my actual physical body, which
was asleep in my bed.

At the instant of this thought, the shadow beings scurried
away, and the little girl was alone in my field of vision. I
watched her and became convinced that I knew her. She
seemed to falter as if she were about to faint. A boundless
wave of affection for her enveloped me.

I tried to speak to her, but I was incapable of uttering sounds.
It became clear to me then that all my dialogues with the emissary had been elicited and accomplished by the emissary's
energy. Left to my own devices, I was helpless. I attempted
next to direct my thoughts to the little girl. It was useless. We
were separated by a membrane of energy I could not pierce.

The little girl seemed to understand my despair and actually
communicated with me, directly into my thoughts. She told
me, essentially, what don Juan had already said: that she was a
scout caught in the webs of that world. Then she added that

she had adopted the shape of a little girl because that shape was familiar to me and to her and that she needed my help as much as I needed hers. She said this to me in one clump of energetic feeling, which was like words that came to me all at once. I had no difficulty understanding her, although this was the first time anything of the sort had happened to me.

I did not know what to do. I tried to convey to her my sensation of incapacity. She seemed to comprehend me instantly. She silently appealed to me with a burning look. She even smiled as if to let me know that she had left it up to me to extricate her from her bonds. When I retorted, in a thought, that I had no abilities whatsoever, she gave me the impression of a hysterical child in the throes of despair.

I frantically tried to talk to her. The little girl actually cried, like a child her age would cry, out of desperation and fear. I couldn't stand it. I charged at her, but with no effective result. My energy mass went through her. My idea was to lift her up and take her with me.

I attempted the same maneuver over and over until I was exhausted. I stopped to consider my next move. I was afraid that my dreaming attention was going to wane, and then I would lose sight of her. I doubted that the inorganic beings would bring me back to that specific part of their realm. It seemed to me that this was going to be my last visit to them: the visit that counted.

Then I did something unthinkable. Before my dreaming attention vanished, I yelled loud and clear my intent to merge my energy with the energy of that prisoner scout and set it free.

▪ 7 ▪

THE BLUE SCOUT

I was dreaming an utterly nonsensical dream. Carol Tiggs was by my side. She was speaking to me, although I could not understand what she said. Don Juan was also in my dream, as were all the members of his party. They seemed to be trying to drag me out of a foggy, yellowish world.

After a serious effort, during which I lost and regained sight of them various times, they succeeded in extricating me from that place. Since I could not conceive the sense of all that endeavor, I finally figured that I was having a normal, incoherent dream.

My surprise was staggering when I woke up and found

myself in bed, in don Juan's house. I was incapable of moving. I had no energy at all. I did not know what to think, although I immediately sensed the gravity of my situation. I had the vague feeling that I had lost my energy because of fatigue caused by dreaming.

Don Juan's companions seemed to be extremely affected by whatever was happening to me. They kept on coming into my room, one at a time. Each stayed for a moment, in complete silence, until someone else showed up. It appeared to me that they were taking turns watching over me. I was too weak to ask them to explain their behavior.

During the subsequent days, I began to feel better, and they started to talk to me about my dreaming. At first, I did not know what they wanted of me. Then it dawned on me, because of their questions, that they were obsessed with the shadow beings. Every one of them appeared to be scared and said to me more or less the same thing. They insisted that they had never been in the shadows' world. Some of them even claimed that they did not know it existed. Their claims and reactions increased my sense of bewilderment and my fear.

The questions everyone asked were, "Who took you into that world? Or how did you even begin to know how to get there?" When I told them that the scouts had shown me that world, they could not believe me. Obviously, they had surmised that I had been there, but since it was not possible for them to use their personal experience as a reference point, they were unable to fathom what I was saying. Yet they still wanted to know all I could tell them about the shadow beings and their realm. I obliged them. All of them, with the exception of don Juan, sat by my bed, hanging on every word I said. However, every time I asked them about my situation, they scurried away, just like the shadow beings.

Another disturbing reaction, which they never had before, was that they frantically avoided any physical contact with me. They kept their distance, as if I were carrying the plague. Their reaction worried me so much that I felt obliged to ask them about it. They denied it. They seemed insulted and even went so far as to insist on proving to me that I was wrong. I laughed heartily at the tense situation that ensued. Their bodies went rigid every time they tried to embrace me.

Florinda Grau, don Juan's closest cohort, was the only member of his party who lavished physical attention on me and tried to explain to me what was going on. She told me that I had been discharged of energy in the inorganic beings' world and charged again, but that my new energetic charge was a bit disturbing to the majority of them.

Florinda used to put me to bed every night, as if I were an invalid. She even spoke to me in baby talk, which all of them celebrated with gales of laughter. But regardless of how she made fun of me, I appreciated her concern, which seemed to be real.

I have written about Florinda before in connection with my meeting her. She was by far the most beautiful woman I had ever met. Once I said to her, and I really meant it, that she could have been a fashion magazine model. "Of a magazine of nineteen ten," she retorted.

Florinda, although she was old, was not old at all. She was young and vibrant. When I asked don Juan about her unusual youthfulness, he replied that sorcery kept her in a vital state. Sorcerers' energy, he remarked, was seen by the eye as youth and vigor.

After satisfying their initial curiosity about the shadows' world, don Juan's companions stopped coming into my room, and their conversation remained at the level of casual inquiries about my health. Every time I tried to get up, however, there was someone around who gently put me back to bed. I did not want their ministrations, yet it seemed that I needed them; I was weak. I accepted that. But what really took its toll on me was not having anyone explain to me what I was doing in Mexico when I had gone to bed to dream in Los Angeles. I asked them repeatedly. Every one of them gave me the same answer, "Ask the nagual. He's the only one who can explain it."

Finally, Florinda broke the ice. "You were lured into a trap; that's what happened to you," she said.

"Where was I lured into a trap?"

"In the world of the inorganic beings, of course. That has been the world you've been dealing with for years. Isn't that so?"

"Most definitely, Florinda. But can you tell me about the kind of trap it was?"

"Not really. All I can tell you is that you lost all your energy there. But you fought very well."

"Why am I sick, Florinda?"

"You are not sick with an illness; you were energetically wounded. You were critical, but now you are only gravely wounded."

"How did all this happen?"

"You entered into a mortal combat with the inorganic beings, and you were defeated."

"I don't remember fighting anyone, Florinda."

"Whether you remember or not is immaterial. You fought and were outclassed. You didn't have a chance against those masterful manipulators."

"I fought the inorganic beings?"

"Yes. You had a mortal encounter with them. I really don't know how you have survived their death blow."

She refused to tell me anything else and hinted that the nagual was coming to see me any day.

The next day don Juan showed up. He was very jovial and supportive. He jokingly announced that he was paying me a visit in his capacity of energy doctor. He examined me by gazing at me from head to toe. "You're almost cured," he concluded.

"What happened to me, don Juan?" I asked.

"You fell into a trap the inorganic beings set for you," he answered.

"How did I end up here?"

"Right there is the big mystery, for sure," he said and smiled jovially, obviously trying to make light of a serious matter. "The inorganic beings snatched you, body and all. First they took your energy body into their realm, when you followed one of their scouts, and then they took your physical body."

Don Juan's companions seemed to be in a state of shock. One of them asked don Juan whether the inorganic beings could abduct anyone. Don Juan answered that they certainly could. He reminded them that the nagual Elias was taken into that universe, and he definitely did not intend to go there.

All of them assented with a nod. Don Juan continued speaking to them, referring to me in the third person. He said that the combined awareness of a group of inorganic beings had first consumed my energy body by forcing an emotional outburst from me: to free the blue scout. Then the combined awareness of the same group of inorganic beings had pulled my inert physical mass into their world. Don Juan added that without the energy body one is merely a lump of organic matter that can be easily manipulated by awareness.

"The inorganic beings are glued together, like the cells of the body," don Juan went on. "When they put their awareness together, they are unbeatable. It's nothing for them to yank us out of our moorings and plunge us into their world. Especially if we make ourselves conspicuous and available, like he did."

Their sighs and gasps echoed against the walls. All of them seemed to be genuinely frightened and concerned.

I wanted to whine and blame don Juan for not stopping me, but I remembered how he had tried to warn me, to deviate me, time and time again, to no avail. Don Juan was definitely aware of what was going on in my mind. He gave a knowing smile.

"The reason you think you're sick," he said, addressing me, "is that the inorganic beings discharged your energy and gave you theirs. That should have been enough to kill anyone. As the nagual, you have extra energy; therefore, you barely survived."

I mentioned to don Juan that I remembered bits and pieces of quite an incoherent dream, in which I was in a yellow-fogged world. He, Carol Tiggs, and his companions were pulling me out.

"The inorganic beings' realm looks like a yellow-fog world to the physical eye," he said. "When you thought you were having an incoherent dream, you were actually looking with your physical eyes, for the first time, at the inorganic beings' universe. And, strange as it may seem to you, it was also the first time for us. We knew about the fog only through sorcerers' stories, not through experience."

Nothing of what he was saying made sense to me. Don Juan assured me that, because of my lack of energy, a more complete explanation was impossible; I had to be satisfied, he said, with what he was telling me and how I understood it.

"I don't understand it at all," I insisted.

"Then you haven't lost anything," he said. "When you get stronger, you yourself will answer your questions."

I confessed to don Juan that I was having hot flashes. My temperature rose suddenly, and, while I felt hot and sweaty, I had extraordinary but disturbing insights into my situation.

Don Juan scanned my entire body with his penetrating gaze. He said that I was in a state of energetic shock. Losing energy had temporarily affected me, and what I interpreted as hot flashes were, in essence, blasts of energy during which I momentarily regained control of my energy body and knew everything that had happened to me.

"Make an effort, and tell me yourself what happened to you in the inorganic beings' world," he ordered me.

I told him that the clear sensation I got, from time to time, was that he and his companions had gone into that world with their physical bodies and had snatched me out of the inorganic beings' clutches.

"Right!" he exclaimed. "You're doing fine. Now, turn that sensation into a view of what happened."

I was unable to do what he wanted, hard as I tried. Failing made me experience an unusual fatigue, which seemed to dry up the inside of my body. Before don Juan left the room, I remarked to him that I was suffering from anxiety.

"That means nothing," he said, unconcerned. "Gain back your energy, and don't worry about nonsense."

More than two weeks went by, during which I slowly gained back my energy. However, I kept on worrying about everything. I worried mainly about being unknown to myself, especially about a streak of coldness in me that I had not noticed before, a sort of indifference, a detachment that I had attributed to my lack of energy until I regained it. Then I realized that it was a new feature of my being, a feature that had me permanently out of synchronization. To elicit the feelings I was accustomed to, I had to summon them up and actually wait a moment until they made their appearance in my mind.

Another new feature of my being was a strange longing that took hold of me from time to time. I longed for someone I did not know; it was such an overpowering and consuming feeling that, when I experienced it, I had to move around the room incessantly to alleviate it. The longing remained with me until I made use of another newcomer in my life: a rigid control of myself, so new and powerful that it only added more fuel to my worrying.

By the end of the fourth week, everybody felt that I was finally cured. They cut down their visits drastically. I spent much of the time alone, sleeping. The rest and relaxation I was getting was so complete that my energy began to increase remarkably. I felt like my old self again. I even began to exercise.

One day around noon, after a light lunch, I returned to my room to take a nap. Just before I sank into a deep sleep, I was tossing in my bed, trying to find a more comfortable spot, when a strange pressure on my temples made me open my eyes. The little girl of the inorganic beings' world was standing by the foot of my bed, peering at me with her cold, steel blue eyes.

I jumped out of bed and screamed so loudly that three of don Juan's companions were in the room before I had stopped my scream. They were aghast. They watched in horror as the little girl came to me and was stopped by the boundaries of my luminous physical being. We looked at each other for an eternity. She was telling me something, which I could not comprehend at first but which in the next moment became as clear as a bell. She said that for me to understand what she was saying, my awareness had to be transferred from my physical body into my energy body.

Don Juan came into the room at that moment. The little girl and don Juan stared at each other. Without a word, don Juan turned around and walked out of the room. The little girl swished past the door after him.

The commotion this scene created among don Juan's companions was indescribable. They lost all their composure. Apparently, all of them had seen the little girl as she left the room with the nagual.

I myself seemed to be on the verge of exploding. I felt faint and had to sit down. I had experienced the presence of the little girl as a blow on my solar plexus. She bore an astonishing likeness to my father. Waves of sentiment hit me. I wondered about the meaning of this until I was actually sick.

When don Juan returned to the room, I had gained minimal control over myself. The expectation of hearing what he had to say about the little girl was making my breathing very difficult. Everybody was as excited as I was. They all talked to don Juan at once and laughed when they realized what they were doing. Their main interest was to find out whether there was any uniformity in the way they had perceived the scout's appearance. Everybody was in agreement that they had seen a little girl, six to seven years old, very thin, with angular, beautiful features. They also agreed that her eyes were steel blue and burning with a mute emotion; her eyes, they said, expressed gratitude and loyalty.

Every detail they described about the little girl I corroborated myself. Her eyes were so bright and overpowering that they had actually caused me something like pain. I had felt the weight of her look on my chest.

A serious query, which don Juan's companions had and which I echoed myself, was about the implications of this event. All agreed that the scout was a portion of foreign energy that had filtered through the walls separating the second attention and the attention of the daily world. They asserted that since they were not dreaming and yet all of them had seen the alien energy projected into the figure of a human child; that child had existence.

They argued that there must have been hundreds, if not thousands, of cases in which foreign energy slips unnoticed through natural barriers into our human world, but that in the history of their lineage there was no mention whatsoever of an event of this nature. What worried them the most was that there were no sorcerers' stories about it.

"Is this the first time in the history of mankind that this has happened?" one of them asked don Juan.

"I think it happens all the time," he replied, "but it has never happened in such an overt, volitional way."

"What does it mean to us?" another one of them asked don Juan.

"Nothing to us, but everything to him," he said and pointed at me.

All of them then entered into a most disturbing silence. Don Juan paced back and forth for a moment. Then he stopped in front of me and peered at me, giving all the indications of someone who cannot find words to express an overwhelming realization.

"I can't even begin to assess the scope of what you've done," don Juan finally said to me in a tone of bewilderment. "You fell into a pitfall, but it wasn't the kind of pitfall I was worrying about. Your pitfall was designed for you alone, and it was deadlier than anything I could have thought of. I worried about your falling prey to flattery and being served. What I never counted on was that the shadow beings would set a trap using your inherent aversion to chains."

Don Juan had once made a comparison of his reaction and mine, in the sorcerers' world, to the things that pressed us the most. He said, without making it sound like a complaint, that although he wanted and tried to, he had never been able to inspire the kind of affection his teacher, the nagual Julian, inspired in people.

"My unbiased reaction, which I am putting on the table for you to examine, is to be able to say, and mean it: it's not my fate to evoke blind and total affection. So be it!

"Your unbiased reaction," he went on, "is that you can't stand chains, and you would forfeit your life to break them."

I sincerely disagreed with him and told him that he was exaggerating. My views were not that clear.

"Don't worry," he said laughing, "sorcery is action. When the time comes, you'll act your passion the same way I act mine. Mine is to acquiesce to my fate, not passively, like an idiot, but actively, like a warrior. Yours is to jump without either capriciousness or premeditation to cut someone else's chains."

Don Juan explained that upon merging my energy with the scout I had truthfully ceased to exist. All my physicalness had then been transported into the inorganic beings' realm and, had it not been for the scout who guided don Juan and his companions to where I was, I would have died or remained in that world, inextricably lost.

"Why did the scout guide you to where I was?" I asked.

"The scout is a sentient being from another dimension," he said. "It's a little girl now, and as such she told me that in order to get the necessary energy to break the barrier that had trapped her in the inorganic beings' world, she had to take all of yours. That's her human part now. Something resembling gratitude drove her to me. When I saw her, I knew instantly that you were done for."

"What did you do then, don Juan?"

"I rounded up everyone I could get hold of, especially Carol Tiggs, and off we went into the inorganic beings' realm."

"Why Carol Tiggs?"

"In the first place, because she has endless energy, and, in the second place, because she had to familiarize herself with the scout. All of us got something invaluable out of this experience. You and Carol Tiggs got the scout. And the rest of us got a reason to round up our physicality and place it on our energy bodies; we became energy."

"How did all of you do that, don Juan?"

"We displaced our assemblage points, in unison. Our impeccable intent to save you did the work. The scout took us, in the blink of an eye, to where you were lying, half dead, and Carol dragged you out."

His explanation made no sense to me. Don Juan laughed when I tried to raise that point.

"How can you understand this when you don't even have enough energy to get out of your bed?" he retorted.

I confided to him that I was certain I knew infinitely more than I rationally admitted but that something was keeping a tight lid on my memory.

"Lack of energy is what has put a tight lid on your memory," he said. "When you have sufficient energy, your memory will work fine."

"Do you mean that I can remember everything if I want to?"

"Not quite. You may want as much as you like, but if your energy level is not on a par with the importance of what you know, you might as well kiss your knowledge good-bye: it'll never be available to you."

"So what's the thing to do, don Juan?"

"Energy tends to be cumulative; if you follow the warrior's

way impeccably, a moment will come when your memory opens up."

I confessed that hearing him talk gave me the absurd sensation that I was indulging in feeling sorry for myself, that there was nothing wrong with me.

"You are not just indulging," he said. "You were actually energetically dead four weeks ago. Now you are merely stunned. Being stunned and lacking energy is what makes you hide your knowledge. You certainly know more than any of us about the inorganic beings' world. That world was the exclusive concern of the old sorcerers. All of us have told you that only through sorcerers' stories do we know about it. I sincerely say that it is more than strange to me that you've become, in your own right, another source of sorcerers' stories for us."

I reiterated that it was impossible for me to believe I had done something he had not. But I could not believe either that he was merely humoring me.

"I am not flattering or humoring you," he said, visibly annoyed. "I am stating a sorcery fact. Knowing more than any of us about that world shouldn't be a reason for feeling pleased. There's no advantage in that knowledge; in fact, in spite of all you know, you couldn't save yourself. We saved you, because we found you. But without the aid of the scout, there was no point in even trying to find you. You were so infinitely lost in that world that I shudder at the mere thought."

In my state of mind, I did not find it strange in the least that I actually saw a ripple of emotion going through all of don Juan's companions and apprentices. The only one who remained unaltered was Carol Tiggs. She seemed to have fully accepted her role. She was one with me.

"You did free the scout," don Juan continued, "but you gave up your life. Or, worse yet, you gave up your freedom. The inorganic beings let the scout go, in exchange for you."

"I can hardly believe that, don Juan. Not that I doubt you, you understand, but you describe such an underhanded maneuver that I am stunned."

"Don't consider it underhanded and you have the whole thing in a nutshell. The inorganic beings are forever in search of awareness and energy; if you supply them with the possibility of both, what do you think they'll do? Blow you kisses from across the street?"

I knew that don Juan was right. However, I could not hold that certainty for too long; clarity kept drifting away from me.

Don Juan's companions continued asking him questions. They wanted to know if he had given any thought to what to do with the scout.

"Yes, I have. It is a most serious problem, which the nagual here has to resolve," he said, pointing at me. "He and Carol Tiggs are the only ones who can free the scout. And he knows it too."

Naturally, I asked him the only possible question, "How can I free it?"

"Instead of my telling you how, there is a much better and more just way of finding out," don Juan said with a big smile. "Ask the emissary. The inorganic beings cannot lie, you know."

·8·

THE THIRD GATE OF

DREAMING

The third gate of dreaming is reached when you find yourself in a dream, staring at someone else who is asleep. And that someone else turns out to be you," don Juan said.

My energy level was so keyed up at the time that I went to work on the third task right away, although he did not offer any more information about it. The first thing I noticed, in my dreaming practices, was that a surge of energy immediately rearranged the focus of my dreaming attention. Its focus was now on waking up in a dream and seeing myself sleeping; journeying to the realm of inorganic beings was no longer an issue for me.

Very soon after, I found myself in a dream looking at myself asleep. I immediately reported it to don Juan. The dream had happened while I was at his house.

"There are two phases to each of the gates of dreaming," he said. "The first, as you know, is to arrive at the gate; the second is to cross it. By dreaming what you've dreamt, that you saw yourself asleep, you arrived at the third gate. The second phase is to move around once you've seen yourself asleep.

"At the third gate of dreaming," he went on, "you begin to deliberately merge your dreaming reality with the reality of the daily world. This is the drill, and sorcerers call it completing the energy body. The merge between the two realities has to be so thorough that you need to be more fluid than ever. Examine everything at the third gate with great care and curiosity."

I complained that his recommendations were too cryptic and were not making any sense to me. "What do you mean by great care and curiosity?" I asked.

"Our tendency at the third gate is to get lost in detail," he replied. "To view things with great care and curiosity means to resist the nearly irresistible temptation to plunge into detail.

"The given drill, at the third gate, as I said, is to consolidate the energy body. Dreamers begin forging the energy body by fulfilling the drills of the first and second gates. When they reach the third gate, the energy body is ready to come out, or perhaps it would be better to say that it is ready to act. Unfortunately, this also means that it's ready to be mesmerized by detail."

"What does it mean to be mesmerized by detail?"

"The energy body is like a child who's been imprisoned all its life. The moment it is free, it soaks up everything it can find, and I mean everything. Every irrelevant, minute detail totally absorbs the energy body."

An awkward silence followed. I had no idea what to say. I had understood him perfectly, I just didn't have anything in my experience to give me an idea of exactly what it all meant.

"The most asinine detail becomes a world for the energy body," don Juan explained. "The effort that dreamers have to make to direct the energy body is staggering. I know that it sounds awkward to tell you to view things with care and curiosity, but that is the best way to describe what you should do. At the third gate, dreamers have to avoid a nearly irresistible impulse to plunge into everything, and they avoid it by being so curious, so desperate to get into everything that they don't let any particular thing imprison them."

Don Juan added that his recommendations, which he knew sounded absurd to the mind, were directly aimed at my energy body. He stressed over and over that my energy body had to unite all its resources in order to act.

"But hasn't my energy body been acting all along?" I asked.

"Part of it has, otherwise you wouldn't have journeyed to the inorganic beings' realm," he replied. "Now your entire energy body has to be engaged to perform the drill of the third gate. Therefore, to make things easier for your energy body, you must hold back your rationality."

"I am afraid you are barking up the wrong tree," I said. "There is very little rationality left in me after all the experiences you've brought into my life."

"Don't say anything. At the third gate, rationality is responsible for the insistence of our energy bodies on being obsessed with superfluous detail. At the third gate, then, we need irrational fluidity, irrational abandon to counteract that insistence."

Don Juan's statement that each gate is an obstacle could not have been more truthful. I labored to fulfill the drill of the third gate of dreaming more intensely than I had on the other two tasks combined. Don Juan put tremendous pressure on me. Besides, something else had been added to my life: a true sense of fear. I had been normally and even excessively afraid of one thing or another throughout my life, but there had been nothing in my experience comparable to the fear I felt after my bout with the inorganic beings. Yet all this wealth of experience was inaccessible to my normal memory. Only in the presence of don Juan were those memories at my disposal.

I asked him about this strange situation once when we were at the National Museum of Anthropology and History in Mexico City. What had prompted my question was that, at the moment, I had the odd ability to remember everything that had happened to me in the course of my association with don Juan. And that made me feel so free, so daring and light-footed that I was practically dancing around.

"It just happens that the presence of the nagual induces a shift of the assemblage point," he said.

He guided me then into one of the display rooms of the museum and said that my question was apropos to what he had been planning to tell me.

"My intention was to explain to you that the position of the assemblage point is like a vault where sorcerers keep their records," he said. "I was tickled pink when your energy body felt my intent and you asked me about it. The energy body knows immensities. Let me show you how much it knows."

He instructed me to enter into total silence. He reminded me that I was already in a special state of awareness, because my assemblage point had been made to shift by his presence. He assured me that entering into total silence was going to allow the sculptures in that room to make me see and hear inconceivable things. He added, apparently to increase my confusion, that some of the archaeological pieces in that room had the capacity to produce, by themselves, a shift of the assemblage point, and that if I reached a state of total silence I would be actually witnessing scenes pertaining to the lives of the people who made those pieces.

He then began the strangest tour of a museum I have ever taken. He went around the room, describing and interpreting astounding details of every one of the large pieces. According to him, every archaeological piece in that room was a purposeful record left by the people of antiquity, a record that don Juan as a sorcerer was reading to me as one would read a book.

"Every piece here is designed to make the assemblage point shift," he went on. "Fix your gaze on any of them, silence your mind, and find out whether or not your assemblage point can be made to shift."

"How would I know that it has shifted?"

"Because you would see and feel things that are beyond your normal reach."

I gazed at the sculptures and saw and heard things that I would be at a loss to explain. In the past, I had examined all those pieces with the bias of anthropology, always bearing in mind the descriptions of scholars in the field. Their descriptions of the functions of those pieces, rooted in modern man's cognition of the world, appeared to me, for the first time, to be utterly prejudiced if not asinine. What don Juan said about those pieces and what I heard and saw myself, gazing at them, was the farthest thing from what I had always read about them.

My discomfort was so great that I felt obliged to apologize to don Juan for what I thought was my suggestibility. He did not laugh or make fun of me. He patiently explained that sorcerers were capable of leaving accurate records of their findings in the position of the assemblage point. He maintained that when it comes to getting to the essence of a written account, we have to use our sense of sympathetic or imaginative participation to go beyond the mere page into the experience itself. However, in the sorcerers' world, since there are no written pages, total records, which can be relived instead of read, are left in the position of the assemblage point.

To illustrate his argument, don Juan talked about the sorcerers' teachings for the second attention. He said that they are given when the apprentice's assemblage point is on a place other than the normal one. The position of the assemblage point becomes, in this manner, the record of the lesson. In order to play the lesson back, the apprentice has to return his assemblage point to the position it occupied when the lesson was given. Don Juan concluded his remarks by reiterating that to return the assemblage point to all the positions it occupied when the lessons were given is an accomplishment of the highest magnitude.

For nearly a year, don Juan did not ask me anything about my third dreaming task. Then one day, quite abruptly, he wanted me to describe to him all the nuances of my dreaming practices.

The first thing I mentioned was a baffling recurrence. For a period of months, I had dreams in which I found myself staring at me, sleeping in my bed. The odd part was the regularity of those dreams; they happened every four days, like clockwork. During the other three days, my dreaming was what it always had been so far: I examined every possible item in my dreams, I changed dreams, and occasionally, driven by a suicidal curiosity, I followed the foreign energy scouts, although I felt extremely guilty doing this. I fancied it to be like having a secret drug addiction. The realness of that world was irresistible to me.

Secretly, I felt somehow exonerated from total responsibility, because don Juan himself had suggested that I ask the dreaming emissary about what to do to free the blue scout trapped among us. He meant for me to pose the question in my everyday practice, but I construed his statement to imply that I had to ask the emissary while I was in its world. The question I really wanted to ask the emissary was whether the inorganic beings had set a trap for me. The emissary not only told me that everything don Juan had said was true but also gave me instructions on what Carol Tiggs and I had to do to liberate the scout.

"The regularity of your dreams is something that I rather expected," don Juan remarked, after listening to me.

"Why did you expect something like that, don Juan?"

"Because of your relationship with the inorganic beings."

"That's over and forgotten, don Juan," I lied, hoping he would not pursue the subject any further.

"You are saying that for my benefit, aren't you? You don't need to; I know the true story. Believe me, once you get to play with them, you are hooked. They'll always be after you. Or, what's worse yet, you'll always be after them."

He stared at me, and my guilt must have been so obvious that it made him laugh.

"The only possible explanation for such regularity is that the inorganic beings are catering to you again," don Juan said in a serious tone.

I hurried to change the subject and told him that another nuance of my dreaming practices worth mentioning was my reaction to the sight of myself lying sound asleep. That view was always so startling that it either glued me to the spot until the dream changed or frightened me so profoundly that it made me wake up, screaming at the top of my voice. I had gotten to the point where I was afraid to go to sleep on the days I knew I was going to have that dream.

"You are not yet ready for a true merging of your dreaming reality and your daily reality," he concluded. "You must recapitulate your life further."

"But I've done all the recapitulating possible," I protested. "I've been recapitulating for years. There is nothing more I can remember about my life."

"There must be much more," he said adamantly, "otherwise, you wouldn't wake up screaming."

I did not like the idea of having to recapitulate again. I had done it, and I believed I had done it so well that I did not need to touch the subject ever again.

"The recapitulation of our lives never ends, no matter how well we've done it once," don Juan said. "The reason average people lack volition in their dreams is that they have never recapitulated and their lives are filled to capacity with heavily loaded emotions like memories, hopes, fears, et cetera, et cetera.

"Sorcerers, in contrast, are relatively free from heavy, binding emotions, because of their recapitulation. And if something stops them, as it has stopped you at this moment, the assumption is that there still is something in them that is not quite clear."

"To recapitulate is too involving, don Juan. Maybe there is something else I can do instead."

"No. There isn't. Recapitulating and dreaming go hand in hand. As we regurgitate our lives, we get more and more airborne."

Don Juan had given me very detailed and explicit instructions about the recapitulation. It consisted of reliving the totality of one's life experiences by remembering every possible minute detail of them. He saw the recapitulation as the essential factor in a dreamer's redefinition and redeployment of energy. "The recapitulation sets free energy imprisoned within us, and without this liberated energy dreaming is not possible." That was his statement.

Years before, don Juan had coached me to make a list of all the people I had met in my life, starting at the present. He helped me to arrange my list in an orderly fashion, breaking it down into areas of activity, such as jobs I had had, schools I had attended. Then he guided me to go, without deviation, from the first person on my list to the last one, reliving every one of my interactions with them.

He explained that recapitulating an event starts with one's mind arranging everything pertinent to what is being recapitulated. Arranging means reconstructing the event, piece by piece, starting by recollecting the physical details of the surroundings, then going to the person with whom one shared the interaction, and then going to oneself, to the examination of one's feelings.

Don Juan taught me that the recapitulation is coupled with a natural, rhythmical breathing. Long exhalations are performed as the head moves gently and slowly from right to left; and long inhalations are taken as the head moves back from left to right. He called this act of moving the head from side to side "fanning the event." The mind examines the event from beginning to end while the body fans, on and on, everything the mind focuses on.

Don Juan said that the sorcerers of antiquity, the inventors of the recapitulation, viewed breathing as a magical, life-giving act and used it, accordingly, as a magical vehicle; the exhalation, to eject the foreign energy left in them during the interaction being recapitulated and the inhalation to pull back the energy that they themselves left behind during the interaction.

Because of my academic training, I took the recapitulation to be the process of analyzing one's life. But don Juan insisted that it was more involved than an intellectual psychoanalysis. He postulated the recapitulation as a sorcerer's ploy to induce a minute but steady displacement of the assemblage point. He said that the assemblage point, under the impact of reviewing past actions and feelings, goes back and forth between its present site and the site it occupied when the event being recapitulated took place.

Don Juan stated that the old sorcerers' rationale behind the recapitulation was their conviction that there is an inconceivable dissolving force in the universe, which makes organisms live by lending them awareness. That force also makes organisms die, in order to extract the same lent awareness, which organisms have enhanced through their life experiences. Don Juan explained the old sorcerers' reasoning. They believed that since it is our life experience this force is after, it is of supreme importance that it can be satisfied with a facsimile of our life experience: the recapitulation. Having had what it seeks, the dissolving force then lets sorcerers go, free to expand their capacity to perceive and reach with it the confines of time and space.

When I started again to recapitulate, it was a great surprise to me that my dreaming practices were automatically suspended the moment my recapitulation began. I asked don Juan about this unwanted recess.

"Dreaming requires every bit of our available energy," he replied. "If there is a deep preoccupation in our life, there is no possibility of dreaming."

"But I have been deeply preoccupied before," I said, "and my practices were never interrupted."

"It must be then that every time you thought you were preoccupied, you were only egomaniacally disturbed," he said, laughing. "To be preoccupied, for sorcerers, means that all your energy sources are taken on. This is the first time you've engaged your energy sources in their totality. The rest of the time, even when you recapitulated before, you were not completely absorbed."

Don Juan gave me this time a new recapitulation pattern. I was supposed to construct a jigsaw puzzle by recapitulating, without any apparent order, different events of my life.

"But it's going to be a mess," I protested.

"No, it won't be," he assured me. "It'll be a mess if you let your pettiness choose the events you are going to recapitulate. Instead, let the spirit decide. Be silent, and then get to the event the spirit points out."

The results of that pattern of recapitulation were shocking to me on many levels. It was very impressive to find out that, whenever I silenced my mind, a seemingly independent force immediately plunged me into a most detailed memory of some event in my life. But it was even more impressive that a very orderly configuration resulted. What I thought was going to be chaotic turned out to be extremely effective.

I asked don Juan why he had not made me recapitulate in this manner from the start. He replied that there are two basic rounds to the recapitulation, that the first is called formality and rigidity, and the second fluidity.

I had no inkling about how different my recapitulation was going to be this time. The ability to concentrate, which I had acquired by means of my dreaming practices, permitted me to examine my life at a depth I would never have imagined possible. It took me over a year to view and review all I could about my life experiences. At the end, I had to agree with don Juan: there had been immensities of loaded emotions hidden so deeply inside me as to be virtually inaccessible.

The result of my second recapitulation was a new, more relaxed attitude. The very day I returned to my dreaming practices, I dreamt I saw myself asleep. I turned around and daringly left my room, penuriously going down a flight of stairs to the street.

I was elated with what I had done and reported it to don Juan. My disappointment was enormous when he did not consider this dream part of my dreaming practices. He argued that I had not gone to the street with my energy body, because if I had I would have had a sensation other than walking down a flight of stairs.

"What kind of sensation are you talking about, don Juan?" I asked, with genuine curiosity.

"You have to establish some valid guide to find out whether you are actually seeing your body asleep in your bed," he said instead of answering my question. "Remember, you must be in your actual room, seeing your actual body. Otherwise, what you are having is merely a dream. If that's the case, control that dream, either by observing its detail or by changing it."

I insisted he tell me more about the valid guide he had referred to, but he cut me short. "Figure out a way to validate the fact that you are looking at yourself," he said.

"Do you have any suggestions as to what can be a valid guide?" I insisted.

"Use your own judgment. We are coming to the end of our time together. You have to be on your own very soon."

He changed the subject then, and I was left with a clear taste of my ineptitude. I was unable to figure out what he wanted or what he meant by a valid guide.

In the next dream in which I saw myself asleep, instead of leaving the room and walking down the stairs, or waking up screaming, I remained glued, for a long time, to the spot from which I watched. Without fretting or despairing, I observed the details of my dream. I noticed then that I was asleep wearing a white T-shirt that was ripped at the shoulder. I tried to come closer and examine the rip, but moving was beyond my capabilities. I felt a heaviness that seemed to be part of my very being. In fact, I was all weight. Not knowing what to do next, I instantly entered into a devastating confusion. I tried to change dreams, but some unaccustomed force kept me staring at my sleeping body.

In the midst of my turmoil, I heard the dreaming emissary saying that not having control to move around was frightening me to the point that I might have to do another recapitulation. The emissary's voice and what it said did not surprise me at all. I had never felt so vividly and terrifyingly unable to move. I did not, however, give in to my terror. I examined it and found out that it was not a psychological terror but a physical sensation of helplessness, despair, and annoyance. It bothered me beyond words that I was not capable of moving my limbs. My annoyance grew in proportion to my realization that something outside me had me brutally pinned down. The effort I made to move my arms or legs was so intense and single-minded that at one moment I actually saw one leg of my body, sleeping on the bed, flung out as if kicking.

My awareness was then pulled into my inert, sleeping body, and I woke up with such a force that it took more than half an hour to calm myself down. My heart was beating almost erratically. I was shivering, and some of the muscles in my legs twitched uncontrollably. I had suffered such a radical loss of body heat that I needed blankets and hot-water bottles to raise my temperature.

Naturally, I went to Mexico to ask don Juan's advice about the sensation of paralysis, and about the fact that I really had been wearing a ripped T-shirt, thus, I had indeed seen myself asleep. Besides, I was deadly afraid of hypothermia. He was reluctant to discuss my predicament. All I got out of him was a caustic remark.

"You like drama," he said flatly. "Of course you really saw yourself asleep. The problem is that you got nervous, because your energy body has never been consciously in one piece before. If you ever get nervous and cold again, hold on to your dick. That will restore your body temperature in a jiffy and without any fuss."

I felt a bit offended by his crassness. However, the advice proved effective. The next time I became frightened, I relaxed and returned to normal in a few minutes, doing what he had prescribed. In this manner, I discovered that if I did not fret and kept my annoyance in check, I did not panic. To remain controlled did not help me move, but it certainly gave me a deep sensation of peace and serenity.

After months of useless efforts at walking, I sought don Juan's comments once again, not so much for his advice this time but because I wanted to concede defeat. I was up against an impassable barrier, and I knew with indisputable certainty that I had failed.

"Dreamers have to be imaginative," don Juan said with a malicious grin. "Imaginative you are not. I didn't warn you about having to use your imagination to move your energy body because I wanted to find out whether you could resolve the riddle by yourself. You didn't, and your friends didn't help you either."

In the past, I had been driven to defend myself viciously whenever he accused me of lacking imagination. I thought I was imaginative, but having don Juan as a teacher had taught me, the hard way, that I am not. Since I was not going to engage my energy in futile defenses of myself, I asked him instead, "What is this riddle you are talking about, don Juan?"

"The riddle of how impossible and yet how easy it is to move the energy body. You are trying to move it as if you were in the daily world. We spend so much time and effort learning to walk that we believe our dreaming bodies should also walk. There is no reason why they should, except that walking is foremost in our minds."

I marveled at the simplicity of the solution. I instantly knew that don Juan was right. I had gotten stuck again at the level of interpretation. He had told me I had to move around once I reached the third gate of dreaming, and to me moving around meant walking. I told him that I understood his point.

"It isn't my point," he curtly answered. "It's a sorcerers' point. Sorcerers say that at the third gate the entire energy body can move like energy moves: fast and directly. Your energy body knows exactly how to move. It can move as it moves in the inorganic beings' world.

"And this brings us to the other issue here," don Juan added with an air of pensiveness. "Why didn't your inorganic being friends help you?"

"Why do you call them my friends, don Juan?"

"They are like the classic friends who are not really thoughtful or kind to us but not mean either. The friends who are just waiting for us to turn our backs so they can stab us there."

I understood him completely and agreed with him one hundred percent.

"What makes me go there? Is it a suicidal tendency?" I asked him, more rhetorically than not.

"You don't have any suicidal tendency," he said. "What you have is a total disbelief that you were near death. Since you were not in physical pain, you can't quite convince yourself you were in mortal danger."

His argument was most reasonable, except that I did believe a deep, unknown fear had been ruling my life since my bout with the inorganic beings. Don Juan listened in silence as I described to him my predicament. I could not discard or explain away my urge to go to the inorganic beings' world, in spite of what I knew about it.

"I have a streak of insanity," I said. "What I do doesn't make sense."

"It does make sense. The inorganic beings are still reeling you in, like a fish hooked at the end of a line," he said. "They throw worthless bait at you from time to time to keep you going. To arrange your dreams to occur every four days without fail is worthless bait. But they didn't teach you how to move your energy body."

"Why do you think they didn't?"

"Because when your energy body learns to move by itself, you'll be thoroughly out of their reach. It was premature of me to believe that you are free from them. You are relatively but not completely free. They are still bidding for your awareness."

I felt a chill in my back. He had touched a sore spot in me. "Tell me what to do, don Juan, and I'll do it," I said.

"Be impeccable. I have told you this dozens of times. To be impeccable means to put your life on the line in order to back up your decisions, and then to do quite a lot more than your best to realize those decisions. When you are not deciding anything, you are merely playing roulette with your life in a helter-skelter way."

Don Juan ended our conversation, urging me to ponder what he had said.

At the first opportunity I had, I put don Juan's suggestion about moving my energy body to the test. When I found myself looking at my body asleep, instead of struggling to walk toward it I simply willed myself to move closer to the bed. Instantly, I was nearly touching my body. I saw my face. In fact, I could see every pore in my skin. I cannot say that I liked what I saw. My view of my own body was too detailed to be aesthetically pleasing. Then something like a wind came into the room, totally disarranged everything, and erased my view.

During subsequent dreams, I entirely corroborated that the only way the energy body can move is to glide or soar. I discussed this with don Juan. He seemed unusually satisfied with what I had done, which certainly surprised me. I was accustomed to his cold reaction to anything I did in my dreaming practices.

"Your energy body is used to moving only when something pulls it," he said. "The inorganic beings have been pulling your energy body right and left, and until now you have never moved it by yourself, with your own volition. It doesn't seem like you've done much, moving the way you did, yet I assure you that I was seriously considering ending your practices. For a while, I believed you were not going to learn how to move on your own."

"Were you considering ending my dreaming practices because I am slow?"

"You're not slow. It takes sorcerers forever to learn to move the energy body. I was going to end your dreaming practices because I have no more time. There are other topics, more pressing than dreaming, on which you can use your energy."

"Now that I've learned how to move my energy body by myself, what else should I do, don Juan?"

"Continue moving. Moving your energy body has opened up a new area for you, an area of extraordinary exploration."

He urged me again to come up with an idea to validate the faithfulness of my dreams; that request did not seem as odd as it had the first time he voiced it.

"As you know, to be transported by a scout is the real dreaming task of the second gate," he explained. "It is a very serious matter, but not as serious as forging and moving the energy body. Therefore, you have to make sure, by some means of your own, whether you are actually seeing yourself asleep or whether you are merely dreaming that you're seeing yourself asleep. Your new extraordinary exploration hinges on really seeing yourself asleep."

After some heavy pondering and wondering, I believed that I had come up with the right plan. Having seen my ripped T-shirt gave me an idea for a valid guide. I started from the assumption that, if I were actually observing myself asleep, I would also be observing whether I had the same sleeping attire I had gone to bed in, an attire that I had decided to change radically every four days. I was confident that I was not going to have any difficulty in remembering, in dreams, what I was wearing when I went to bed; the discipline I had acquired through my dreaming practices made me think that I had the ability to record things like this in my mind and remember them in dreams.

I engaged my best efforts to follow this guide, but the results did not pan out as I thought they would. I lacked the necessary control over my dreaming attention, and I could not quite remember the details of my sleeping attire. Yet something else was definitely at work; somehow I always knew whether my dreams were ordinary dreams or not. The outstanding aspect of the dreams that were not just ordinary dreams was that my body lay asleep in bed while my consciousness observed it.

A notable feature of these dreams was my room. It was never like my room in the daily world but an enormous empty hall with my bed at one end. I used to soar over a considerable distance to be at the side of the bed where my body lay. The moment I was next to it, a windlike force used to make me hover over it, like a hummingbird. At times the room used to vanish; disappear piece by piece until only my body and the bed were left. At other times, I used to experience a complete loss of volition. My dreaming attention seemed then to function independently of me. Either it was completely absorbed by the first item it encountered in the room or it seemed unable to decide what to do. In those instances, I had the sensation that I was helplessly floating, going from item to item.

The voice of the dreaming emissary explained to me once that all the elements of the dreams, which were not just commonplace dreams, were really energy configurations different from those of our normal world. The emissary's voice pointed out that, for example, the walls were liquid. It urged me then to plunge into one of them.

Without thinking twice, I dived into a wall as if I were diving into a huge lake. I did not feel the waterlike wall; what I felt was not a physical sensation of plunging into a body of water either. It was more like the thought of diving and the visual sensation of going through liquid matter. I was going, headfirst, into something that opened up, like water does, as I kept moving downward.

The sensation of going down, headfirst, was so real that I began to wonder how long or how deep or how far I was diving. From my point of view, I spent an eternity in there. I saw clouds and rocklike masses of matter suspended in a waterlike substance. There were some glowing, geometric objects that resembled crystals, and blobs of the deepest primary colors I had ever seen. There were also zones of intense light and others of pitch blackness. Everything went by me, either slowly or at a fast speed. I had the thought that I was viewing the cosmos. At the instant of that thought, my speed increased so immensely that everything became blurred, and all of a sudden, I found myself awake with my nose smack against the wall of my room.

Some hidden fear urged me to consult with don Juan. He listened to me, hanging on every word.

"You need to do some drastic maneuvering at this point," he said. "The dreaming emissary has no business interfering with your dreaming practices. Or rather, you should not, under any conditions, permit it to do so."

"How can I stop it?"

"Perform a simple but difficult maneuver. Upon entering into dreaming, voice out loud your desire not to have the dreaming emissary anymore."

"Does that mean, don Juan, that I will never hear it again?"

"Positively. You'll get rid of it forever."

"But is it advisable to get rid of it forever?"

"It most certainly is, at this point."

With those words, don Juan involved me in a most disturbing dilemma. I did not want to put an end to my relationship with the emissary, but, at the same time, I wanted to follow don Juan's advice. He noticed my hesitation.

"I know it's a very difficult affair," he conceded, "but if you don't do it, the inorganic beings will always have a line on you. If you want to avoid this, do what I said, and do it now."

During my next dreaming session, as I prepared myself to utter my intent, the emissary's voice interrupted me. It said, "If you refrain from stating your request, I promise you never to interfere with your dreaming practices and talk to you only if you ask me direct questions."

I instantly accepted its proposition and sincerely felt that it was a good deal. I was even relieved it had turned out this way. I was afraid, however, that don Juan was going to be disappointed.

"It was a good maneuver," he remarked and laughed. "You were sincere; you really intended to voice your request. To be sincere is all that was required. There was, essentially, no need for you to eliminate the emissary. What you wanted was to corner it into proposing an alternative way, convenient to you. I am sure the emissary won't interfere anymore."

He was right. I continued my dreaming practices without any meddling from the emissary. The remarkable consequence was that I began to have dreams in which my dream rooms were my room in the daily world, with one difference: in the dreams, my room was always so slanted, so distorted that it looked like a giant cubist painting; obtuse and acute angles were the rule instead of the normal right angles of walls, ceiling, and floor. In my lopsided room, the very slant, created by the acute or obtuse angles, was a device to display prominently some absurd, superfluous, but real detail; for example, intricate lines in the hardwood floor, or weather discolorations in the wall paint, or dust spots on the ceiling, or smudged finger-prints on the edge of a door.

In those dreams, I unavoidably got lost in the waterlike universes of the detail pointed out by the slant. During my entire dreaming practices, the profusion of detail in my room was so immense and its pull so intense that it instantly made me dive into it.

At the first free moment I had, I was at don Juan's place, consulting him about this state. "I can't overcome my room," I said to him after I had given him the details of my dreaming practices.

"What gives you the idea you have to overcome it?" he asked with a grin.

"I feel that I have to move beyond my room, don Juan."

"But you are moving beyond your room. Perhaps you should ask yourself whether you are caught again in interpretations. What do you think moving means in this case?"

I told him walking from my room to the street had been such a haunting dream for me that I felt a real need to do it again.

"But you are doing greater things than that," he protested. "You are going to unbelievable regions. What else do you want?"

I tried to explain to him that I had a physical urge to move away from the trap of detail. What upset me the most was my incapacity to free myself from whatever caught my attention. To have a modicum of volition was the bottom line for me.

A very long silence followed. I waited to hear more about the trap of detail. After all, he had warned me about its dangers. "You are doing fine," he finally said. "Dreamers take a very long time to perfect their energy bodies. And this is exactly what's at stake here: perfecting your energy body."

Don Juan explained that the reason my energy body was compelled to examine detail and get inextricably stuck in it was its inexperience, its incompleteness. He said that sorcerers spend a lifetime consolidating the energy body by letting it sponge up everything possible.

"Until the energy body is complete and mature, it is self-absorbed," don Juan went on. "It can't get free from the compulsion to be absorbed by everything. But if one takes this into consideration, instead of fighting the energy body, as you're doing now, one can lend it a hand."

"How can I do that, don Juan?"

"By directing its behavior, that is to say, by stalking it."

He explained that since everything related to the energy body depends on the appropriate position of the assemblage point, and since dreaming is nothing else but the means to displace it, stalking is, consequently, the way to make the assemblage point stay put on the perfect position, in this case, the position where the energy body can become consolidated and from which it can finally emerge.

Don Juan said that the moment the energy body can move on its own, sorcerers assume that the optimum position of the assemblage point has been reached. The next step is to stalk it, that is, to fixate it on that position in order to complete the energy body. He remarked that the procedure is simplicity itself. One intends to stalk it.

Silence and looks of expectation followed that statement. I expected him to say more, and he expected me to have understood what he had said. I had not.

"Let your energy body intend to reach the optimum dreaming position," he explained. "Then, let your energy body intend to stay at that position and you will be stalking."

He paused and, with his eyes, urged me to consider his statement. "Intending is the secret, but you already know that," he said. "Sorcerers displace their assemblage points through intending and fixate them, equally, through intending. And there is no technique for intending. One intends through usage."

To have another of my wild assumptions about my worth as

a sorcerer was unavoidable at that point. I had boundless confidence that something was going to put me on the right track to intend the fixation of my assemblage point on the ideal spot. I had accomplished in the past all kinds of successful maneuvers without knowing how I performed them. Don Juan himself had marveled at my ability or my luck, and I was sure this was going to be one of those instances. I was gravely mistaken. No matter what I did, or how long I waited, I had no success whatsoever in fixing my assemblage point on any spot, much less on the ideal one.

After months of serious but unsuccessful struggling, I gave up. "I really believed I could do it," I said to don Juan, the moment I was in his house. "I am afraid that nowadays I am more of an egomaniac than ever."

"Not really," he said with a smile. "What happens is that you are caught in another of your routinary misinterpretations of terms. You want to find the ideal spot, as if you were finding your lost car keys. Then you want to tie your assemblage point, as if you were tying your shoes. The ideal spot and the fixation of the assemblage point are metaphors. They have nothing to do with the words used to describe them."

He asked me then to tell him the latest events of any dreaming practices. The first thing I mentioned was that my urge to be absorbed by detail had subsided notably. I said that perhaps because I moved in my dreams, compulsively and incessantly, the movement might have been what always managed to stop me before I plunged into the detail I was observing. To be stopped in that fashion gave me the opportunity to examine the act of being absorbed by detail. I came to the conclusion that inanimate matter actually possesses an immobilizing force, which I saw as a beam of dull light that kept me pinned down. For example, many times some minute mark on the walls or in the wood lines of the hardwood floor of my room used to send a line of light that transfixed me; from the moment my dreaming attention was focused on that light, the whole dream rotated around that minute mark. I saw it enlarged perhaps to the size of the cosmos. That view used to last until I woke up, usually with my nose pressed against the wall or the wood floor. My own observations were that, in the first place, the detail was real, and, in the second place, I seemed to have been observing it while I was asleep.

Don Juan smiled and said, "All this is happening to you because the forging of your energy body was completed the moment it moved by itself. I didn't tell you that, but I insinuated it. I wanted to know whether or not you were capable of finding it out by yourself, which, of course, you did."

I had no idea what he meant. Don Juan scrutinized me in his usual manner. His penetrating gaze scanned my body.

"What exactly did I find out by myself, don Juan?" I was forced to ask.

"You found out that your energy body had been completed," he answered.

"I didn't find out anything of the kind, I assure you."

"Yes, you did. It started some time ago, when you couldn't find a guide to validate the realness of your dreams, but then something went to work for you and let you know whether you were having a regular dream. That something was your energy body. Now, you despair that you couldn't find the ideal spot to fix your assemblage point. And I tell you that you did. The proof is that, by moving around, your energy body curtailed its obsession with detail."

I was nonplussed. I could not even ask one of my feeble questions.

"What comes next for you is a sorcerers' gem," don Juan went on. "You are going to practice *seeing* energy, in your dreaming. You have fulfilled the drill for the third gate of dreaming: moving your energy body by itself. Now you are going to perform the real task: *seeing* energy with your energy body.

"You have *seen* energy before," he went on, "many times, in fact. But each of those times, *seeing* was a fluke. Now you are going to do it deliberately.

"Dreamers have a rule of thumb," he continued. "If their energy body is complete, they *see* energy every time they gaze at an item in the daily world. In dreams, if they *see* the energy of an item, they know they are dealing with a real world, no matter how distorted that world may appear to their dreaming attention. If they can't *see* the energy of an item, they are in an ordinary dream and not in a real world."

"What is a real world, don Juan?"

"A world that generates energy; the opposite of a phantom world of projections, where nothing generates energy, like most of our dreams, where nothing has an energetic effect."

Don Juan then gave me another definition of dreaming: a process by which dreamers isolate dream conditions in which they can find energy-generating elements. He must have noticed my bewilderment. He laughed and gave another, even more convoluted definition: dreaming is the process by which we intend to find adequate positions of the assemblage point, positions that permit us to perceive energy-generating items in dreamlike states.

He explained that the energy body is also capable of perceiving energy that is quite different from the energy of our own world, as in the case of items of the inorganic beings' realm, which the energy body perceives as sizzling energy. He added that in our world nothing sizzles; everything here wavers.

"From now on," he said, "the issue of your dreaming is going to be to determine whether the items on which you focus your dreaming attention are energy generating, mere phantom projections, or generators of foreign energy."

Don Juan admitted that he had hoped I was going to come up with the idea of *seeing* energy as the gauge to determine whether or not I was observing my real body asleep. He laughed at my spurious device of putting on elaborate sleeping attire, every four days. He said that I'd had, at my fingertips, all the information necessary to deduce what was the real task of the third gate of dreaming and to come up with the right idea but that my interpretation system had forced me to seek contrived solutions that lacked the simplicity and directness of sorcery.

·9·

THE NEW AREA OF

EXPLORATION

Don Juan told me that in order to *see* in dreaming not only did I have to intend *seeing* but I had to put my intent into loud words. For reasons he refused to explain, he insisted that I had to speak up. He conceded that there are other means to accomplish the same result, but he asserted that voicing one's intent is the simplest and most direct way.

The first time I put into words my intent to *see*, I was dreaming of a church bazaar. There were so many articles that I could not make up my mind which one to gaze at. A giant, conspicuous vase in a corner made up my mind for me. I gazed at it, voicing my intent to *see*. The vase remained in my view for an instant, then it changed into another object.

I gazed at as many things as I could in that dream. After I voiced my intent to *see*, every item I had chosen to gaze at vanished or turned into something else, as had happened all along in my dreaming practices. My dreaming attention was finally exhausted, and I woke up tremendously frustrated, almost angry.

For months on end, I actually gazed at hundreds of items in my dreams and deliberately voiced my intent to *see*, but nothing ever happened. Tired of waiting, I finally had to ask don Juan about it.

"You need to have patience. You are learning to do something extraordinary," he remarked. "You are learning to intend to *see* in your dreams. Someday you will not have to voice your intent; you'll simply will it, silently."

"I think I have not understood the function of whatever I am doing," I said. "Nothing happens when I shout my intent to *see*. What does that mean?"

"It means that your dreams, so far, have been ordinary dreams; they have been phantom projections; images that have life only in your dreaming attention."

He wanted to know exactly what had happened to the items on which I had focused my gaze. I said that they had vanished or changed shape or even produced vortexes that eventually changed my dreams.

"It has been like that in all my daily dreaming practices," I said. "The only thing out of the ordinary is that I am learning to yell in my dreams, at the top of my voice."

My last statement threw don Juan into a genuine fit of belly laughter, which I found disconcerting. I failed to find the humor of my statement or the reason for his reaction.

"Someday you'll appreciate how funny all this is," he said as an answer to my silent protest. "In the meantime, don't give up or get discouraged. Keep on trying. Sooner or later, you'll hit the right note."

As usual, he was right. A couple of months later, I hit the jackpot. I had a most unusual dream. It started with the appearance of a scout from the inorganic beings' world. The scouts as well as the dreaming emissary had been strangely absent from my dreams. I had not missed them or pondered their disappearance. In fact, I was so at ease without them I had even forgotten to ask don Juan about their absence.

In that dream, the scout had been, at first, a gigantic yellow topaz, which I had found stuck in the back of a drawer. The moment I voiced my intent to *see*, the topaz turned into a blob of sizzling energy. I feared that I would be compelled to follow it, so I moved my gaze away from the scout and focused it on an aquarium with tropical fish. I voiced my intent to *see* and got a tremendous surprise. The aquarium emitted a low, greenish glow and changed into a large surrealist portrait of a bejeweled woman. The portrait emitted the same greenish glow when I voiced my intent to *see*.

As I gazed at that glow, the whole dream changed. I was walking then on a street in a town that seemed familiar to me; it might have been Tucson. I gazed at a display of women's clothes in a store window and spoke out loud my intent to *see*. Instantly, a black mannequin, prominently displayed, began to glow. I gazed next at a saleslady who came at that moment to rearrange the window. She looked at me. After voicing my intent, I *saw* her glow. It was so stupendous that I was afraid some detail in her splendorous glow would trap me, but the woman moved inside the store before I had time to focus my total attention on her. I certainly intended to follow her inside; however, my dreaming attention was caught by a moving glow. It came to me charging, filled with hatred. There was loathing in it and viciousness. I jumped backward. The glow stopped its charge; a black substance swallowed me, and I woke up.

These images were so vivid that I firmly believed I had *seen* energy and my dream had been one of those conditions that don Juan had called dreamlike, energy-generating. The idea that dreams can take place in the consensual reality of our daily world intrigued me, just as the dream images of the inorganic beings' realm had intrigued me.

"This time, you not only *saw* energy but crossed a dangerous boundary," don Juan said, after hearing my account.

He reiterated that the drill for the third gate of dreaming is to make the energy body move on its own. In my last session, he said, I had unwittingly superseded the effect of that drill and crossed into another world.

"Your energy body moved," he said. "It journeyed, by itself. That kind of journeying is beyond your abilities at this moment, and something attacked you."

"What do you think it was, don Juan?"

"This is a predatorial universe. It could have been one of thousands of things existing out there."

"Why do you think it attacked me?"

"For the same reason the inorganic beings attacked you: because you made yourself available."

"Is it that clear-cut, don Juan?"

"Certainly. It's as clear-cut as what you would do if a strange-looking spider crept across your desk while you were writing. You'd squash it, out of fright, rather than admire it or examine it."

I was at a loss and searched for words to ask the proper question. I wanted to ask him where my dream had taken place, or what world I was in in that dream. But those questions did not make any sense; I could gather that myself. Don Juan was very understanding.

"You want to know where your dreaming attention was focused, don't you?" he asked with a grin.

This was exactly how I wanted to word my question. I reasoned that in the dream under consideration, I must have been looking at some real object. Just like what had happened when I saw in dreams the minute details on the floor or the walls or the door of my room, details that I later had corroborated existed.

Don Juan said that in special dreams, like the one I'd had, our dreaming attention focuses on the daily world, and that it moves instantly from one real object to another in the world. What makes this movement possible is that the assemblage point is on the proper dreaming position. From that position, the assemblage point gives the dreaming attention such fluidity that it can move in a split second over incredible distances, and in doing so it produces a perception so fast, so fleeting that it resembles an ordinary dream.

Don Juan explained that in my dream I had *seen* a real vase and then my dreaming attention had moved over distances to *see* a real surrealist painting of a bejeweled woman. The result, with the exception of *seeing* energy, had been very close to an ordinary dream, in which items, when gazed at, quickly turn into something else.

"I know how disturbing this is," he went on, definitely aware of my bewilderment. "For some reason pertinent to the mind, to *see* energy in dreaming is more upsetting than anything one can think of."

I remarked that I had *seen* energy in dreaming before, yet it had never affected me like this.

"Now your energy body is complete and functioning," he said. "Therefore, the implication that you *see* energy in your dream is that you are perceiving a real world, through the veil of a dream. That's the importance of the journey you took. It was real. It involved energy-generating items that nearly ended your life."

"Was it that serious, don Juan?"

"You bet! The creature that attacked you was made of pure awareness and was as deadly as anything can be. You *saw* its energy. I am sure that you realize by now that unless we *see* in dreaming, we can't tell a real, energy-generating thing from a phantom projection. So, even though you battled the inorganic beings and indeed *saw* the scouts and the tunnels, your energy body doesn't know for sure if they were real, meaning energy generating. You are ninety-nine but not one hundred percent sure."

Don Juan insisted on talking about the journey I had taken. For inexplicable reasons, I was reluctant to deal with that subject. What he was saying produced an instantaneous reaction in me. I found myself trying to come to grips with a deep, strange fear; it was dark and obsessive in a nagging, visceral way.

"You definitely went into another layer of the onion," don Juan said, finishing a statement to which I had not paid attention.

"What is this other layer of the onion, don Juan?"

"The world is like an onion, it has many skins. The world we know is but one of them. Sometimes, we cross boundaries and enter into another skin: another world, very much like this one, but not the same. And you entered into one, all by yourself."

"How is this journey you're talking about possible, don Juan?"

"That is a meaningless question, because no one can answer it. In the view of sorcerers, the universe is constructed in layers, which the energy body can cross. Do you know where the old sorcerers are still existing to this day? In another layer, in another skin of the onion."

"For me, the idea of a real, pragmatic journey, taken in dreams, is very difficult to understand or to accept, don Juan."

"We have discussed this topic to exhaustion. I was convinced you understood that the journey of the energy body depends exclusively on the position of the assemblage point."

"You've told me that. And I have been mulling it over and over; still, saying that the journey is in the position of the assemblage point doesn't say anything to me."

"Your problem is your cynicism. I was just like you. Cynicism doesn't allow us to make drastic changes in our understanding of the world. It also forces us to feel that we are always right."

I understood his point to perfection, but I reminded him about my fight against all that.

"I propose that you do one nonsensical thing that might turn the tide," he said. "Repeat to yourself incessantly that the hinge of sorcery is the mystery of the assemblage point. If you repeat this to yourself long enough, some unseen force takes over and makes the appropriate changes in you."

Don Juan did not give me any indication that he was being facetious. I knew he meant every word of it. What bothered me was his insistence that I repeat the formula ceaselessly to myself. I caught myself thinking that all of it was asinine.

"Cut your cynical attitude," he snapped at me. "Repeat this in a bona fide manner.

"The mystery of the assemblage point is everything in sorcery," he continued, without looking at me. "Or rather, everything in sorcery rests on the manipulation of the assemblage point. You know all this, but you have to repeat it."

For an instant, as I heard his remarks, I thought I was going to die of anguish. An incredible sense of physical sadness gripped my chest and made me scream with pain. My stomach and diaphragm seemed to be pushing up, moving into my chest cavity. The push was so intense that my awareness changed levels, and I entered into my normal state. Whatever we had been talking about became a vague thought about something that might have happened but actually had not, according to the mundane reasoning of my everyday-life consciousness.

The next time don Juan and I talked about dreaming, we discussed the reasons I had been unable to proceed with my dreaming practices for months on end. Don Juan warned me that to explain my situation he had to go in a roundabout way. He pointed out, first, that there is an enormous difference between the thoughts and deeds of the men of antiquity and those of modern men. Then he pointed out that the men of ancient times had a very realistic view of perception and awareness because their view stemmed from their observations of the universe around them. Modern men, in contrast, have an absurdly unrealistic view of perception and awareness because their view stems from their observations of the social order and from their dealings with it.

"Why are you telling me this?" I asked.

"Because you are a modern man involved with the views and observations of men of antiquity," he replied. "And none of those views and observations are familiar to you. Now more than ever you need sobriety and aplomb. I am trying to make a solid bridge, a bridge you can walk on, between the views of men of ancient times and those of modern men."

He remarked that of all the transcendental observations of the men of ancient times, the only one with which I was familiar, because it had filtered down to our day, was the idea of selling our souls to the devil in exchange for immortality, which he admitted sounded to him like something coming straight out of the relationship of the old sorcerers with the inorganic beings. He reminded me how the dreaming emissary had tried to induce me to stay in its realm by offering me the possibility of maintaining my individuality and self-awareness for nearly an eternity.

"As you know, succumbing to the lure of the inorganic beings is not just an idea; it's real," don Juan went on. "But you haven't yet fully realized the implication of that realness. Dreaming, likewise, is real; it is an energy-generating condition. You hear my statements and you certainly understand what I mean, but your awareness hasn't caught up with the total implication of it yet."

Don Juan said that my rationality knew the import of a realization of this nature, and during our last talk it had forced my awareness to change levels. I ended up in my normal awareness before I could deal with the nuances of my dream. My rationality had further protected itself by suspending my dreaming practices.

"I assure you that I am fully aware of what an energy-generating condition means," I said.

"And I assure you that you are not," he retorted. "If you were, you would measure dreaming with greater care and deliberation. Since you believe you are just dreaming, you take blind chances. Your faulty reasoning tells you that no matter what happens, at a given moment the dream will be over and you will wake up."

He was right. In spite of all the things I had witnessed in my dreaming practices, somehow I still retained the general sense that all of it had been a dream.

"I am talking to you about the views of men of antiquity and the views of modern man," don Juan went on, "because your awareness, which is the awareness of modern man, prefers to deal with an unfamiliar concept as if it were an empty ideality.

"If I left it up to you, you'd regard dreaming as an idea. Of course, I'm sure you take dreaming seriously, but you don't quite believe in the reality of dreaming."

"I understand what you are saying, don Juan, but I don't understand why you are saying it."

"I am saying all this because you are now, for the first time, in the proper position to understand that dreaming is an energy-generating condition. For the first time, you can understand now that ordinary dreams are the honing devices used to train the assemblage point to reach the position that creates this energy-generating condition we call dreaming."

He warned me that, since dreamers touch and enter real worlds of all-inclusive effects, they ought to be in a permanent state of the most intense and sustained alertness; any deviation from total alertness imperils the dreamer in ways more than dreadful.

I began again, at this point, to experience a movement in my chest cavity, exactly as I had felt the day my awareness changed levels by itself. Don Juan forcibly shook me by the arm.

"Regard dreaming as something extremely dangerous!" he commanded me. "And begin that now! Don't start any of your weird maneuvers."

His tone of voice was so urgent that I stopped whatever I was, unconsciously, doing.

"What is going on with me, don Juan?" I asked.

"What's going on with you is that you can displace your assemblage point quickly and easily," he said. "Yet that ease has the tendency to make the displacement erratic. Bring your ease to order. And don't allow yourself even a fraction of an inch leeway."

I could easily have argued that I did not know what he was talking about, but I knew. I also knew I had only a few seconds to round up my energy and change my attitude, and I did.

This was the end of our exchange that day. I went home, and for nearly a year I faithfully and daily repeated what don Juan had asked me to say. The results of my litany-like invocation were incredible. I was firmly convinced that it had the same effect on my awareness that exercise has on the muscles of the body. My assemblage point became more agile, which meant that *seeing* energy in dreaming became the sole goal of my practices. My skill at intending to *see* grew in proportion to my efforts. A moment came when I was able just to intend *seeing*, without saying a word, and actually experience the same result as when I voiced out loud my intent to *see*.

Don Juan congratulated me on my accomplishment. I, naturally, assumed he was being facetious. He assured me that he meant it, but beseeched me to continue shouting, at least whenever I was at a loss. His request did not seem odd to me. On my own, I had been yelling in my dreams at the top of my voice every time I deemed it necessary.

I discovered that the energy of our world wavers. It scintillates. Not only living beings but everything in our world glimmers with an inner light of its own. Don Juan explained that the energy of our world consists of layers of shimmering hues.

The top layer is whitish; another, immediately adjacent to it, is chartreuse; and another one, more distant yet, is amber.

I found all those hues, or rather I *saw* glimmers of them whenever items that I encountered in my dreamlike states changed shapes. However, a whitish glow was always the initial impact of *seeing* anything that generated energy.

"Are there only three different hues?" I asked don Juan.

"There is an endless number of them," he replied, "but for the purposes of a beginning order, you should be concerned with those three. Later on, you can get as sophisticated as you want and isolate dozens of hues, if you are able to do it.

"The whitish layer is the hue of the present position of mankind's assemblage point," don Juan continued. "Let's say that it is a modern hue. Sorcerers believe that everything man does nowadays is tinted with that whitish glow. At another time, the position of mankind's assemblage point made the hue of the ruling energy in the world chartreuse; and at another time, more distant yet, it made it amber. The color of sorcerers' energy is amber, which means that they are energetically associated with the men who existed in a distant past."

"Do you think, don Juan, that the present whitish hue will change someday?"

"If man is capable of evolving. The grand task of sorcerers is to bring forth the idea that, in order to evolve, man must first free his awareness from its bindings to the social order. Once awareness is free, intent will redirect it into a new evolutionary path."

"Do you think sorcerers will succeed in that task?"

"They have already succeeded. They themselves are the proof. To convince others of the value and import of evolving is another matter."

The other kind of energy I found present in our world but alien to it was the scouts' energy, the energy don Juan had called sizzling. I encountered scores of items in my dreams that, once I *saw* them, turned into blobs of energy that seemed to be frying, bubbling with some heatlike inner activity.

"Bear in mind that not every scout you are going to find belongs to the realm of inorganic beings," don Juan remarked. "Every scout you have found so far, except for the blue scout, has been from that realm, but that was because the inorganic beings were catering to you. They were directing the show. Now you are on your own. Some of the scouts you will encounter are going to be not from the inorganic beings' realm but from other, even more distant levels of awareness."

"Are the scouts aware of themselves?" I asked.

"Most certainly," he replied.

"Then why don't they make contact with us when we are awake?"

"They do. But our great misfortune is to have our consciousness so fully engaged that we don't have time to pay attention. In our sleep, however, the two-way-traffic trapdoor opens: we dream. And in our dreams, we make contact."

"Is there any way to tell whether the scouts are from a level besides the inorganic beings' world?"

"The greater their sizzling, the farther they come from. It sounds simplistic, but you have to let your energy body tell you what is what. I assure you, it'll make very fine distinctions and unerring judgments when faced with alien energy."

He was right again. Without much ado, my energy body distinguished two general types of alien energy. The first was the scouts from the inorganic beings' realm. Their energy fizzled mildly. There was no sound to it, but it had all the overt appearance of effervescence, or of water that is starting to boil.

The energy of the second general type of scouts gave me the impression of considerably more power. Those scouts seemed to be just about to burn. They vibrated from within as if they were filled with pressurized gas.

My encounters with the alien energy were always fleeting because I paid total attention to what don Juan recommended. He said, "Unless you know exactly what you are doing and what you want out of alien energy, you have to be content with a brief glance. Anything beyond a glance is as dangerous and as stupid as petting a rattlesnake."

"Why is it dangerous, don Juan?" I asked.

"Scouts are always very aggressive and extremely daring," he said. "They have to be that way in order to prevail in their explorations. Sustaining our dreaming attention on them is tantamount to soliciting their awareness to focus on us. Once they focus their attention on us, we are compelled to go with them. And that, of course, is the danger. We may end up in worlds beyond our energetic possibilities."

Don Juan explained that there are many more types of scouts than the two I had classified, but that at my present level of energy I could only focus on three. He described the first two types as the easiest to spot. Their disguises in our dreams are so outlandish, he said, that they immediately attract our dreaming attention. He depicted the scouts of the third type as the most dangerous, in terms of aggressiveness and power, and because they hide behind subtle disguises.

"One of the strangest things dreamers find, which you yourself will find presently," don Juan continued, "is this third type of scout. So far, you have found samples of only the first two types, but that's because you haven't looked in the right place."

"And what is the right place, don Juan?"

"You have again fallen prey to words; this time the culprit word is 'items,' which you have taken to mean only things, objects. Well, the most ferocious scout hides behind people in our dreams. A formidable surprise was in store for me, in my dreaming, when I focused my gaze on the dream image of my mother. After I voiced my intent to see, she turned into a ferocious, frightening bubble of sizzling energy."

Don Juan paused to let his statements sink in. I felt stupid for being disturbed at the possibility of finding a scout behind the dream image of my mother.

"It's annoying that they are always associated with the dream images of our parents or close friends," he went on.

"Perhaps that's why we often feel ill at ease when we dream of them." His grin gave me the impression that he was enjoying my turmoil. "A rule of thumb for dreamers is to assume that the third type of scout is present whenever they feel perturbed by their parents or friends in a dream. Sound advice is to avoid those dream images. They are sheer poison."

"Where does the blue scout stand in relation to the other scouts?" I asked.

"Blue energy doesn't sizzle," he replied. "It is like ours; it wavers, but it is blue instead of white. Blue energy doesn't exist in a natural state in our world.

"And this brings us to something we've never talked about. What color were the scouts you've *seen* so far?"

Until the moment he mentioned it, I had never thought about this. I told don Juan that the scouts I had *seen* were either pink or reddish. And he said that the deadly scouts of the third type were bright orange.

I found out myself that the third type of scout is outright scary. Every time I found one of them, it was behind the dream images of my parents, especially of my mother. *Seeing* it always reminded me of the blob of energy that had attacked me in my first deliberate *seeing* dream. Every time I found it, the alien exploring energy actually seemed about to jump on me. My energy body used to react with horror even before I *saw* it.

During our next discussion of dreaming, I queried don Juan about the total absence of inorganic beings in my dreaming practices. "Why don't they show up anymore?" I asked.

"They only show themselves at the beginning," he explained. "After their scouts take us to their world, there is no necessity for the inorganic beings' projections. If we want to *see* the inorganic beings, a scout takes us there. For no one, and I mean no one, can journey by himself to their realm."

"Why is that so, don Juan?"

"Their world is sealed. No one can enter or leave without the consent of the inorganic beings. The only thing you can do by yourself once you are inside is, of course, voice your intent to stay. To say it out loud means to set in motion currents of energy that are irreversible. In olden times, words were incredibly powerful. Now they are not. In the inorganic beings' realm, they haven't lost their power."

Don Juan laughed and said that he had no business saying anything about the inorganic beings' world because I really knew more about it than he and all his companions combined.

"There is one last issue related to that world that we haven't discussed," he said. He paused for a long while, as if searching for the appropriate words. "In the final analysis," he began, "my aversion to the old sorcerers' activities is very personal. As a nagual, I detest what they did. They cowardly sought refuge in the inorganic beings' world. They argued that in a predatorial universe, poised to rip us apart, the only possible haven for us is in that realm."

"Why did they believe that?" I asked.

"Because it's true," he said. "Since the inorganic beings can't lie, the sales pitch of the dreaming emissary is all true. That world can give us shelter and prolong our awareness for nearly an eternity."

"The emissary's sales pitch, even if it's the truth, has no appeal to me," I said.

"Do you mean you will chance a road that might rip you apart?" he asked with a note of bewilderment in his voice.

I assured don Juan that I did not want the inorganic beings' world no matter what advantages it offered. My statement seemed to please him to no end.

"You are ready then for one final statement about that world. The most dreadful statement I can make," he said, and tried to smile but did not quite make it.

Don Juan searched in my eyes, I suppose for a glimmer of agreement or comprehension. He was silent for a moment.

"The energy necessary to move the assemblage points of sorcerers comes from the realm of inorganic beings," he said, as if he were hurrying to get it over with.

My heart nearly stopped. I felt a vertigo and had to stomp my feet on the ground not to faint.

"This is the truth," don Juan went on, "and the legacy of the old sorcerers to us. They have us pinned down to this day. This is the reason I don't like them. I resent having to dip into one source alone. Personally, I refuse to do it. And I have tried to steer you away from it. But with no success, because something pulls you to that world, like a magnet."

I understood don Juan better than I could have thought. Journeying to that world had always meant to me, at an energetic level, a boost of dark energy. I had even thought of it in those terms, long before don Juan voiced his statement.

"What can we do about it?" I asked.

"We can't have dealings with them," he answered, "and yet we can't stay away from them. My solution has been to take their energy but not give in to their influence. This is known as the ultimate stalking. It is done by sustaining the unbending intent of freedom, even though no sorcerer knows what freedom really is."

"Can you explain to me, don Juan, why sorcerers have to take energy from the realm of inorganic beings?"

"There is no other viable energy for sorcerers. In order to maneuver the assemblage point in the manner they do, sorcerers need an inordinate amount of energy."

I reminded him of his own statement: that a redeployment of energy is necessary in order to do dreaming.

"That is correct," he replied. "To start dreaming sorcerers need to redefine their premises and save their energy, but that redefining is valid only to have the necessary energy to set up dreaming. To fly into other realms, to *see* energy, to forge the energy body, et cetera, et cetera, is another matter. For those maneuvers, sorcerers need loads of dark, alien energy."

"But how do they take it from the inorganic beings' world?"

"By the mere act of going to that world. All the sorcerers of our line have to do this. However, none of us is idiotic enough to do what you've done. But this is because none of us has your proclivities."

Don Juan sent me home to ponder what he had revealed to me. I had endless questions, but he did not want to hear any of them.

"All the questions you have, you can answer yourself," he said as he waved good-bye to me.

· 10 ·

STALKING THE STALKERS

At home, I soon realized that it was impossible for me to answer any of my questions. In fact, I could not even formulate them. Perhaps that was because the boundary of the second attention had begun to collapse on me; this was when I met Florinda Grau and Carol Tiggs in the world of everyday life. The confusion of not knowing them at all yet knowing them so intimately that I would have died for them at the drop of a hat was most deleterious to me. I had met Taisha Abelar a few years before, and I was just beginning to get used to the confounded feeling of knowing her without having the vaguest idea of how. To add two more people to my overloaded system proved too much for me. I got ill out of fatigue and had to seek don Juan's aid. I went to the town in southern Mexico where he and his companions lived.

Don Juan and his fellow sorcerers laughed uproariously at the mere mention of my turmoils. Don Juan explained to me that they were not really laughing at me but at themselves. My cognitive problems reminded them of the ones they had had when the boundary of the second attention had collapsed on them, just as it had on me. Their awareness, like mine, had not been prepared for it, he said.

"Every sorcerer goes through the same agony," don Juan went on. "Awareness is an endless area of exploration for sorcerers and man in general. In order to enhance awareness, there is no risk we should not run, no means we should refuse. Bear in mind, however, that only in soundness of mind can awareness be enhanced."

Don Juan reiterated, then, that his time was coming to an end and that I had to use my resources wisely to cover as much ground as I could before he left. Talk like that used to throw me into states of profound depression. But as the time of his departure approached, I had begun to react with more resignation. I no longer felt depressed, but I still panicked.

Nothing else was said after that. The next day, at his request, I drove don Juan to Mexico City. We arrived around noon and went directly to the hotel del Prado, in the Paseo Alameda, the place he usually lodged when he was in the city. Don Juan had an appointment with a lawyer that day, at four in the afternoon. Since we had plenty of time, we went to have lunch in the famous Café Tacuba, a restaurant in the heart of downtown where it was purported that real meals were served.

Don Juan was not hungry. He ordered only two sweet tamales, while I gorged myself on a sumptuous feast. He laughed at me and made signs of silent despair at my healthy appetite.

"I'm going to propose a line of action for you," he said in a curt tone when we had finished our lunch. "It's the last task of the third gate of dreaming, and it consists of stalking the stalkers, a most mysterious maneuver. To stalk the stalkers means to deliberately draw energy from the inorganic beings' realm in order to perform a sorcery feat."

"What kind of sorcery feat, don Juan?"

"A journey, a journey that uses awareness as an element of the environment," he explained. "In the world of daily life, water is an element of the environment that we use for traveling. Imagine awareness being a similar element that can be used for traveling. Through the medium of awareness, scouts from all over the universe come to us, and vice versa; via awareness, sorcerers go to the ends of the universe."

There had been certain concepts, among the hosts of concepts don Juan had made me aware of in the course of his teachings, that attracted my full interest without any coaxing. This was one.

"The idea that awareness is a physical element is revolutionary," I said in awe.

"I didn't say it's a physical element," he corrected me. "It's an energetic element. You have to make that distinction. For sorcerers who *see*, awareness is a glow. They can hitch their energy body to that glow and go with it."

"What's the difference between a physical and an energetic element?" I asked.

"The difference is that physical elements are part of our interpretation system, but energetic elements are not. Energetic elements, like awareness, exist in our universe. But we, as average people, perceive only the physical elements because we were taught to do so. Sorcerers perceive the energetic elements for the same reason: they were taught to do so."

Don Juan explained that the use of awareness as an energetic element of our environment is the essence of sorcery, that in terms of practicalities, the trajectory of sorcery is, first, to free the existing energy in us by impeccably following the sorcerers' path; second, to use that energy to develop the energy body by means of dreaming; and, third, to use awareness as an element of the environment in order to enter with the energy body and all our physicality into other worlds.

"There are two kinds of energy journeys into other worlds," he went on. "One is when awareness picks up the sorcerer's energy body and takes it wherever it may, and the other is when the sorcerer decides, in full consciousness, to use the avenue of awareness to make a journey. You've done the first kind of journeying. It takes an enormous discipline to do the second."

After a long silence, don Juan stated that in the life of sorcerers there are issues that require masterful handling, and that dealing with awareness, as an energetic element open to the energy body, is the most important, vital, and dangerous of those issues.

I had no comment. I was suddenly on pins and needles, hanging on every one of his words.

"By yourself, you don't have enough energy to perform the last task of the third gate of dreaming," he went on, "but you and Carol Tiggs together can certainly do what I have in mind."

He paused, deliberately egging me on with his silence to ask what he had in mind. I did. His laughter only increased the ominous mood.

"I want you two to break the boundaries of the normal world and, using awareness as an energetic element, enter into another," he said. "This breaking and entering amounts to stalking the stalkers. Using awareness as an element of the environment bypasses the influence of the inorganic beings, but it still uses their energy."

He did not want to give me any more information, in order not to influence me, he said. His belief was that the less I knew beforehand the better off I would be. I disagreed, but he assured me that, in a pinch, my energy body was perfectly capable of taking care of itself.

We went from the restaurant to the lawyer's office. Don Juan quickly concluded his business, and we were, in no time at all, in a taxi on our way to the airport. Don Juan informed me that Carol Tiggs was arriving on a flight from Los Angeles, and that she was coming to Mexico City exclusively to fulfill this last dreaming task with me.

"The valley of Mexico is a superb place to perform the kind of sorcery feat you are after," he commented.

"You haven't told me yet what the exact steps to follow are," I said.

He didn't answer me. We did not speak any more, but while we waited for the plane to land, he explained the procedure I had to follow. I had to go to Carol's room at the Regis Hotel, across the street from our hotel, and, after getting into a state of total inner silence, with her I had to slip gently into dreaming, voicing our intent to go to the realm of the inorganic beings.

I interrupted to remind him that I always had to wait for a scout to show up before I could manifest out loud my intent to go to the inorganic beings' world.

Don Juan chuckled and said, "You haven't dreamt with Carol Tiggs yet. You'll find out that it's a treat. Sorceresses don't need any props. They just go to that world whenever they want to; for them, there is a scout on permanent call."

I could not bring myself to believe that a sorceress would be able to do what he was asserting. I thought I had a degree of expertise in handling the inorganic beings' world. When I mentioned to him what was going through my mind, he retorted that I had no expertise whatsoever when it came to what sorceresses are capable of.

"Why do you think I had Carol Tiggs with me to pull you bodily out of that world?" he asked. "Do you think it was because she's beautiful?"

"Why was it, don Juan?"

"Because I couldn't do it myself; and for her, it was nothing. She has a knack for that world."

"Is she an exceptional case, don Juan?"

"Women in general have a natural bent for that realm; sorceresses are, of course, the champions, but Carol Tiggs is better than anyone I know because she, as the nagual woman, has superb energy."

I thought I had caught don Juan in a serious contradiction. He had told me that the inorganic beings were not interested at all in women. Now he was asserting the opposite.

"No. I'm not asserting the opposite," he remarked when I confronted him. "I've said to you that the inorganic beings don't pursue females; they only go after males. But I've also said to you that the inorganic beings are female, and that the entire universe is female to a large degree. So draw your own conclusions."

Since I had no way to draw any conclusions, Don Juan explained to me that sorceresses, in theory, come and go as they please in that world because of their enhanced awareness and their femaleness.

"Do you know this for a fact?" I asked.

"The women of my party have never done that," he confessed, "not because they can't but because I dissuaded them. The women of your party, on the other hand, do it like changing skirts."

I felt a vacuum in my stomach. I really did not know anything about the women of my party. Don Juan consoled me, saying that my circumstances were different from his, as was my role as a nagual. He assured me that I did not have it in me to dissuade any of the women of my party, even if I stood on my head.

As the taxi drove us to her hotel, Carol delighted don Juan and me with her impersonations of people we knew. I tried to be serious and questioned her about our task. She mumbled some apologies for not being able to answer me with the seriousness I deserved. Don Juan laughed uproariously when she mimicked my solemn tone of voice.

After registering Carol at the hotel, the three of us meandered around downtown, looking for secondhand bookstores. We ate a light dinner at the Sanborn's restaurant in the House of Tiles. About ten o'clock, we walked to the Regis Hotel. We went directly to the elevator. My fear had sharpened my capacity to perceive details. The hotel building was old and massive. The furniture in the lobby had obviously seen better days. Yet there was still, all around us, something left of an old glory that had a definite appeal. I could easily understand why Carol liked that hotel so much.

Before we got into the elevator, my anxiety mounted to such heights that I had to ask don Juan for last-minute instructions. "Tell me again how we are going to proceed," I begged.

Don Juan pulled us to the huge, ancient stuffed chairs in the lobby and patiently explained to us that, once we were in the world of the inorganic beings, we had to voice our intent to transfer our normal awareness to our energy bodies. He suggested that Carol and I voice our intent together, although that part was not really important. What was important, he said, was that each of us intend the transfer of the total awareness of our daily world to our energy body.

"How do we do this transference of awareness?" I asked.

"Transferring awareness is purely a matter of voicing our intent and having the necessary amount of energy," he said. "Carol knows all this. She's done it before. She entered physically into the inorganic beings' world when she pulled you out of it, remember? Her energy will do the trick. It'll tip the scales."

"What does it mean to tip the scales? I am in limbo, don Juan."

Don Juan explained that to tip the scales meant to add one's total physical mass to the energy body. He said that using awareness as a medium to make the journey into another world is not the result of applying any techniques but the corollary of intending and having enough energy. The bulk of energy from

Carol Tiggs added to mine, or the bulk of my energy added to Carol's, was going to make us into one single entity, energetically capable of pulling our physicality and placing it on the energy body in order to make that journey.

"What exactly do we have to do in order to enter into that other world?" Carol asked. Her question scared me half to death; I thought she knew what was going on.

"Your total physical mass has to be added to your energy body," don Juan replied, looking into her eyes. "The great difficulty of this maneuver is to discipline the energy body, a thing the two of you have already done. Lack of discipline is the only reason the two of you may fail in performing this feat of ultimate stalking. Sometimes, as a fluke, an average person ends up performing it and entering into another world. But this is immediately explained away as insanity or hallucination."

I would have given anything in the world for don Juan to continue talking. But he put us in the elevator, and we went up to the second floor, to Carol's room, despite my protests and my rational need to know. Deep down, however, my turmoil was not so much that I needed to know; the bottom line was my fear. Somehow, this sorcerers' maneuver was more frightening to me than anything I had done so far.

Don Juan's parting words to us were "Forget the self and you will fear nothing." His grin and the nodding of his head were invitations to ponder the statement.

Carol laughed and began to clown, imitating don Juan's voice as he gave us his cryptic instructions. Her lisping added quite a bit of color to what don Juan had said. Sometimes I found her lisping adorable. Most of the time, I detested it. Fortunately, that night her lisping was hardly noticeable.

We went to her room and sat down on the edge of the bed. My last conscious thought was that the bed was a relic from the beginning of the century. Before I had time to utter a single word, I found myself in a strange-looking bed. Carol was with me. She half sat up at the same time I did. We were naked, each covered with a thin blanket.

"What's going on?" she asked in a feeble voice.

"Are you awake?" I asked inanely.

"Of course I am awake," she said in an impatient tone.

"Do you remember where we were?" I asked.

There was a long silence, as she obviously tried to put her thoughts in order. "I think I am real, but you are not," she finally said. "I know where I was before this. And you want to trick me."

I thought she was doing the same thing herself. She knew what was going on and was testing me or pulling my leg. Don Juan had told me that her demons and mine were caginess and distrust. I was having a grand sample of that.

"I refuse to be part of any shit where you are in control," she said. She looked at me with venom in her eyes. "I am talking to you, whoever you are."

She took one of the blankets we had been covered with and wrapped herself with it. "I am going to lie here and go back to where I came from," she said, with an air of finality. "You and the nagual go and play with each other."

"You have to stop this nonsense," I said forcefully. "We are in another world."

She didn't pay any attention and turned her back to me like an annoyed, pampered child. I did not want to waste my dreaming attention in futile discussions of realness. I began to examine my surroundings. The only light in the room was moonlight shining through the window directly in front of us. We were in a small room, on a high bed. I noticed that the bed was primitively constructed. Four thick posts had been planted in the ground, and the bed frame was a lattice, made of long poles attached to the posts. The bed had a thick mattress, or rather a compact mattress. There were no sheets or pillows. Filled burlap sacks were stacked up against the walls. Two sacks by the foot of the bed, staggered one on top of the other, served as a stepladder to climb onto it.

Looking for a light switch, I became aware that the high bed was in a corner, against the wall. Our heads were to the wall; I was on the outside of the bed and Carol on the inside. When I sat on the edge of the bed, I realized that it was perhaps over three feet above the ground.

Carol sat up suddenly and said with a heavy lisp, "This is disgusting! The nagual certainly didn't tell me I was going to end up like this."

"I didn't know it either," I said. I wanted to say more and start a conversation, but my anxiety had grown to extravagant proportions.

"You shut up," she snapped at me, her voice cracking with anger. "You don't exist. You're a ghost. Disappear! Disappear!"

Her lisping was actually cute and distracted me from my obsessive fear. I shook her by the shoulders. She yelled, not so much in pain as in surprise or annoyance.

"I'm not a ghost," I said. "We made the journey because we joined our energy."

Carol Tiggs was famous among us for her speed in adapting to any situation. In no time at all she was convinced of the realness of our predicament and began to look for her clothes in the semidarkness. I marveled at the fact that she was not afraid. She became busy, reasoning out loud where she might have put her clothes had she gone to bed in that room.

"Do you see any chair?" she asked.

I faintly saw a stack of three sacks that might have served as a table or high bench. She got out of the bed, went to it, and found her clothes and mine, neatly folded, the way she always handled garments. She handed my clothes to me; they were my clothes, but not the ones I had been wearing a few minutes before, in Carol's room at the Regis Hotel.

"These are not my clothes," she lisped. "And yet they are mine. How strange!"

We dressed in silence. I wanted to tell her that I was about to burst with anxiety. I also wanted to comment on the speed of our journey, but, in the time I had taken to dress, the thought of our journey had become very vague. I could hardly remember where we had been before waking up in that room. It was as if I had dreamt the hotel room. I made a supreme effort to recollect, to push away the vagueness that had begun to envelop me. I succeeded in dispelling the fog, but that act exhausted all my energy. I ended up panting and sweating.

"Something nearly, nearly got me," Carol said. I looked at her. She, like me, was covered with perspiration. "It nearly got you too. What do you think it is?"

"The position of the assemblage point," I said with absolute certainty.

She did not agree with me. "It's the inorganic beings collecting their dues," she said shivering. "The nagual told me it was going to be horrible, but I never imagined anything this horrible."

I was in total agreement with her; we were in a horrifying mess, yet I could not conceive what the horror of that situation was. Carol and I were not novices; we had seen and done endless things, some of them outright terrifying. But there was something in that dream room that chilled me beyond belief.

"We are dreaming, aren't we?" Carol asked.

Without hesitation, I reassured her that we were, although I would have given anything to have don Juan there to reassure me of the same thing.

"Why am I so frightened?" she asked me, as if I were capable of rationally explaining it.

Before I could formulate a thought about it, she answered her question herself. She said that what frightened her was to realize, at a body level, that perceiving is an all-inclusive act when the assemblage point has been immobilized on one position. She reminded me that don Juan had told us that the power our daily world has over us is a result of the fact that our assemblage point is immobile on its habitual position. This immobility is what makes our perception of the world so inclusive and overpowering that we cannot escape from it. Carol also reminded me about another thing the nagual had said: that if we want to break this totally inclusive force, all we have to do is dispel the fog, that is to say, displace the assemblage point by intending its displacement.

I had never really understood what don Juan meant until the moment I had to bring my assemblage point to another position, in order to dispel that world's fog, which had begun to swallow me.

Carol and I, without saying another word, went to the window and looked out. We were in the country. The moonlight revealed some low, dark shapes of dwelling structures. By all indications, we were in the utility or supply room of a farm or a big country house.

"Do you remember going to bed here?" Carol asked.

"I almost do," I said and meant it. I told her I had to fight to keep the image of her hotel room in my mind, as a point of reference.

"I have to do the same," she said in a frightened whisper. "I know that if we let go of that memory, we are goners."

Then she asked me if I wanted us to leave that shack and venture outside. I did not. My apprehension was so acute that I was unable to voice my words. I could only give her a signal with my head.

"You are so very right not to want to go out," she said. "I have the feeling that if we leave this shack, we'll never make it back."

I was going to open the door and just look outside, but she stopped me. "Don't do that," she said. "You might let the outside in."

The thought that crossed my mind at that instant was that we had been placed inside a frail cage. Anything, such as opening the door, might upset the precarious balance of that cage. At the moment I had that thought, both of us had the same urge. We took off our clothes as if our lives depended on that;

we then jumped into the high bed without using the two sack steps, only to jump down from it in the next instant.

It was evident that Carol and I had the same realization at the same time. She confirmed my assumption when she said, "Anything that we use belonging to this world can only weaken us. If I stand here naked and away from the bed and away from the window, I don't have any problem remembering where I came from. But if I lie in that bed or wear those clothes or look out the window, I am done for."

We stood in the center of the room for a long time, huddled together. A weird suspicion began to fester in my mind. "How are we going to return to our world?" I asked, expecting her to know.

"The reentry into our world is automatic if we don't let the fog set in," she said with the air of a foremost authority, which was her trademark.

And she was right. Carol and I woke up, at the same time, in the bed of her room in the Regis Hotel. It was so obvious we were back in the world of daily life that we didn't ask questions or make comments about it. The sunlight was nearly blinding.

"How did we get back?" Carol asked. "Or rather, when did we get back?"

I had no idea what to say or what to think. I was too numb to speculate, which was all I could have done.

"Do you think that we just returned?" Carol insisted. "Or maybe we've been asleep here all night. Look! We're naked. When did we take our clothes off?"

"We took them off in that other world," I said and surprised myself with the sound of my voice.

My answer seemed to stump Carol. She looked uncomprehendingly at me and then at her own naked body.

We sat there without moving for an endless time. Both of us seemed to be deprived of volition. But then, quite abruptly, we had the same thought at exactly the same time. We got dressed in record time, ran out of the room, went down two flights of stairs, crossed the street, and rushed into don Juan's hotel.

Inexplicably and excessively out of breath, since we had not really exerted ourselves physically, we took turns explaining to him what we had done.

He confirmed our conjectures. "What you two did was about the most dangerous thing one can imagine," he said.

He addressed Carol and told her that our attempt had been both a total success and a fiasco. We had succeeded in transferring our awareness of the daily world to our energy bodies, thus making the journey with all our physicality, but we had failed in avoiding the influence of the inorganic beings. He said that ordinarily dreamers experience the whole maneuver as a series of slow transitions, and that they have to voice their intent to use awareness as an element. In our case, all those steps were dispensed with. Because of the intervention of the inorganic beings, the two of us had actually been hurled into a deadly world with a most terrifying speed.

"It wasn't your combined energy that made your journey possible," he continued. "Something else did that. It even selected adequate clothes for you."

"Do you mean, nagual, that the clothes and the bed and the room happened only because we were being run by the inorganic beings?" Carol asked.

"You bet your life," he replied. "Ordinarily, dreamers are merely voyeurs. The way your journey turned out, you two got a ringside seat and lived the old sorcerers' damnation. What happened to them was precisely what happened to you. The inorganic beings took them to worlds from which they could not return. I should have known, but it didn't even enter my mind, that the inorganic beings would take over and try to set up the same trap for you two."

"Do you mean they wanted to keep us there?" Carol asked.

"If you had gotten outside that shack, you'd now be meandering hopelessly in that world," don Juan said.

He explained that since we entered into that world with all our physicality, the fixation of our assemblage points on the position preselected by the inorganic beings was so overpowering that it created a sort of fog that obliterated any memory of the world we came from. He added that the natural consequence of such an immobility, as in the case of the sorcerers of antiquity, is that the dreamer's assemblage point cannot return to its habitual position.

"Think about this," he urged us. "Perhaps this is exactly what is happening to all of us in the world of daily life. We are here, and the fixation of our assemblage point is so overpowering that it has made us forget where we came from, and what our purpose was for coming here."

Don Juan did not want to say any more about our journey. I felt that he was sparing us further discomfort and fear. He took us to eat a late lunch. By the time we reached the restaurant, a couple of blocks down Francisco Madero Avenue, it was six o'clock in the afternoon. Carol and I had slept, if that is what we did, about eighteen hours.

Only don Juan was hungry. Carol remarked with a touch of anger that he was eating like a pig. Quite a few heads turned in our direction on hearing don Juan's laughter.

It was a warm night. The sky was clear. There was a soft, caressing breeze as we sat down on a bench in the Paseo Alameda.

"There is a question that's burning me," Carol said to don Juan. "We didn't use awareness as a medium for traveling, right?"

"That's true," don Juan said and sighed deeply. "The task was to sneak by the inorganic beings, not be run by them."

"What's going to happen now?" she asked.

"You are going to postpone stalking the stalkers until you two are stronger," he said. "Or perhaps you'll never accomplish it. It doesn't really matter; if one thing doesn't work, another will. Sorcery is an endless challenge."

He explained to us again, as if he were trying to fix his explanation in our minds, that in order to use awareness as an element of the environment, dreamers first have to make a journey to the inorganic beings' realm. Then they have to use that journey as a springboard, and, while they are in possession of the necessary dark energy, they have to intend to be hurled through the medium of awareness into another world.

"The failure of your trip was that you didn't have time to use awareness as an element for traveling," he went on. "Before you even got to the inorganic beings' world, you two were already in another world."

"What do you recommend we do?" Carol asked.

"I recommend that you see as little of each other as possible," he said. "I'm sure the inorganic beings will not pass up the opportunity to get you two, especially if you join forces."

So Carol Tiggs and I deliberately stayed away from each other from then on. The prospect that we might inadvertently elicit a similar journey was too great a risk for us. Don Juan encouraged our decision by repeating over and over that we had enough combined energy to tempt the inorganic beings to lure us again.

Don Juan brought my dreaming practices back to *seeing* energy in energy-generating dreamlike states. In the course of time, I *saw* everything that presented itself to me. I entered in this manner into a most peculiar state: I became incapable of rendering intelligently what I *saw*. My sensation was always that I had reached states of perception for which I had no lexicon.

Don Juan explained my incomprehensible and indescribable visions as my energy body using awareness as an element not for journeying, because I never had enough energy, but for entering into the energy fields of inanimate matter or of living beings.

THE TENANT

There were no more dreaming practices for me, as I was accustomed to having them. The next time I saw don Juan, he put me under the guidance of two women of his party: Florinda and Zuleica, his two closest cohorts. Their instruction was not at all about the gates of dreaming but about different ways to use the energy body, and it did not last long enough to be influential. They gave me the impression that they were more interested in checking me out than in teaching me anything.

"There is nothing else I can teach you about dreaming," don Juan said when I questioned him about this state of affairs.

"My time on this earth is up. But Florinda will stay. She's the one who will direct, not only you but all my other apprentices."

"Will she continue my dreaming practices?"

"I don't know that, and neither does she. It's all up to the spirit. The real player. We are not players ourselves. We are mere pawns in its hands. Following the commands of the spirit, I have to tell you what the fourth gate of dreaming is, although I can't guide you anymore."

"What's the point of whetting my appetite? I'd rather not know."

"The spirit is not leaving that up to me or to you. I have to outline the fourth gate of dreaming for you, whether I like it or not."

Don Juan explained that, at the fourth gate of dreaming, the energy body travels to specific, concrete places and that there are three ways of using the fourth gate: one, to travel to concrete places in this world; two, to travel to concrete places out of this world; and, three, to travel to places that exist only in the intent of others. He stated that the last one is the most difficult and dangerous of the three and was, by far, the old sorcerers' predilection.

"What do you want me to do with this knowledge?" I asked.

"Nothing for the moment. File it away until you need it."

"Do you mean that I can cross the fourth gate by myself, without help?"

"Whether or not you can do that is up to the spirit."

He abruptly dropped the subject, but he did not leave me with the sensation that I should try to reach and cross the fourth gate by myself.

Don Juan then made one last appointment with me to give me, he said, a sorcerers' send-off: the concluding touch of my dreaming practices. He told me to meet him in the small town in southern Mexico where he and his sorcerer companions lived.

I arrived there in the late afternoon. Don Juan and I sat in the patio of his house on some uncomfortable wicker chairs fitted with thick, oversize pillows. Don Juan laughed and winked at me. The chairs were a gift from one of the women members of his party, and we simply had to sit as if nothing was bothering us, especially him. The chairs had been bought for him in Phoenix, Arizona, and with great difficulty brought into Mexico.

Don Juan asked me to read to him a poem by Dylan Thomas, which he said had the most pertinent meaning for me at that point in time.

> *I have longed to move away*
> *From the hissing of the spent lie*
> *And the old terrors' continual cry*
> *Growing more terrible as the day*
> *Goes over the hill into the deep sea. . . .*
>
> *I have longed to move away but am afraid;*
> *Some life, yet unspent, might explode*
> *Out of the old lie burning on the ground,*
> *And, crackling into the air, leave me half-blind.*

Don Juan stood up and said that he was going for a walk in the plaza, in the center of town. He asked me to come along. I immediately assumed that the poem had evoked a negative response in him and he needed to dispel it.

We reached the square plaza without having said a word. We walked around it a couple of times, still not talking. There were quite a number of people, milling around the stores on the streets facing the east and north sides of the park. All the streets around the plaza were unevenly paved. The houses were massive, one-story adobe buildings, with tiled roofs, whitewashed walls, and blue or brown painted doors. On a side street, a block away from the plaza, the high walls of the enormous colonial church, which looked like a Moorish mosque, loomed ominously over the roof of the only hotel in town. On the south side, there were two restaurants, which inexplicably coexisted side by side, doing good business, serving practically the same menu at the same prices.

I broke the silence and asked don Juan whether he also found it odd that both restaurants were just about the same.

"Everything is possible in this town," he replied.

The way he said it made me feel uneasy.

"Why are you so nervous?" he asked, with a serious expression. "Do you know something you're not telling me?"

"Why am I nervous? That's a laugh. I am always nervous around you, don Juan. Sometimes more so than others."

He seemed to be making a serious effort not to laugh. "Naguals are not really the most friendly beings on earth," he said in a tone of apology. "I learned this the hard way, being pitted against my teacher, the terrible nagual Julian. His mere presence used to scare the daylights out of me. And when he used to zero in on me, I always thought my life wasn't worth a plug nickel."

"Unquestionably, don Juan, you have the same effect on me."

He laughed openly. "No, no. You are definitely exaggerating. I'm an angel in comparison."

"You may be an angel in comparison, except that I don't have the nagual Julian to compare you with."

He laughed for a moment, then became serious again.

"I don't know why, but I definitely feel scared," I explained.

"Do you feel you have reason to be scared?" he asked and stopped walking to peer at me.

His tone of voice and his raised eyebrows gave me the impression he suspected that I knew something I was not revealing to him. He was clearly expecting a disclosure on my part.

"Your insistence makes me wonder," I said. "Are you sure you are not the one who has something up his sleeve?"

"I do have something up my sleeve," he admitted and grinned. "But that's not the issue. The issue is that there is something in this town awaiting you. And you don't quite know what it is or you do know what it is but don't dare to tell me, or you don't know anything about it at all."

"What's waiting for me here?"

Instead of answering me, don Juan briskly resumed his walking, and we kept going around the plaza in complete silence. We circled it quite a few times, looking for a place to sit. Then, a group of young women got up from a bench and left.

"For years now, I have been describing to you the aberrant practices of the sorcerers of ancient Mexico," don Juan said as he sat down on the bench and gestured for me to sit by him.

With the fervor of someone who has never said it before, he began to tell me again what he had told me many times, that those sorcerers, guided by extremely selfish interests, put all their efforts into perfecting practices that pushed them further and further away from sobriety or mental balance, and that they were finally exterminated when their complex edifices of beliefs and practices became so cumbersome that they could no longer support them.

"The sorcerers of antiquity, of course, lived and proliferated in this area," he said, watching my reaction. "Here in this town. This town was built on the actual foundations of one of their towns. Here in this area, the sorcerers of antiquity carried on all their dealings."

"Do you know this for a fact, don Juan?"

"I do, and so will you, very soon."

My mounting anxiety was forcing me to do something I detested: to focus on myself. Don Juan, sensing my frustration, egged me on.

"Very soon, we'll know whether or not you're really like the old sorcerers or like the new ones," he said.

"You are driving me nuts with all this strange and ominous talk," I protested.

Being with don Juan for thirteen years had conditioned me, above everything else, to conceive of panic as something that was just around the corner at all times, ready to be released.

Don Juan seemed to vacillate. I noticed his furtive glances in the direction of the church. He was even distracted. When I talked to him, he was not listening. I had to repeat my question. "Are you waiting for someone?"

"Yes, I am," he said. "Most certainly I am. I was just sensing the surroundings. You caught me in the act of scanning the area with my energy body."

"What did you sense, don Juan?"

"My energy body senses that everything is in place. The play is on tonight. You are the main protagonist. I am a character actor with a small but meaningful role. I exit in the first act."

"What in the world are you talking about?"

He did not answer me. He smiled knowingly. "I'm preparing the ground," he said. "Warming you up, so to speak, harping on the idea that modern-day sorcerers have learned a hard lesson. They have realized that only if they remain totally detached can they have the energy to be free. Theirs is a peculiar type of detachment, which is born not out of fear or indolence but out of conviction."

Don Juan paused and stood up, stretched his arms in front of him, to his sides, and then behind him. "Do the same," he advised me. "It relaxes the body, and you have to be very relaxed to face what's coming to you tonight." He smiled broadly. "Either total detachment or utter indulging is coming to you tonight. It is a choice that every nagual in my line has to make." He sat down again and took a deep breath. What he had said seemed to have taken all his energy.

"I think I can understand detachment and indulging," he went on, "because I had the privilege of knowing two naguals: my benefactor, the nagual Julian, and his benefactor, the nagual Elias. I witnessed the difference between the two. The nagual Elias was detached to the point that he could put aside a gift of power. The nagual Julian was also detached, but not enough to put aside such a gift."

"Judging by the way you're talking," I said, "I would say that you are going to spring some sort of test on me tonight. Is that true?"

"I don't have the power to spring tests of any sort on you, but the spirit does." He said this with a grin, then added, "I am merely its agent."

"What is the spirit going to do to me, don Juan?"

"All I can say is that tonight you're going to get a lesson in dreaming, the way lessons in dreaming used to be, but you are not going to get that lesson from me. Someone else is going to be your teacher and guide you tonight."

"Who is going to be my teacher and guide?"

"A visitor, who might be a horrendous surprise to you or no surprise at all."

"And what's the lesson in dreaming I am going to get?"

"It's a lesson about the fourth gate of dreaming. And it is in two parts. The first part I'll explain to you presently. The second part nobody can explain to you, because it is something that pertains only to you. All the naguals of my line got this two-part lesson, but no two of those lessons were alike; they were tailored to fit those naguals' personal bents of character."

"Your explanation doesn't help me at all, don Juan. I am getting more and more nervous."

We remained quiet for a long moment. I was shaken up and fidgety and did not know what else to say without actually nagging.

"As you already know, for modern-day sorcerers to perceive energy directly is a matter of personal attainment," don Juan said. "We maneuver the assemblage point through self-discipline. For the old sorcerers, the displacement of the assemblage point was a consequence of their subjugation to others, their teachers, who accomplished those displacements through dark operations and gave them to their disciples as gifts of power.

"It's possible for someone with greater energy than ours to do anything to us," he went on. "For example, the nagual Julian could have turned me into anything he wanted, a fiend or a saint. But he was an impeccable nagual and let me be myself. The old sorcerers were not that impeccable, and, by means of their ceaseless efforts to gain control over others, they created a situation of darkness and terror that was passed on from teacher to disciple."

He stood up and swept his gaze all around us. "As you can see, this town isn't much," he continued, "but it has a unique fascination for the warriors of my line. Here lies the source of what we are and the source of what we don't want to be.

"Since I am at the end of my time, I must pass on to you certain ideas, recount to you certain stories, put you in touch with certain beings, right here in this town, exactly as my benefactor did with me."

Don Juan said that he was reiterating something I already was familiar with, that whatever he was and everything he knew were a legacy from his teacher, the nagual Julian. He in turn inherited everything from his teacher, the nagual Elias. The nagual Elias from the nagual Rosendo; he from the nagual Lujan; the nagual Lujan from the nagual Santisteban; and the nagual Santisteban from the nagual Sebastian.

He told me again, in a very formal tone, something he had explained to me many times before, that there were eight naguals before the nagual Sebastian, but that they were quite different. They had a different attitude toward sorcery, a different concept of it, although they were still directly related to his sorcery lineage.

"You must recollect now, and repeat to me, everything I've told you about the nagual Sebastian," he demanded.

His request seemed odd to me, but I repeated everything I had been told by him or by any of his companions about the nagual Sebastian and the mythical old sorcerer, the death defier, known to them as the tenant.

"You know that the death defier makes us gifts of power every generation," don Juan said. "And the specific nature of those gifts of power is what changed the course of our lineage."

He explained that the tenant, being a sorcerer from the old school, had learned from his teachers all the intricacies of shifting his assemblage point. Since he had perhaps thousands of years of strange life and awareness—ample time to perfect anything—he knew now how to reach and hold hundreds, if not thousands, of positions of the assemblage point. His gifts were like both maps for shifting the assemblage point to specific spots and manuals on how to immobilize it on any of those positions and thus acquire cohesion.

Don Juan was at the peak of his raconteur's form. I had never seen him more dramatic. If I had not known him better, I would have sworn that his voice had the deep and worried inflection of someone gripped by fear or preoccupation. His gestures gave me the impression of a good actor portraying nervousness and concern to perfection.

Don Juan peered at me, and, in the tone and manner of someone making a painful revelation, he said that, for instance, the nagual Lujan received from the tenant a gift of fifty positions. He shook his head rhythmically, as if he were silently asking me to consider what he had just said. I kept quiet.

"Fifty positions!" he exclaimed in wonder. "For a gift, one or, at the most, two positions of the assemblage point should be more than adequate."

He shrugged his shoulders, gesturing bewilderment. "I was told that the tenant liked the nagual Lujan immensely," he continued. "They struck up such a close friendship that they were practically inseparable. I was told that the nagual Lujan and the tenant used to stroll into the church over there every morning for early mass."

"Right here, in this town?" I asked, in total surprise.

"Right here," he replied. "Possibly they sat down on this very spot, on another bench, over a hundred years ago."

"The nagual Lujan and the tenant really walked in this plaza?" I asked again, unable to overcome my surprise.

"You bet!" he exclaimed. "I brought you here tonight because the poem you were reading to me cued me that it was time for you to meet the tenant."

Panic overtook me with the speed of wildfire. I had to breathe through my mouth for a moment.

"We have been discussing the strange accomplishments of the sorcerers of ancient times," don Juan continued. "But it's always hard when one has to talk exclusively in idealities, without any firsthand knowledge. I can repeat to you from now until doomsday something that is crystal clear to me but impossible for you to understand or believe, because you don't have any practical knowledge of it."

He stood up and gazed at me from head to toe. "Let's go to church," he said. "The tenant likes the church and its surroundings. I'm positive this is the moment to go there."

Very few times in the course of my association with don Juan had I felt such apprehension. I was numb. My entire body trembled when I stood up. My stomach was tied in knots, yet I followed him without a word when he headed for the church, my knees wobbling and sagging involuntarily every time I took a step. By the time we had walked the short block from the plaza to the limestone steps of the church portico, I was about to faint. Don Juan put his arm around my shoulders to prop me up.

"There's the tenant," he said as casually as if he had just spotted an old friend.

I looked in the direction he was pointing and saw a group of five women and three men at the far end of the portico. My fast and panicked glance did not register anything unusual about those people. I couldn't even tell whether they were going into the church or coming out of it. I noticed, though, that they seemed to be congregated there accidentally. They were not together.

By the time don Juan and I reached the small door, cut out in the church's massive wooden portals, three women had entered the church. The three men and the other two women were walking away. I experienced a moment of confusion and looked at don Juan for directions. He pointed with a movement of his chin to the holy water font.

"We must observe the rules and cross ourselves," he whispered.

"Where's the tenant?" I asked, also in a whisper.

Don Juan dipped the tips of his fingers in the basin and made the sign of the cross. With an imperative gesture of the chin, he urged me to do the same.

"Was the tenant one of the three men who left?" I whispered nearly in his ear.

"No," he whispered back. "The tenant is one of the three women who stayed. The one in the back row."

At that moment, a woman in the back row turned her head toward me, smiled, and nodded at me.

I reached the door in one jump and ran out.

Don Juan ran after me. With incredible agility, he overtook me and held me by the arm.

"Where are you going?" he asked, his face and body contorting with laughter.

He held me firmly by the arm as I took big gulps of air. I was veritably choking. Peals of laughter came out of him, like ocean waves. I forcefully pulled away and walked toward the plaza. He followed me.

"I never imagined you were going to get so upset," he said, as new waves of laughter shook his body.

"Why didn't you tell me that the tenant is a woman?"

"That sorcerer in there is the death defier," he said solemnly. "For such a sorcerer, so versed in the shifts of the assemblage point, to be a man or a woman is a matter of choice or convenience. This is the first part of the lesson in dreaming I said you were going to get. And the death defier is the mysterious visitor who's going to guide you through it."

He held his sides as laughter made him cough. I was speechless. Then a sudden fury possessed me. I was not mad at don Juan or myself or anyone in particular. It was a cold fury, which made me feel as if my chest and all my neck muscles were going to explode.

"Let's go back to the church," I shouted, and I didn't recognize my own voice.

"Now, now," he said softly. "You don't have to jump into the fire just like that. Think. Deliberate. Measure things up. Cool that mind of yours. Never in your life have you been put to such a test. You need calmness now.

"I can't tell you what to do," he continued. "I can only, like any other nagual, put you in front of your challenge, after telling you, in quite oblique terms, everything that is pertinent. This is another of the nagual's maneuvers: to say everything without saying it or to ask without asking."

I wanted to get it over with quickly. But don Juan said that a moment's pause would restore whatever was left of my self-assurance. My knees were about to give in. Solicitously, don Juan made me sit down on the curb. He sat next to me.

"The first part of the dreaming lesson in question is that maleness and femaleness are not final states but are the result of a specific act of positioning the assemblage point," he said. "And this act is, naturally, a matter of volition and training. Since it was a subject close to the old sorcerers' hearts, they are the only ones who can shed light on it."

Perhaps because it was the only rational thing to do, I began to argue with don Juan. "I can't accept or believe what you are saying," I said. I felt heat rising to my face.

"But you saw the woman," don Juan retorted. "Do you think that all of this is a trick?"

"I don't know what to think."

"That being in the church is a real woman," he said forcefully. "Why should that be so disturbing to you? The fact that she was born a man attests only to the power of the old sorcerers' machinations. This shouldn't surprise you. You have already embodied all the principles of sorcery."

My insides were about to burst with tension. In an accusing tone, don Juan said that I was just being argumentative. With forced patience but real pomposity, I explained to him the biological foundation of maleness and femaleness.

"I understand all that," he said. "And you're right in what you're saying. Your flaw is to try to make your assessments universal."

"What we're talking about are basic principles," I shouted. "They'll be pertinent to man here or in any other place in the universe."

"True. True," he said in a quiet voice. "Everything you say is true as long as our assemblage point remains on its habitual position. But the moment it is displaced beyond certain boundaries and our daily world is no longer in function, none of the principles you cherish has the total value you're talking about.

"Your mistake is to forget that the death defier has transcended those boundaries thousands upon thousands of times. It doesn't take a genius to realize that the tenant is no longer bound by the same forces that bind you now."

I told him that my quarrel, if it could be called a quarrel, was not with him but with accepting the practical side of sorcery, which, up to that moment, had been so farfetched that it had never posed a real problem to me. I reiterated that, as a dreamer, it was within my experience to attest that in dreaming anything is possible. I reminded him that he himself had sponsored and cultivated this conviction, together with the ultimate necessity for soundness of mind. What he was proposing as the tenant's case was not sane. It was a subject only for dreaming, certainly not for the daily world. I let him know that to me it was an abhorrent and untenable proposition.

"Why this violent reaction?" he asked with a smile.

His question caught me off guard. I felt embarrassed. "I think it threatens me at the core," I admitted. And I meant it. To think that the woman in the church was a man was somehow nause-ating to me.

A thought played in my mind: perhaps the tenant is a transvestite. I queried don Juan, in earnest, about this possibility. He laughed so hard he seemed about to get ill.

"That's too mundane a possibility," he said. "Maybe your old friends would do such a thing. Your new ones are more resourceful and less masturbatory. I repeat. That being in the church is a woman. It is a she. And she has all the organs and attributes of a female." He smiled maliciously. "You've always been attracted to women, haven't you? It seems that this situation has been tailored just for you."

His mirth was so intense and childlike that it was conta-gious. We both laughed. He, with total abandon. I, with total apprehension.

I came to a decision then. I stood up and said out loud that I had no desire to deal with the tenant in any form or shape. My choice was to bypass all this business and go back to don Juan's house and then home.

Don Juan said that my decision was perfectly all right with him, and we started back to his house. My thoughts raced wildly. Am I doing the right thing? Am I running away out of fear? Of course, I immediately rationalized my decision as the right and unavoidable one. After all, I assured myself, I was not interested in acquisitions, and the tenant's gifts were like acquiring property. Then doubt and curiosity hit me. There were so many questions I could have asked the death defier.

My heart began to pound so intensely I felt it beating against my stomach. The pounding suddenly changed into the emis-sary's voice. It broke its promise not to interfere and said that an incredible force was accelerating my heart beat in order to drive me back to the church; to walk toward don Juan's house was to walk toward my death.

I stopped walking and hurriedly confronted don Juan with the emissary's words. "Is this true?" I asked.

"I am afraid it is," he admitted sheepishly.

"Why didn't you tell me yourself, don Juan? Were you going to let me die because you think I am a coward?" I asked in a furious mood.

"You were not going to die just like that. Your energy body has endless resources. And it had never occurred to me to think you're a coward. I respect your decisions, and I don't give a damn about what motivates them.

"You are at the end of the road, just like me. So be a true nagual. Don't be ashamed of what you are. If you were a coward, I think you would have died of fright years ago. But if you're too afraid to meet the death defier, then die rather than face him. There is no shame in that."

"Let's go back to the church," I said, as calmly as I could.

"Now we're getting to the crux of the matter!" don Juan exclaimed. "But first, let's go back to the park and sit down on a bench and carefully consider your options. We can spare the time; besides, it's too early for the business at hand."

We walked back to the park and immediately found an unoccupied bench and sat down.

"You have to understand that only you, yourself, can make the decision to meet or not to meet the tenant or to accept or reject his gifts of power," don Juan said. "But your decision has to be voiced to the woman in the church, face to face and alone; otherwise it won't be valid."

Don Juan said that the tenant's gifts were extraordinary but that the price for them was tremendous. And that he himself did not approve of either, the gifts or the price.

"Before you make your real decision," don Juan continued, "you have to know all the details of our transactions with that sorcerer."

"I'd rather not hear about this anymore, don Juan," I pleaded.

"It's your duty to know," he said. "How else are you going to make up your mind?"

"Don't you think that the less I know about the tenant the better off I'll be?"

"No. This is not a matter of hiding until the danger is over. This is the moment of truth. Everything you've done and experienced in the sorcerers' world has channeled you to this spot. I didn't want to say it, because I knew your energy body was going to tell you, but there is no way to get out of this appointment. Not even by dying. Do you understand?" He shook me by the shoulders. "Do you understand?" he repeated.

I understood so well that I asked him if it would be possible for him to make me change levels of awareness in order to alleviate my fear and discomfort. He nearly made me jump with the explosion of his no.

"You must face the death defier in coldness and with ultimate premeditation," he went on. "And you can't do this by proxy."

Don Juan calmly began to repeat everything he had already told me about the death defier. As he talked, I realized that part of my confusion was the result of his use of words. He rendered "death defier" in Spanish as *el desafiante de la muerte,* and "tenant" as *el inquilino,* both of which automatically denote a male. But in describing the relationship between the tenant and the naguals of his line, don Juan kept on mixing the Spanish-language male and female gender denotation, creating a great confusion in me.

He said that the tenant was supposed to pay for the energy *he* took from the naguals of our lineage, but that whatever *he* paid has bound those sorcerers for generations. As payment for the energy taken from all those naguals, the woman in the church taught them exactly what to do to displace their assemblage point to some specific positions, which *she* herself had chosen. In other words, *she* bound every one of those men with a gift of power consisting of a preselected, specific position of the assemblage point and all its implications.

"What do you mean by 'all its implications,' don Juan?"

"I mean the negative results of those gifts. The woman in the church knows only of indulging. There is no frugality, no temperance in that woman. For instance, she taught the nagual Julian how to arrange his assemblage point to be, just like her, a woman. Teaching this to my benefactor, who was an incurable voluptuary, was like giving booze to a drunkard."

"But isn't it up to each one of us to be responsible for what we do?"

"Yes, indeed. However, some of us have more difficulty than others in being responsible. To augment that difficulty deliberately, as that woman does, is to put too much unnecessary pressure on us."

"How do you know the woman in the church does this deliberately?"

"She has done it to every one of the naguals of my line. If we look at ourselves fairly and squarely, we have to admit that the death defier has made us, with his gifts, into a line of very indulging, dependent sorcerers."

I could not overlook his inconsistency of language usage any longer, and I complained to him. "You have to speak about that sorcerer as either a male or a female, but not as both," I said harshly. "I'm too stiff, and your arbitrary use of gender makes me all the more uneasy."

"I am very uneasy myself," he confessed. "But the truth is that the death defier is both: male and female. I've never been able to take that sorcerer's change with grace. I was sure you would feel the same way, having seen him as a man first."

Don Juan reminded me of a time, years before, when he took me to meet the death defier and I met a man, a strange Indian who was not old but not young either and was very slightly built. I remember mostly his strange accent and his use of one odd metaphor when describing things he allegedly had seen. He said, *mis ojos se pasearon*, my eyes walked on. For instance, he said, "My eyes walked on the helmets of the Spanish conquerors."

The event was so fleeting in my mind that I had always thought the meeting had lasted only a few minutes. Don Juan later told me that I had been gone with the death defier for a whole day.

"The reason I was trying to find out from you earlier whether you knew what was going on," don Juan continued, "was because I thought that years ago you had made an appointment with the death defier yourself."

"You were giving me undue credit, don Juan. In this instance, I really don't know whether I am coming or going. But what gave you the idea that I knew?"

"The death defier seemed to have taken a liking to you. And that meant to me that he might have already given you a gift of power, although you didn't remember it. Or he might have set up your appointment with him, as a woman. I even suspected she had given you precise directions."

Don Juan remarked that the death defier, being definitely a creature of ritual habits, always met the naguals of his line first as a man, as it had happened with the nagual Sebastian, and subsequently as a woman.

"Why do you call the death defier's gifts, gifts of power? And why the mystery?" I asked. "You yourself can displace your assemblage point to whatever spot you want, isn't that so?"

"They are called gifts of power because they are products of the specialized knowledge of the sorcerers of antiquity," he said. "The mystery about the gifts is that no one on this earth, with the exception of the death defier, can give us a sample of that knowledge. And, of course, I can displace my assemblage point to whatever spot I want, inside or outside man's energy shape. But what I can't do, and only the death defier can, is to know what to do with my energy body in each one of those spots in order to get total perception, total cohesion."

He explained, then, that modern-day sorcerers do not know the details of the thousands upon thousands of possible positions of the assemblage point.

"What do you mean by details?" I asked.

"Particular ways of treating the energy body in order to maintain the assemblage point fixed on specific positions," he replied.

He took himself as an example. He said that the death defier's gift of power to him had been the position of the assemblage point of a crow and the procedures to manipulate his energy body to get the total perception of a crow. Don Juan explained that total perception, total cohesion was what the old sorcerers sought at any cost, and that, in the case of his own gift of power, total perception came to him by means of a deliberate process he had to learn, step by step, as one learns to work a very complex machine.

Don Juan further explained that most of the shifts modern-day sorcerers experience are mild shifts within a thin bundle of energetic luminous filaments inside the luminous egg, a bundle called the band of man, or the purely human aspect of the universe's energy. Beyond that band, but still within the luminous egg, lies the realm of the grand shifts. When the assemblage point shifts to any spot on that area, perception is still comprehensible to us, but extremely detailed procedures are required for perception to be total.

"The inorganic beings tricked you and Carol Tiggs in your last journey by helping you two to get total cohesion on a grand shift," don Juan said. "They displaced your assemblage points to the farthest possible spot, then helped you perceive there as if you were in your daily world. A nearly impossible thing. To do that type of perceiving a sorcerer needs pragmatic knowledge, or influential friends.

"Your friends would have betrayed you in the end and left you and Carol to fend for yourselves and learn pragmatic measures in order to survive in that world. You two would have ended filled to the brim with pragmatic procedures, just like those most knowledgeable old sorcerers.

"Every grand shift has different inner workings," he continued, "which modern sorcerers could learn if they knew how to fixate the assemblage point long enough at any grand shift. Only the sorcerers of ancient times had the specific knowledge required to do this."

Don Juan went on to say that the knowledge of specific procedures involved in shifts was not available to the eight naguals who preceded the nagual Sebastian, and that the tenant showed the nagual Sebastian how to achieve total perception on ten new positions of the assemblage point. The nagual Santisteban received seven, the nagual Lujan fifty, the nagual Rosendo six, the nagual Elias four, the nagual Julian sixteen, and he was shown two; that made a total of ninety-five specific positions of the assemblage point that his lineage knew about. He said that if I asked him whether he considered this an advantage to his lineage, he would have to say no, because the weight of those gifts put them closer to the old sorcerers' mood.

"Now it's your turn to meet the tenant," he continued. "Perhaps the gifts he will give you will offset our total balance and our lineage will plunge into the darkness that finished off the old sorcerers."

"This is so horribly serious, it's sickening," I said.

"I most sincerely sympathize with you," he retorted with a serious expression. "I know it's no consolation to you if I say that this is the toughest trial of a modern nagual. To face something so old and mysterious as the tenant is not awe-inspiring but revolting. At least it was to me, and still is."

"Why do I have to continue with it, don Juan?"

"Because, without knowing it, you accepted the death defier's challenge. I drew an acceptance from you in the course of your apprenticeship, in the same manner my teacher drew one from me, surreptitiously.

"I went through the same horror, only a little more brutally than you." He began to chuckle. "The nagual Julian was given to playing horrendous jokes. He told me that there was a very beautiful and passionate widow who was madly in love with me. The nagual used to take me to church often, and I had seen the woman staring at me. I thought she was a good-looking woman. And I was a horny young man. When the nagual said that she liked me, I fell for it. My awakening was very rude."

I had to fight not to laugh at don Juan's gesture of lost innocence. Then the idea of his predicament hit me, as being not funny but ghastly.

"Are you sure, don Juan, that that woman is the tenant?" I asked, hoping that perhaps it was a mistake or a bad joke.

"I am very, very sure," he said. "Besides, even if I were so dumb as to forget the tenant, my *seeing* can't fail me."

"Do you mean, don Juan, that the tenant has a different type of energy?"

"No, not a different type of energy, but certainly different energy features than a normal person."

"Are you absolutely sure, don Juan, that that woman is the tenant?" I insisted, driven by a strange revulsion and fear.

"That woman is the tenant!" don Juan exclaimed in a voice that admitted no doubts.

We remained quiet. I waited for the next move in the midst of a panic beyond description.

"I have already said to you that to be a natural man or a natural woman is a matter of positioning the assemblage point," don Juan said. "By natural I mean someone who was born either male or female. To a seer, the shiniest part of the assemblage point faces outward, in the case of females and inward, in the case of males. The tenant's assemblage point was originally facing inward, but he changed it by twisting it around and making his egglike energy shape look like a shell that has curled up on itself."

· 12 ·

THE WOMAN IN

THE CHURCH

Don Juan and I sat in silence. I had run out of questions, and he seemed to have said to me all that was pertinent. It could not have been more than seven o'clock, but the plaza was unusually deserted. It was a warm night. In the evenings in that town, people usually meandered around the plaza until ten or eleven.

I took a moment to reconsider what was happening to me. My time with don Juan was coming to an end. He and his party were going to fulfill the sorcerers' dream of leaving this world and entering into inconceivable dimensions. On the basis of my limited success in dreaming, I believed that their claims were not illusory but extremely sober, although contrary to reason. They were seeking to perceive the unknown, and they had made it.

Don Juan was right in saying that, by inducing a systematic displacement of the assemblage point, dreaming liberates perception, enlarging the scope of what can be perceived. For the sorcerers of his party, dreaming had not only opened the doors of other perceivable worlds but prepared them for entering into those realms in full awareness. Dreaming, for them, had become ineffable, unprecedented, something whose nature and scope could only be alluded to, as when don Juan said that it is the gateway to the light and to the darkness of the universe.

There was only one thing pending for them: my encounter with the death defier. I regretted that don Juan had not given me notice so that I could prepare myself better. But he was a nagual who did everything of importance on the spur of the moment, without any warning.

For a moment, I seemed to be doing fine, sitting with don Juan in that park, waiting for things to develop. But then my emotional stability suffered a downward swing and, in the twinkling of an eye, I was in the midst of a dark despair. I was assailed by petty considerations about my safety, my goals, my hopes in the world, my worries. Upon examination, however, I had to admit that perhaps the only true worry I had was about my three cohorts in don Juan's world. Yet, if I thought it out, even that was no real worry to me. Don Juan had taught them to be the kind of sorceresses who always knew what to do, and, most important, he had prepared them always to know what to do with what they knew.

Having had all the possible worldly reasons for feeling anguish stripped off me a long time ago, all I had been left with was concern for myself. And I gave myself to it shamelessly. One last indulging for the road: the fear of dying at the hands of the death defier. I became so afraid that I got sick to my stomach. I tried to apologize, but don Juan laughed.

"You're not in any way unique at barfing out of fear," he said. "When I met the death defier, I wet my pants. Believe me."

I waited in silence for a long, unbearable moment. "Are you ready?" he asked. I said yes. And he added, standing up, "Let's go then and find out how you are going to stand up in the firing line."

He led the way back to the church. To the best of my ability, all I remember of that walk, to this day, is that he had to drag me bodily the whole way. I do not remember arriving at the church or entering it. The next thing I knew, I was kneeling on a long, worn-out wooden pew next to the woman I had seen earlier. She was smiling at me. Desperately, I looked around, trying to spot don Juan, but he was nowhere in sight. I would have flown like a bat out of hell had the woman not restrained me by grabbing my arm.

"Why should you be so afraid of poor little me?" the woman asked me in English.

I stayed glued to the spot where I was kneeling. What had taken me entirely and instantaneously was her voice. I cannot describe what it was about its raspy sound that called out the most recondite memories in me. It was as if I had always known that voice.

I remained there immobile, mesmerized by that sound. She asked me something else in English, but I could not make out what she was saying. She smiled at me, knowingly. "It's all right," she whispered in Spanish. She was kneeling to my right. "I understand real fear. I live with it."

I was about to talk to her when I heard the emissary's voice in my ear. "It's the voice of Hermelinda, your wet nurse," it said. The only thing I had ever known about Hermelinda was the story I was told of her being accidentally killed by a runaway truck. That the woman's voice would stir such deep, old memories was shocking to me. I experienced a momentary agonizing anxiety.

"I am your wet nurse!" the woman exclaimed softly. "How

extraordinary! Do you want my breast?" Laughter convulsed her body.

I made a supreme effort to remain calm, yet I knew that I was quickly losing ground and in no time at all was going to take leave of my senses.

"Don't mind my joking," the woman said in a low voice. "The truth is that I like you very much. You are bustling with energy. And we are going to get along fine."

Two older men knelt down right in front of us. One of them turned curiously to look at us. She paid no attention to him and kept on whispering in my ear.

"Let me hold your hand," she pleaded. But her plea was like a command. I surrendered my hand to her, unable to say no. "Thank you. Thank you for your confidence and your trust in me," she whispered.

The sound of her voice was driving me mad. Its raspiness was so exotic, so utterly feminine. Not under any circumstances would I have taken it for a man's voice laboring to sound womanly. It was a raspy voice, but not a throaty or harsh-sounding one. It was more like the sound of bare feet softly walking on gravel.

I made a tremendous effort to break an invisible sheet of energy that seemed to have enveloped me. I thought I succeeded. I stood up, ready to leave, and I would have had not the woman also stood up and whispered in my ear, "Don't run away. There is so much I have to tell you."

I automatically sat down, stopped by curiosity. Strangely, my anxiety was suddenly gone, and so was my fear. I even had enough presence to ask the woman, "Are you really a woman?"

She chuckled softly, like a young girl. Then she voiced a convoluted sentence. "If you dare to think that I would transform myself into a fearsome man and cause you harm, you are gravely mistaken," she said, accentuating even more that strange, mesmeric voice. "You are my benefactor. I am your servant, as I have been the servant of all the naguals who preceded you."

Gathering all the energy I could, I spoke my mind to her. "You are welcome to my energy," I said. "It's a gift from me to you, but I don't want any gifts of power from you. And I really mean this."

"I can't take your energy for free," she whispered. "I pay for what I get, that's the deal. It's foolish to give your energy for free."

"I've been a fool all my life. Believe me," I said. "I can surely afford to make you a gift. I have no problem with it. You need the energy, take it. But I don't need to be saddled with unnecessaries. I have nothing and I love it."

"Perhaps," she said pensively.

Aggressively, I asked her whether she meant that perhaps she would take my energy or that she did not believe I had nothing and loved it.

She giggled with delight and said that she might take my energy since I was so generously offering it but that she had to make a payment. She had to give me a thing of similar value.

As I heard her speak, I became aware that she spoke Spanish with a most extravagant foreign accent. She added an extra phoneme to the middle syllable of every word. Never in my life had I heard anyone speak like that.

"Your accent is quite extraordinary," I said. "Where is it from?"

"From nearly eternity," she said and sighed.

We had begun to connect. I understood why she sighed. She was the closest thing to permanent, while I was temporary. That was my advantage. The death defier had worked herself into a corner, and I was free.

I examined her closely. She seemed to be between thirty-five and forty years old. She was a dark, thoroughly Indian woman, almost husky, but not fat or even hefty. I could see that the skin of her forearms and hands was smooth, the muscles, firm and youthful. I judged that she was five feet, six or seven inches tall. She wore a long dress, a black shawl, and guaraches. In her kneeling position, I could also see her smooth heels and part of her powerful calves. Her midsection was lean. She had big breasts that she could not or perhaps did not want to hide under her shawl. Her hair was jet black and tied in a long braid. She was not beautiful, but she was not homely either. Her features were in no way outstanding. I felt that she could not possibly have attracted anybody's attention, except for her eyes, which she kept low, hidden beneath downcast eyelids. Her eyes were magnificent, clear, peaceful. Apart from don Juan's, I had never seen eyes more brilliant, more alive.

Her eyes put me completely at ease. Eyes like that could not be malevolent. I had a surge of trust and optimism and the feeling that I had known her all my life. But I was also very conscious of something else: my emotional instability. It had always plagued me in don Juan's world, forcing me to be like a yo-yo. I had moments of total trust and insight only to be followed by abject doubts and distrust. This event was not going to be different. My suspicious mind suddenly came up with the warning thought that I was falling under the woman's spell.

"You learned Spanish late in life, didn't you?" I said, just to get out from under my thoughts and to avoid her reading them.

"Only yesterday," she retorted and broke into a crystalline laughter, her small, strangely white teeth, shining like a row of pearls.

People turned to look at us. I lowered my forehead as if in deep prayer. The woman moved closer to me.

"Is there a place where we could talk?" I asked.

"We are talking here," she said. "I have talked here with all the naguals of your line. If you whisper, no one will know we are talking."

I was dying to ask her about her age. But a sobering memory came to my rescue. I remembered a friend of mine who for years had been setting up all kinds of traps to make me confess my age to him. I detested his petty concern, and now I was about to engage in the same behavior. I dropped it instantly.

I wanted to tell her about it, just to keep the conversation going. She seemed to know what was going through my mind. She squeezed my arm in a friendly gesture, as if to say that we had shared a thought.

"Instead of giving me a gift, can you tell me something that would help me in my way?" I asked her.

She shook her head. "No," she whispered. "We are extremely different. More different than I believed possible."

She got up and slid sideways out of the pew. She deftly genuflected as she faced the main altar. She crossed herself and signaled me to follow her to a large side altar to our left.

We knelt in front of a life-size crucifix. Before I had time to say anything, she spoke. "I've been alive for a very, very long time," she said. "The reason I have had this long life is that I control the shifts and movements of my assemblage point. Also, I don't stay here in your world too long. I have to save the energy I get from the naguals of your line."

"What is it like to exist in other worlds?" I asked.

"It's like in your dreaming, except that I have more mobility. And I can stay longer anywhere I want. Just like if you would stay as long as you wanted in any of your dreams."

"When you are in this world, are you pinned down to this area alone?"

"No. I go everywhere I want."

"Do you always go as a woman?"

"I've been a woman longer than a man. Definitely, I like it much better. I think I've nearly forgotten how to be a man. I am all female!"

She took my hand and made me touch her crotch. My heart was pounding in my throat. She was indeed a female.

"I can't just take your energy," she said, changing the subject. "We have to strike another kind of agreement."

Another wave of mundane reasoning hit me then. I wanted to ask her where she lived when she was in this world. I did not need to voice my question to get an answer.

"You're much, much younger than I," she said, "and you already have difficulty telling people where you live. And even if you take them to the house you own or pay rent on, that's not where you live."

"There are so many things I want to ask you, but all I do is think stupid thoughts," I said.

"You don't need to ask me anything," she went on. "You already know what I know. All you needed was a jolt in order to claim what you already know. I am giving you that jolt."

Not only did I think stupid thoughts but I was in a state of such suggestibility that no sooner had she finished saying that I knew what she knew than I felt I knew everything, and I no longer needed to ask any more questions. Laughingly, I told her about my gullibility.

"You're not gullible," she assured me with authority. "You know everything, because you're now totally in the second attention. Look around!"

For a moment, I could not focus my sight. It was exactly as if water had gotten into my eyes. When I arranged my view, I knew that something portentous had happened. The church was different, darker, more ominous, and somehow harder. I stood up and took a couple of steps toward the nave. What caught my eye were the pews; they were made not out of lumber but out of thin, twisted poles. These were homemade pews, set inside a magnificent stone building. Also, the light in the church was different. It was yellowish, and its dim glow cast the blackest shadows I had ever seen. It came from the candles of the many altars. I had an insight about how well candlelight mixed with the massive stone walls and ornaments of a colonial church.

The woman was staring at me; the brightness of her eyes was most remarkable. I knew then that I was dreaming and she was directing the dream. But I was not afraid of her or of the dream.

I moved away from the side altar and looked again at the nave of the church. There were people kneeling in prayer there.

Lots of them, strangely small, dark, hard people. I could see their bowed heads all the way to the foot of the main altar. The ones who were close to me stared at me, obviously, in disapproval. I was gaping at them and at everything else. I could not hear any noise, though. People moved, but there was no sound.

"I can't hear anything," I said to the woman, and my voice boomed, echoing as if the church were a hollow shell.

Nearly all the heads turned to look at me. The woman pulled me back into the darkness of the side altar.

"You will hear if you don't listen with your ears," she said. "Listen with your dreaming attention."

It appeared that all I needed was her insinuation. I was suddenly flooded by the droning sound of a multitude in prayer. I was instantly swept up by it. I found it the most exquisite sound I had ever heard. I wanted to rave about it to the woman, but she was not by my side. I looked for her. She had nearly reached the door. She turned there to signal me to follow her. I caught up with her at the portico. The streetlights were gone. The only illumination was moonlight. The facade of the church was also different; it was unfinished. Square blocks of limestone lay everywhere. There were no houses or buildings around the church. In the moonlight the scene was eerie.

"Where are we going?" I asked her.

"Nowhere," she replied. "We simply came out here to have more space, more privacy. Here we can talk our little heads off."

She urged me to sit down on a quarried, half-chiseled piece of limestone. "The second attention has endless treasures to be discovered," she began. "The initial position in which the dreamer places his body is of key importance. And right there is the secret of the ancient sorcerers, who were already ancient in my time. Think about it."

She sat so close to me that I felt the heat of her body. She put an arm around my shoulder and pressed me against her bosom. Her body had a most peculiar fragrance; it reminded me of trees or sage. It was not that she was wearing perfume; her whole being seemed to exude that characteristic odor of pine forests. Also the heat of her body was not like mine or like that of anyone else I knew. Hers was a cool, mentholated heat, even, balanced. The thought that came to my mind was that her heat would press on relentlessly but knew no hurry.

She began then to whisper in my left ear. She said that the gifts she had given to the naguals of my line had to do with what the old sorcerers used to call the twin positions. That is to say, the initial position in which a dreamer holds his physical body to begin dreaming is mirrored by the position in which he holds his energy body, in dreams, to fixate his assemblage point on any spot of his choosing. The two positions make a unit, she said, and it took the old sorcerers thousands of years to find out the perfect relationship between any two positions. She commented, with a giggle, that the sorcerers of today will never have the time or the disposition to do all that work, and that the men and women of my line were indeed lucky to have her to give them such gifts. Her laughter had a most remarkable, crystalline sound.

I had not quite understood her explanation of the twin positions. Boldly, I told her that I did not want to practice those things but only know about them as intellectual possibilities.

"What exactly do you want to know?" she asked softly.

"Explain to me what you mean by the twin positions, or the initial position in which a dreamer holds his body to start dreaming." I said.

"How do you lie down to start your dreaming?" she asked.

"Any which way. I don't have a pattern. Don Juan never stressed this point."

"Well, I do stress it," she said and stood up.

She changed positions. She sat down to my right and whispered in my other ear that, in accordance with what she knew, the position in which one places the body is of utmost importance. She proposed a way of testing this by performing an extremely delicate but simple exercise.

"Start your dreaming by lying on your right side, with your knees a bit bent," she said. "The discipline is to maintain that position and fall asleep in it. In dreaming, then, the exercise is to dream that you lie down in exactly the same position and fall asleep again."

"What does that do?" I asked.

"It makes the assemblage point stay put, and I mean really stay put, in whatever position it is at the instant of that second falling asleep."

"What are the results of this exercise?"

"Total perception. I am sure your teachers have already told you that my gifts are gifts of total perception."

"Yes. But I think I am not clear about what total perception means," I lied.

She ignored me and went on to tell me that the four variations of the exercise were to fall asleep lying on the right side, the left, the back, and the stomach. Then in dreaming the exercise was to dream of falling asleep a second time in the same position as the dreaming had been started. She promised me extraordinary results, which she said were not possible to foretell.

She abruptly changed the subject and asked me, "What's the gift you want for yourself?"

"No gift for me. I've told you that already."

"I insist. I must offer you a gift, and you must accept it. That is our agreement."

"Our agreement is that we give you energy. So take it from me. This one is on me. My gift to you."

The woman seemed dumbfounded. And I persisted in telling her it was all right with me that she took my energy. I even told her that I liked her immensely. Naturally, I meant it. There was something supremely sad and, at the same time, supremely appealing about her.

"Let's go back inside the church," she muttered.

"If you really want to make me a gift," I said, "take me for a stroll in this town, in the moonlight."

She shook her head affirmatively. "Provided that you don't say a word," she said.

"Why not?" I asked, but I already knew the answer.

"Because we are dreaming," she said. "I'll be taking you deeper into my dream."

She explained that as long as we stayed in the church, I had enough energy to think and converse, but that beyond the boundaries of that church it was a different situation.

"Why is that?" I asked daringly.

In a most serious tone, which not only increased her eeriness but terrified me, the woman said, "Because there is no out there. This is a dream. You are at the fourth gate of dreaming, dreaming my dream."

She told me that her art was to be capable of projecting her intent, and that everything I saw around me was her intent. She said in a whisper that the church and the town were the results of her intent; they did not exist, yet they did. She added, looking into my eyes, that this is one of the mysteries of intending in the second attention the twin positions of dreaming. It can be done, but it cannot be explained or comprehended.

She told me then that she came from a line of sorcerers who knew how to move about in the second attention by projecting their intent. Her story was that the sorcerers of her line practiced the art of projecting their thoughts in dreaming in order to accomplish the truthful reproduction of any object or structure or landmark or scenery of their choice.

She said that the sorcerers of her line used to start by gazing at a simple object and memorizing every detail of it. They would then close their eyes and visualize the object and correct their visualization against the true object until they could see it, in its completeness, with their eyes shut.

The next thing in their developing scheme was to dream with

the object and create in the dream, from the point of view of their own perception, a total materialization of the object. This act, the woman said, was called the first step to total perception.

From a simple object, those sorcerers went on to take more and more complex items. Their final aim was for all of them together to visualize a total world, then dream that world and thus re-create a totally veritable realm where they could exist.

"When any of the sorcerers of my line were able to do that," the woman went on, "they could easily pull anyone into their intent, into their dream. This is what I am doing to you now, and what I did to all the naguals of your line."

The woman giggled. "You better believe it," she said, as if I did not. "Whole populations disappeared dreaming like that. This is the reason I said to you that this church and this town are one of the mysteries of intending in the second attention."

"You say that whole populations disappeared that way. How was it possible?" I asked.

"They visualized and then re-created in dreaming the same scenery," she replied. "You've never visualized anything, so it's very dangerous for you to go into my dream."

She warned me, then, that to cross the fourth gate and travel to places that exist only in someone else's intent was perilous, since every item in such a dream had to be an ultimately personal item.

"Do you still want to go?" she asked.

I said yes. Then she told me more about the twin positions. The essence of her explanation was that if I were, for instance, dreaming of my hometown and my dream had started when I lay down on my right side, I could very easily stay in the town of my dream if I would lie on my right side, in the dream, and dream that I had fallen asleep. The second dream not only would necessarily be a dream of my hometown, but would be the most concrete dream one can imagine.

She was confident that in my dreaming training I had gotten countless dreams of great concreteness, but she assured me that every one of them had to be a fluke. For the only way to have absolute control of dreams was to use the technique of the twin positions.

"And don't ask me why," she added. "It just happens. Like everything else."

She made me stand up and admonished me again not to talk or stray from her. She took my hand gently, as if I were a child, and headed toward a clump of dark silhouettes of houses. We were on a cobbled street. Hard river rocks had been pounded edgewise into the dirt. Uneven pressure had created uneven surfaces. It seemed that the cobblers had followed the contours of the ground without bothering to level it.

The houses were big, whitewashed, one-story, dusty buildings with tiled roofs. There were people meandering quietly. Dark shadows inside the houses gave me the feeling of curious but frightened neighbors gossiping behind doors. I could also see the flat mountains around the town.

Contrary to what had happened to me all along in my dreaming, my mental processes were unimpaired. My thoughts were not pushed away by the force of the events in the dream. And my mental calculations told me I was in the dream version of the town where don Juan lived, but at a different time. My curiosity was at its peak. I was actually with the death defier in her dream. But was it a dream? She herself had said it was a dream. I wanted to watch everything, to be superalert. I wanted to test everything by *seeing* energy. I felt embarrassed, but the woman tightened her grip on my hand as if to signal me that she agreed with me.

Still feeling absurdly bashful, I automatically stated out loud my intent to *see*. In my dreaming practices, I had been using all along the phrase "I want to *see* energy." Sometimes, I had to say it over and over until I got results. This time, in the woman's dream town, as I began to repeat it in my usual manner, the woman began to laugh. Her laughter was like don Juan's: a deep, abandoned belly laugh.

"What's so funny?" I asked, somehow contaminated by her mirth.

"Juan Matus doesn't like the old sorcerers in general and me in particular," the woman said between fits of laughter. "All we have to do, in order to *see* in our dreams, is to point with our little finger at the item we want to *see*. To make you yell in my dream is his way to send me his message. You have to admit that he's really clever." She paused for a moment, then said in the tone of a revelation, "Of course, to yell like an asshole works too."

The sorcerers' sense of humor bewildered me beyond measure. She laughed so hard she seemed to be unable to proceed with our walk. I felt stupid. When she calmed down and was perfectly poised again, she politely told me that I could point at anything I wanted in her dream, including herself.

I pointed at a house with the little finger of my left hand. There was no energy in that house. The house was like any other item of a regular dream. I pointed at everything around me with the same result.

"Point at me," she urged me. "You must corroborate that this is the method dreamers follow in order to *see*."

She was thoroughly right. That was the method. The instant I pointed my finger at her, she was a blob of energy. A very peculiar blob of energy, I may add. Her energetic shape was exactly as don Juan had described it; it looked like an enormous seashell, curled inwardly along a cleavage that ran its length.

"I am the only energy-generating being in this dream," she said. "So the proper thing for you to do is just watch everything."

At that moment I was struck, for the first time, by the immensity of don Juan's joke. He had actually contrived to have me learn to yell in my dreaming so that I could yell in the privacy of the death defier's dream. I found that touch so funny that laughter spilled out of me in suffocating waves.

"Let's continue our walk," the woman said softly when I had no more laughter in me.

There were only two streets that intersected; each had three blocks of houses. We walked the length of both streets, not once but four times. I looked at everything and listened with my dreaming attention for any noises. There were very few, only dogs barking in the distance, or people speaking in whispers as we went by.

The dogs barking brought me an unknown and profound longing. I had to stop walking. I sought relief by leaning my shoulder against a wall. The contact with the wall was shocking to me, not because the wall was unusual but because what I had leaned on was a solid wall, like any other wall I had ever touched. I felt it with my free hand. I ran my fingers on its rough surface. It was indeed a wall!

Its stunning realness put an immediate end to my longing and renewed my interest in watching everything. I was looking, specifically, for features that could be correlated with the town of my day. However, no matter how intently I observed, I had no success. There was a plaza in that town, but it was in front of the church, facing the portico.

In the moonlight the mountains around the town were clearly visible and almost recognizable. I tried to orient myself, observing the moon and the stars, as if I were in the consensual reality of everyday life. It was a waning moon, perhaps a day after full. It was high over the horizon. It must have been between eight and nine in the evening. I could see Orion to the right of the moon; its two main stars, Betelgeuse and Rigel, were on a horizontal straight line with the moon. I estimated it to be early December. My time was May. In May, Orion is nowhere in sight at that time. I gazed at the moon as long as I could. Nothing shifted. It was the moon as far as I could tell. The disparity in time got me very excited.

As I reexamined the southern horizon, I thought I could distinguish the bell-like peak visible from don Juan's patio. I tried next to figure out where his house might have been. For one instant I thought I found it. I became so enthralled that I pulled my hand out of the woman's grip. Instantly, a tremendous anxiety possessed me. I knew that I had to go back to the church, because if I did not I would simply drop dead on the spot. I turned around and bolted for the church. The woman quickly grabbed my hand and followed me.

As we approached the church at a running pace, I became aware that the town in that dreaming was behind the church. Had I taken this into consideration, orientation might have been possible. As it was, I had no more dreaming attention. I focused all of it on the architectural and ornamental details on the back of the church. I had never seen that part of the building in the world of everyday life, and I thought that if I could record its features in my memory, I could check them later against the details of the real church.

That was the plan I concocted on the spur of the moment. Something inside me, however, scorned my efforts at validation. During all my apprenticeship, I had been plagued by the need for objectivity, which had forced me to check and recheck everything about don Juan's world. Yet it was not validation per se that was always at stake but the need to use this drive for objectivity as a crutch to give me protection at the moments of most intense cognitive disruption; when it was time to check what I had validated, I never went through with it.

Inside the church, the woman and I knelt in front of the small altar on the left side, where we had been, and the next instant, I woke up in the well-illuminated church of my day.

The woman crossed herself and stood up. I did the same automatically. She took my arm and began to walk toward the door.

"Wait, wait," I said and was surprised that I could talk. I could not think clearly, yet I wanted to ask her a convoluted question. What I wanted to know was how anyone could have the energy to visualize every detail of a whole town.

Smiling, the woman answered my unvoiced question; she said that she was very good at visualizing because after a lifetime of doing it, she had many, many lifetimes to perfect it. She added that the town I had visited and the church where we had talked were examples of her recent visualizations. The church was the same church where Sebastian had been a sexton. She had given herself the task of memorizing every detail of every corner of that church and that town, for that matter, out of a need to survive.

She ended her talk with a most disturbing afterthought. "Since you know quite a bit about this town, even though you've never tried to visualize it," she said, "you are now helping me to intend it. I bet you won't believe me if I tell you that this town you are looking at now doesn't really exist, outside your intent and mine."

She peered at me and laughed at my sense of horror, for I had just fully realized what she was saying. "Are we still dreaming?" I asked, astonished.

"We are," she said. "But this dreaming is more real than the other, because you're helping me. It is not possible to explain it beyond saying that it is happening. Like everything else." She pointed all around her. "There is no way to tell how it happens, but it does. Remember always what I've told you: this is the mystery of intending in the second attention."

She gently pulled me closer to her. "Let's stroll to the plaza of this dream," she said. "But perhaps I should fix myself a little bit so you'll be more at ease."

I looked at her uncomprehendingly as she expertly changed her appearance. She did this with very simple, mundane maneuvers. She undid her long skirt, revealing the very average midcalf skirt she was wearing underneath. She then twisted her long braid into a chignon and changed from her guaraches into inch-heel shoes she had in a small cloth sack.

She turned over her reversible black shawl to reveal a beige stole. She looked like a typical middle-class Mexican woman from the city, perhaps on a visit to that town.

She took my arm with a woman's aplomb and led the way to the plaza.

"What happened to your tongue?" she said in English. "Did the cat eat it?"

I was totally engrossed in the unthinkable possibility that I was still in a dream; what is more, I was beginning to believe that if it were true, I ran the risk of never waking up.

In a nonchalant tone that I could not recognize as mine, I said, "I didn't realize until now that you spoke in English to me before. Where did you learn it?"

"In the world out there. I speak many languages." She paused and scrutinized me. "I've had plenty of time to learn them. Since we're going to spend a lot of time together, I'll teach you my own language sometime." She giggled, no doubt at my look of despair.

I stopped walking. "Are we going to spend a lot of time together?" I asked, betraying my feelings.

"Of course," she replied in a joyful tone. "You are, and I should say very generously, going to give me your energy, for free. You said that yourself, didn't you?"

I was aghast.

"What's the problem?" the woman asked, shifting back into Spanish. "Don't tell me that you regret your decision. We are sorcerers. It's too late to change your mind. You are not afraid, are you?"

I was again more than terrified, but, if I had been put on the spot to describe what terrified me, I would not have known. I was certainly not afraid of being with the death defier in another dream or of losing my mind or even my life. Was I afraid of evil? I asked myself. But the thought of evil could not withstand examination. As a result of all those years on the sorcerers' path, I knew without the shadow of a doubt

that in the universe only energy exists; evil is merely a con-
catenation of the human mind, overwhelmed by the fixation
of the assemblage point on its habitual position. Logically,
there was really nothing for me to be afraid of. I knew that,
but I also knew that my real weakness was to lack the fluidity
to fix my assemblage point instantly on any new position to
which it was displaced. The contact with the death defier was
displacing my assemblage point at a tremendous rate, and I
did not have the prowess to keep up with the push. The end
result was a vague pseudo-sensation of fearing that I might
not be able to wake up.

"There is no problem," I said. "Let's continue our dream
walk."

She linked her arm with mine, and we reached the park in
silence. It was not at all a forced silence. But my mind was running in circles. How strange, I thought; only a while ago I had
walked with don Juan from the park to the church, in the midst
of the most terrifying normal fear. Now I was walking back
from the church to the park with the object of my fear, and I
was more terrified than ever, but in a different, more mature,
more deadly manner.

To fend off my worries, I began to look around. If this was a
dream, as I believed it was, there was a way to prove or dis-
prove it. I pointed my finger at the houses, at the church, at the
pavement in the street. I pointed at people. I pointed at everything. Daringly, I even grabbed a couple of people, whom I
seemed to scare considerably. I felt their mass. They were as
real as anything I consider real, except that they did not gener-
ate energy. Nothing in that town generated energy. Everything
seemed real and normal, yet it was a dream.

I turned to the woman, who was holding on to my arm, and
questioned her about it.

"We are dreaming," she said in her raspy voice and giggled.

"But how can people and things around us to be so real, so
three-dimensional?"

"The mystery of intending in the second attention!" she exclaimed reverently. "Those people out there are so real that they even have thoughts."

That was the last stroke. I did not want to question anything else. I wanted to abandon myself to that dream. A considerable jolt on my arm brought me back to the moment. We had reached the plaza. The woman had stopped walking and was pulling me to sit down on a bench. I knew I was in trouble when I did not feel the bench underneath me as I sat down. I began to spin. I thought I was ascending. I caught a most fleeting glimpse of the park, as if I were looking at it from above.

"This is it!" I yelled. I thought I was dying. The spinning ascension turned into a twirling descent into blackness.

FLYING ON THE WINGS

OF INTENT

ake an effort, nagual," a woman's voice urged me. "Don't sink. Surface, surface. Use your dreaming techniques!"

My mind began to work. I thought it was the voice of an English speaker, and I also thought that if I were to use dreaming techniques, I had to find a point of departure to energize myself.

"Open your eyes," the voice said. "Open them now. Use the first thing you see as a point of departure."

I made a supreme effort and opened my eyes. I saw trees and blue sky. It was daytime! A blurry face was peering at me. But I could not focus my eyes. I thought that it was the woman in the church looking at me.

"Use my face," the voice said. It was a familiar voice, but I could not identify it. "Make my face your home base; then look at everything," the voice went on.

My ears were clearing up, and so were my eyes. I gazed at the woman's face, then at the trees in the park, at the wrought-iron bench, at people walking by, and back again at her face.

In spite of the fact that her face changed every time I gazed at her, I began to experience a minimum of control. When I was more in possession of my faculties, I realized that a woman was sitting on the bench, holding my head on her lap. And she was not the woman in the church; she was Carol Tiggs.

"What are you doing here?" I gasped.

My fright and surprise were so intense that I wanted to jump up and run, but my body was not ruled at all by my mental awareness. Anguishing moments followed, in which I tried desperately but uselessly to get up. The world around me was too clear for me to believe I was still dreaming, yet my impaired motor control made me suspect that this was really a dream. Besides, Carol's presence was too abrupt; there were no antecedents to justify it.

Cautiously, I attempted to will myself to get up, as I had done hundreds of times in dreaming, but nothing happened. If I ever needed to be objective, this was the time. As carefully as I could, I began to look at everything within my field of vision with one eye first. I repeated the process with the other eye. I took the consistency between the images of my two eyes as an indication that I was in the consensual reality of everyday life.

Next, I examined Carol. I noticed at that moment that I could move my arms. It was only my lower body that was veritably paralyzed. I touched Carol's face and hands; I embraced her. She was solid and, I believed, the real Carol Tiggs. My relief was enormous, because for a moment I'd had the dark suspicion that she was the death defier masquerading as Carol.

With utmost care, Carol helped me to sit up on the bench. I had been sprawled on my back, half on the bench and half on the ground. I noticed then something totally out of the norm. I was wearing faded blue Levi's and worn brown leather boots. I also had on a Levi's jacket and a denim shirt.

"Wait a minute," I said to Carol. "Look at me! Are these my clothes? Am I myself?"

Carol laughed and shook me by the shoulders, the way she always did to denote camaraderie, manliness, that she was one of the boys.

"I'm looking at your beautiful self," she said in her funny forced falsetto. "Oh massa, who else could it possibly be?"

"How in the hell can I be wearing Levi's and boots?" I insisted. "I don't own any."

"Those are my clothes you are wearing. I found you naked!"

"Where? When?"

"Around the church, about an hour ago. I came to the plaza here to look for you. The nagual sent me to see if I could find you. I brought the clothes, just in case."

I told her that I felt terribly vulnerable and embarrassed to have wandered around without my clothes.

"Strangely enough, there was no one around," she assured me, but I felt she was saying it just to ease my discomfort. Her playful smile told me so.

"I must have been with the death defier all last night, maybe even longer," I said. "What day is it today?"

"Don't worry about dates," she said, laughing. "When you are more centered, you'll count the days yourself."

"Don't humor me, Carol Tiggs. What day is it today?" My voice was a gruff, no-nonsense voice that did not seem to belong to me.

"It's the day after the big fiesta," she said and slapped me gently on my shoulder. "We all have been looking for you since last night."

"But what am I doing here?"

"I took you to the hotel across the plaza. I couldn't carry you all the way to the nagual's house; you ran out of the room a few minutes ago, and we ended up here."

"Why didn't you ask the nagual for help?"

"Because this is an affair that concerns only you and me. We must solve it together."

That shut me up. She made perfect sense to me. I asked her one more nagging question. "What did I say when you found me?"

"You said that you had been so deeply into the second attention and for such a long time that you were not quite rational yet. All you wanted to do was to fall asleep."

"When did I lose my motor control?"

"Only a moment ago. You'll get it back. You yourself know that it is quite normal, when you enter into the second attention and receive a considerable energy jolt, to lose control of your speech or of your limbs."

"And when did you lose your lisping, Carol?"

I caught her totally by surprise. She peered at me and broke into a hearty laugh. "I've been working on it for a long time," she confessed. "I think that it's terribly annoying to hear a grown woman lisping. Besides, you hate it."

Admitting that I detested her lisping was not difficult. Don Juan and I had tried to cure her, but we had concluded she was not interested in getting cured. Her lisping made her extremely cute to everyone, and don Juan's feelings were that she loved it and was not going to give it up. Hearing her speak without lisping was tremendously rewarding and exciting to me. It proved to me that she was capable of radical changes on her own, a thing neither don Juan nor I was ever sure about.

"What else did the nagual say to you when he sent you to look for me?" I asked.

"He said you were having a bout with the death defier."

In a confidential tone, I revealed to Carol that the death defier was a woman. Nonchalantly, she said that she knew it.

"How can you know it?" I shouted. "No one has ever known this, apart from don Juan. Did he tell you that himself?"

"Of course he did," she replied, unperturbed by my shouting. "What you have overlooked is that I also met the woman in the church. I met her before you did. We amiably chatted in the church for quite a while."

I believed Carol was telling me the truth. What she was describing was very much what don Juan would do. He would in all likelihood send Carol as a scout in order to draw conclusions.

"When did you see the death defier?" I asked.

"A couple of weeks ago," she replied in a matter-of-fact tone. "It was no great event for me. I had no energy to give her, or at least not the energy that woman wants."

"Why did you see her then? Is dealing with the nagual woman also part of the death defier's and sorcerers' agreement?"

"I saw her because the nagual said that you and I are interchangeable, and for no other reason. Our energy bodies have merged many times. Don't you remember? The woman and I talked about the ease with which we merge. I stayed with her maybe three or four hours, until the nagual came in and got me out."

"Did you stay in the church all that time?" I asked, because I could hardly believe that they had knelt in there for three or four hours only talking about the merging of our energy bodies.

"She took me into another facet of her intent," Carol conceded after a moment's thought. "She made me see how she actually escaped her captors."

Carol related then a most intriguing story. She said that according to what the woman in the church had made her see, every sorcerer of antiquity fell, inescapably, prey to the inorganic beings. The inorganic beings, after capturing them, gave them power to be the intermediaries between our world and their realm, which people called the netherworld.

The death defier was unavoidably caught in the nets of the inorganic beings. Carol estimated that he spent perhaps thousands of years as a captive, until the moment he was capable of transforming himself into a woman. He had clearly seen this as his way out of that world the day he found out that the inorganic beings regard the female principle as imperishable. They believe that the female principle has such a pliability and its scope is so vast that its members are impervious to traps and setups and can hardly be held captive. The death defier's transformation was so complete and so detailed that she was instantly spewed out of the inorganic beings' realm.

"Did she tell you that the inorganic beings are still after her?" I asked.

"Naturally they are after her," Carol assured me. "The woman told me she has to fend off her pursuers every moment of her life."

"What can they do to her?"

"Realize she was a man and pull her back to captivity, I suppose. I think she fears them more than you can think it's possible to fear anything."

Nonchalantly, Carol told me that the woman in the church was thoroughly aware of my run-in with the inorganic beings and that she also knew about the blue scout.

"She knows everything about you and me," Carol continued. "And not because I told her anything, but because she is part of our lives and our lineage. She mentioned that she had always followed all of us, you and me in particular."

Carol related to me the instances that the woman knew in which Carol and I had acted together. As she spoke, I began to experience a unique nostalgia for the very person who was in front of me: Carol Tiggs. I wished desperately to embrace her. I reached out to her, but I lost my balance and fell off the bench.

Carol helped me up from the pavement and anxiously examined my legs and the pupils of my eyes, my neck and my lower back. She said that I was still suffering from an energetic jolt.

She propped my head on her bosom and caressed me as if I were a malingering child she was humoring.

After a while I did feel better; I even began to regain my motor control.

"How do you like the clothes I am wearing?" Carol asked me all of a sudden. "Am I overdressed for the occasion? Do I look all right to you?"

Carol was always exquisitely dressed. If there was anything certain about her, it was her impeccable taste in clothes. In fact, as long as I had known her, it had been a running joke between don Juan and the rest of us that her only virtue was her expertise at buying beautiful clothes and wearing them with grace and style.

I found her question very odd and made a comment. "Why would you be insecure about your appearance? It has never bothered you before. Are you trying to impress someone?"

"I'm trying to impress you, of course," she said.

"But this is not the time," I protested. "What's going on with the death defier is the important matter, not your appearance."

"You'd be surprised how important my appearance is." She laughed. "My appearance is a matter of life or death for both of us."

"What are you talking about? You remind me of the nagual setting up my meeting with the death defier. He nearly drove me nuts with his mysterious talk."

"Was his mysterious talk justified?" Carol asked with a deadly serious expression.

"It most certainly was," I admitted.

"So is my appearance. Humor me. How do you find me? Appealing, unappealing, attractive, average, disgusting, over-powering, bossy?"

I thought for a moment and made my assessment. I found Carol very appealing. This was quite strange to me. I had never consciously thought about her appeal. "I find you divinely beautiful," I said. "In fact, you're downright stunning."

"Then this must be the right appearance." She sighed.

I was trying to figure out her meanings, when she spoke again. She asked, "What was your time with the death defier like?"

I succinctly told her about my experience, mainly about the first dream. I said that I believed the death defier had made me see that town, but at another time in the past.

"But that's not possible," she blurted out. "There is no past or future in the universe. There is only the moment."

"I know that it was the past," I said. "It was the same church, but a different town."

"Think for a moment," she insisted. "In the universe there is only energy, and energy has only a here and now, an endless and ever-present here and now."

"So what do you think happened to me, Carol?"

"With the death defier's help, you crossed the fourth gate of dreaming," she said. "The woman in the church took you into her dream, into her intent. She took you into her visualization of this town. Obviously, she visualized it in the past, and that visualization is still intact in her. As her present visualization of this town must be there too."

After a long silence she asked me another question. "What else did the woman do with you?"

I told Carol about the second dream. The dream of the town as it stands today.

"There you are," she said. "Not only did the woman take you into her past intent but she further helped you cross the fourth gate by making your energy body journey to another place that exists today, only in her intent."

Carol paused and asked me whether the woman in the church had explained to me what intending in the second attention meant.

I did remember her mentioning but not really explaining what it meant to intend in the second attention. Carol was dealing with concepts don Juan had never spoken about.

"Where did you get all these novel ideas?" I asked, truly marveling at how lucid she was.

In a noncommittal tone, Carol assured me that the woman in the church had explained to her a great deal about those intricacies.

"We are intending in the second attention now," she continued. "The woman in the church made us fall asleep; you here, and I in Tucson. And then we fell asleep again in our dream. But you don't remember that part, while I do. The secret of the twin positions. Remember what the woman told you; the second dream is intending in the second attention: the only way to cross the fourth gate of dreaming."

After a long pause, during which I could not articulate one word, she said, "I think the woman in the church really made you a gift, although you didn't want to receive one. Her gift was to add her energy to ours in order to move backward and forward on the here-and-now energy of the universe."

I got extremely excited. Carol's words were precise, apropos. She had defined for me something I considered undefinable, although I did not know what it was that she had defined. If I could have moved, I would have leapt to hug her. She smiled beatifically as I kept on ranting nervously about the sense her words made to me. I commented rhetorically that don Juan had never told me anything similar.

"Maybe he doesn't know," Carol said, not offensively but conciliatorily.

I did not argue with her. I remained quiet for a while, strangely void of thoughts. Then my thoughts and words erupted out of me like a volcano. People went around the plaza, staring at us every so often or stopping in front of us to watch us. And we must have been a sight: Carol Tiggs kissing and caressing my face while I ranted on and on about her lucidity and my encounter with the death defier.

When I was able to walk, she guided me across the plaza to the only hotel in town. She assured me that I did not yet have the energy to go to don Juan's house but that everybody there knew our whereabouts.

"How would they know our whereabouts?" I asked.

"The nagual is a very crafty old sorcerer," she replied, laughing. "He's the one who told me that if I found you energetically mangled, I should put you in the hotel rather than risk crossing the town with you in tow."

Her words and especially her smile made me feel so relieved that I kept on walking in a state of bliss. We went around the corner to the hotel's entrance, half a block down the street, right in front of the church. We went through the bleak lobby, up the cement stairway to the second floor, directly to an unfriendly room I had never seen before. Carol said that I had been there; however, I had no recollection of the hotel or the room. I was so tired, though, that I could not think about it. I just sank into the bed, face down. All I wanted to do was sleep, yet I was too keyed up. There were too many loose ends, although everything seemed so orderly. I had a sudden surge of nervous excitation and sat up.

"I never told you that I hadn't accepted the death defier's gift," I said, facing Carol. "How did you know I didn't?"

"Oh, but you told me that yourself," she protested as she sat down next to me. "You were so proud of it. That was the first thing you blurted out when I found you."

This was the only answer, so far, that did not quite satisfy me. What she was reporting did not sound like my statement.

"I think you read me wrong," I said. "I just didn't want to get anything that would deviate me from my goal."

"Do you mean you didn't feel proud of refusing?"

"No. I didn't feel anything. I am no longer capable of feeling anything, except fear."

I stretched my legs and put my head on the pillow. I felt that if I closed my eyes or did not keep on talking I would be asleep in an instant. I told Carol how I had argued with don Juan, at the beginning of my association with him, about his confessed motive for staying on the warrior's path. He had said that fear kept him going in a straight line, and that what he feared the most was to lose the nagual, the abstract, the spirit.

"Compared with losing the nagual, death is nothing," he had said with a note of true passion in his voice. "My fear of losing the nagual is the only real thing I have, because without it I would be worse than dead."

I said to Carol that I had immediately contradicted don Juan and bragged that since I was impervious to fear, if I had to stay within the confines of one path, the moving force for me had to be love.

Don Juan had retorted that when the real pull comes, fear is the only worthwhile condition for a warrior. I secretly resented him for what I thought was his covert narrow-mindedness.

"The wheel has done a full turn," I said to Carol, "and look at me now. I can swear to you that the only thing that keeps me going is the fear of losing the nagual."

Carol stared at me with a strange look I had never seen in her. "I dare to disagree," she said softly. "Fear is nothing compared with affection. Fear makes you run wildly; love makes you move intelligently."

"What are you saying, Carol Tiggs? Are sorcerers people in love now?"

She did not answer. She lay next to me and put her head on my shoulder. We stayed there, in that strange, unfriendly room, for a long time, in total silence.

"I feel what you feel," Carol said abruptly. "Now, try to feel what I feel. You can do it. But let's do it in the dark."

Carol stretched her arm up and turned off the light above the bed. I sat up straight in one single motion. A jolt of fright had gone through me like electricity. As soon as Carol turned off the light, it was nighttime inside that room. In the middle of great agitation, I asked Carol about it.

"You're not all together yet," she said reassuringly. "You had a bout of monumental proportions. Going so deeply into the second attention has left you a little mangled, so to speak. Of course, it's daytime, but your eyes can't yet adjust properly to the dim light inside this room."

More or less convinced, I lay down again. Carol kept on talking, but I was not listening. I felt the sheets. They were real sheets. I ran my hands on the bed. It was a bed! I leaned over and ran the palms of my hands on the cold tiles of the floor. I got out of bed and checked every item in the room and in the bathroom. Everything was perfectly normal, perfectly real. I told Carol that when she turned off the light, I had the clear sensation I was dreaming.

"Give yourself a break," she said. "Cut this investigatory nonsense and come to bed and rest."

I opened the curtains of the window to the street. It was daytime outside, but the moment I closed them it was nighttime inside. Carol begged me to come back to bed. She feared that I might run away and end up in the street, as I had done before. She made sense. I went back to bed without noticing that not even for a second had it entered my mind to point at things. It was as if that knowledge had been erased from my memory.

The darkness in that hotel room was most extraordinary. It brought me a delicious sense of peace and harmony. It brought me also a profound sadness, a longing for human warmth, for companionship. I felt more than bewildered. Never had anything like this happened to me. I lay in bed, trying to remember if that longing was something I knew. It was not. The longings I knew were not for human companionship; they were abstract; they were rather a sort of sadness for not reaching something undefined.

"I am coming apart," I said to Carol. "I am about to weep for people."

I thought she would understand my statement as being funny. I intended it as a joke. But she did not say anything; she seemed to agree with me. She sighed. Being in an unstable state of mind, I became instantly swayed toward emotionality. I faced her in the darkness and muttered something that in a more lucid moment would have been quite irrational to me. "I absolutely adore you," I said.

Talk like that among the sorcerers of don Juan's line was unthinkable. Carol Tiggs was the nagual woman. Between the two of us, there was no need for demonstrations of affection. In fact, we did not even know what we felt for each other. We had been taught by don Juan that among sorcerers there was no need or time for such feelings.

Carol smiled at me and embraced me. And I was filled with such a consuming affection for her that I began to weep involuntarily.

"Your energy body is moving forward on the universe's luminous filaments of energy," she whispered in my ear. "We are being carried by the death defier's gift of intent."

I had enough energy to understand what she was saying. I even questioned her about whether she, herself, understood what it all meant. She hushed me and whispered in my ear. "I do understand; the death defier's gift to you was the wings of intent. And with them, you and I are dreaming ourselves in another time. In a time yet to come."

I pushed her away and sat up. The way Carol was voicing those complex sorcerers' thoughts was unsettling to me. She was not given to take conceptual thinking seriously. We had always joked among ourselves that she did not have a philosopher's mind.

"What's the matter with you?" I asked. "Yours is a new development for me: Carol the sorceress-philosopher. You are talking like don Juan."

"Not yet." She laughed. "But it's coming. It's rolling, and when it finally hits me, it'll be the easiest thing in the world for me to be a sorceress-philosopher. You'll see. And no one will be able to explain it because it will just happen."

An alarm bell rang in my mind. "You're not Carol!" I shouted. "You're the death defier masquerading as Carol. I knew it."

Carol laughed, undisturbed by my accusation. "Don't be absurd," she said. "You're going to miss the lesson. I knew that, sooner or later, you were going to give in to your indulging. Believe me, I am Carol. But we're doing something we've never done: we are intending in the second attention, as the sorcerers of antiquity used to do."

I was not convinced, but I had no more energy to pursue my argument, for something like the great vortexes of my dreaming was beginning to pull me in. I heard Carol's voice faintly, saying in my ear, "We are dreaming ourselves. Dream your intent of me. Intend me forward! Intend me forward!"

With great effort, I voiced my innermost thought. "Stay here with me forever," I said with the slowness of a tape recorder on the blink. She responded with something incomprehensible. I wanted to laugh at my voice, but then the vortex swallowed me.

When I woke up, I was alone in the hotel room. I had no idea how long I had slept. I felt extremely disappointed at not finding Carol by my side. I hurriedly dressed and went down to the lobby to look for her. Besides, I wanted to shake off some strange sleepiness that had clung to me.

At the desk, the manager told me that the American woman who had rented the room had just left a moment ago. I ran out to the street, hoping to catch her, but there was no sign of her. It was midday; the sun was shining in a cloudless sky. It was a bit warm.

I walked to the church. My surprise was genuine but dull at finding out that I had indeed seen the detail of its architectural structure in that dream. Uninterestedly, I played my own devil's advocate and gave myself the benefit of the doubt. Perhaps don Juan and I had examined the back of the church and I did not remember it. I thought about it. It did not matter. My validation scheme had no meaning for me anyway. I was too sleepy to care.

From there I slowly walked to don Juan's house, still looking for Carol. I was sure I was going to find her there, waiting for me. Don Juan received me as if I had come back from the dead.

He and his companions were in the throes of agitation as they examined me with undisguised curiosity.

"Where have you been?" don Juan demanded.

I could not comprehend the reason for all the fuss. I told him that I had spent the night with Carol in the hotel by the plaza, because I had no energy to walk back from the church to their house, but that they already knew this.

"We knew nothing of the sort," he snapped.

"Didn't Carol tell you she was with me?" I asked in the midst of a dull suspicion, which, if I had not been so exhausted, would have been alarming.

No one answered. They looked at one another, searchingly. I faced don Juan and told him I was under the impression he had sent Carol to find me. Don Juan paced the room up and down without saying a word.

"Carol Tiggs hasn't been with us at all," he said. "And you've been gone for nine days."

My fatigue prevented me from being blasted by those statements. His tone of voice and the concern the others showed were ample proof that they were serious. But I was so numb that there was nothing for me to say.

Don Juan asked me to tell them, in all possible detail, what had transpired between the death defier and me. I was shocked at being able to remember so much, and at being able to convey all of it in spite of my fatigue. A moment of levity broke the tension when I told them how hard the woman had laughed at my inane yelling in her dream, my intent to *see*.

"Pointing the little finger works better," I said to don Juan, but without any feeling of recrimination.

Don Juan asked if the woman had any other reaction to my yelling besides laughing. I had no memory of one, except her mirth and the fact that she had commented how intensely he disliked her.

"I don't dislike her," don Juan protested. "I just don't like the old sorcerers' coerciveness."

Addressing everybody, I said that I personally had liked that woman immensely and unbiasedly. And that I had loved Carol Tiggs as I never thought I could love anyone. They did not seem to appreciate what I was saying. They looked at one another as if I had suddenly gone crazy. I wanted to say more, to explain myself. But don Juan, I believed just to stop me from babbling idiocies, practically dragged me out of the house and back to the hotel.

The same manager I had spoken to earlier obligingly listened to our description of Carol Tiggs, but he flatly denied ever having seen her or me before. He even called the hotel maids; they corroborated his statements.

"What can the meaning of all this be?" don Juan asked out loud. It seemed to be a question addressed to himself. He gently ushered me out of the hotel. "Let's get out of this confounded place," he said.

When we were outside, he ordered me not to turn around to look at the hotel or at the church across the street, but to keep my head down. I looked at my shoes and instantly realized I was no longer wearing Carol's clothes but my own. I could not remember, however, no matter how hard I tried, when I had changed clothes. I figured that it must have been when I woke up in the hotel room. I must have put on my own clothes then, although my memory was blank.

By then we had reached the plaza. Before we crossed it to head off to don Juan's house, I explained to him about my clothes. He shook his head rhythmically, listening to every word. Then he sat down on a bench, and, in a voice that conveyed genuine concern, he warned me that, at the moment, I had no way of knowing what had transpired in the second attention between the woman in the church and my energy body. My interaction with the Carol Tiggs of the hotel had been just the tip of the iceberg.

"It's horrendous to think that you were in the second attention for nine days," don Juan went on. "Nine days is just a second for the death defier, but an eternity for us." Before I could protest or explain or say anything, he stopped me with a comment. "Consider this," he said. "If you still can't remember all the things I taught you and did with you in the second attention, imagine how much more difficult it must be to remember what the death defier taught you and did with you. I only made you change levels of awareness; the death defier made you change universes."

I felt meek and defeated. Don Juan and his two companions urged me to make a titanic effort and try to remember when I changed my clothes. I could not. There was nothing in my mind: no feelings, no memories. Somehow, I was not totally there with them.

The nervous agitation of don Juan and his two companions reached a peak. Never had I seen him so discombobulated. There had always been a touch of fun, of not quite taking himself seriously in everything he did or said to me. Not this time, though.

Again, I tried to think, bring forth some memory that would shed light on all this; and again I failed, but I did not feel defeated; an improbable surge of optimism overtook me. I felt that everything was coming along as it should.

Don Juan's expressed concern was that he knew nothing about the dreaming I had done with the woman in the church. To create a dream hotel, a dream town, a dream Carol Tiggs was to him only a sample of the old sorcerers' dreaming prowess, the total scope of which defied human imagination.

Don Juan opened his arms expansively and finally smiled with his usual delight. "We can only deduce that the woman in the church showed you how to do it," he said in a slow, deliberate tone. "It's going to be a giant task for you to make comprehensible an incomprehensible maneuver. It has been a masterful movement on the chessboard, performed by the death defier as the woman in the church. She has used Carol's energy body and yours to lift off, to break away from her moorings. She took you up on your offer of free energy."

What he was saying had no meaning to me; apparently, it meant a great deal to his two companions. They became immensely agitated. Addressing them, don Juan explained that the death defier and the woman in the church were different expressions of the same energy; the woman in the church was the more powerful and complex of the two. Upon taking control, she made use of Carol Tiggs's energy body, in some obscure, ominous fashion congruous with the old sorcerers' machinations, and created the Carol Tiggs of the hotel, a Carol Tiggs of sheer intent. Don Juan added that Carol and the woman may have arrived at some sort of energetic agreement during their meeting.

At that instant, a thought seemed to find its way to don Juan. He stared at his two companions, unbelievingly. Their eyes darted around, going from one to the other. I was sure they were not merely looking for agreement, for they seemed to have realized something in unison.

"All our speculations are useless," don Juan said in a quiet, even tone. "I believe there is no longer any Carol Tiggs. There isn't any woman in the church either; both have merged and flown away on the wings of intent, I believe, forward.

"The reason the Carol Tiggs of the hotel was so worried about her appearance was because she was the woman in the church, making you dream a Carol Tiggs of another kind; an infinitely more powerful Carol Tiggs. Don't you remember what she said? 'Dream your intent of me. Intend me forward.'"

"What does this mean, don Juan?" I asked stunned.

"It means that the death defier has seen her total way out. She has caught a ride with you. Your fate is her fate."

"Meaning what, don Juan?"

"Meaning that if you reach freedom so will she."

"How is she going to do that?"

"Through Carol Tiggs. But don't worry about Carol." He said this before I voiced my apprehension. "She's capable of that maneuver and much more."

Immensities were piling up on me. I already felt their crushing weight. I had a moment of lucidity and asked don Juan, "What is going to be the outcome of all this?"

He did not answer. He gazed at me, scanning me from head to toe. Then he slowly and deliberately said, "The death defier's gift consists of endless dreaming possibilities. One of them was your dream of Carol Tiggs in another time, in another world; a more vast world, open-ended; a world where the impossible might even be feasible. The implication was not only that you will live those possibilities but that one day you will comprehend them."

He stood up, and we started to walk in silence toward his house. My thoughts began to race wildly. They were not thoughts, actually, but images, a mixture of memories of the woman in the church and of Carol Tiggs, talking to me in the darkness in the dream hotel room. A couple of times I was near to condensing those images into a feeling of my usual self, but I had to give it up; I had no energy for such a task.

Before we arrived at the house, don Juan stopped walking and faced me. He again scrutinized me carefully, as if he were looking for signs in my body. I then felt obliged to set him straight on a subject I believed he was deadly wrong about.

"I was with the real Carol Tiggs at the hotel," I said. "For a moment, I myself believed she was the death defier, but after careful evaluation, I can't hold on to that belief. She was Carol. In some obscure, awesome way she was at the hotel, as I was there at the hotel myself."

"Of course she was Carol," don Juan agreed. "But not the Carol you and I know. This one was a dream Carol, I've told you, a Carol made out of pure intent. You helped the woman in the church spin that dream. Her art was to make that dream an all-inclusive reality: the art of the old sorcerers, the most frightening thing there is. I told you that you were going to get the crowning lesson in dreaming, didn't I?"

"What do you think happened to Carol Tiggs?" I asked.

"Carol Tiggs is gone," he replied. "But someday you will find the new Carol Tiggs, the one in the dream hotel room."

"What do you mean she's gone?"

"She's gone from the world," he said.

I felt a surge of nervousness cut through my solar plexus. I was awakening. The awareness of myself had started to become familiar to me, but I was not yet fully in control of it. It had begun, though, to break through the fog of the dream; it had begun as a mixture of not knowing what was going on and the foreboding sensation that the incommensurable was just around the corner.

I must have had an expression of disbelief, because don Juan added in a forceful tone, "This is dreaming. You should know by now that its transactions are final. Carol Tiggs is gone."

"But where do you think she went, don Juan?"

"Wherever the sorcerers of antiquity went. I told you that the death defier's gift was endless dreaming possibilities. You didn't want anything concrete, so the woman in the church gave you an abstract gift: the possibility of flying on the wings of intent."